Toward a Multicultural Configuration of Spain

Toward a Multicultural Configuration of Spain

Local Cities, Global Spaces

Edited by Ana Corbalán and Ellen Mayock

FAIRLEIGH DICKINSON UNIVERSITY PRESS
Madison • Teaneck

Published by Fairleigh Dickinson University Press
Copublished by The Rowman & Littlefield Publishing Group, Inc.
4501 Forbes Boulevard, Suite 200, Lanham, Maryland 20706
www.rowman.com

16 Carlisle Street, London W1D 3BT, United Kingdom

British Library Cataloguing in Publication Information Available

Library of Congress Cataloging-in-Publication Data

Toward a multicultural configuration of Spain: local cities, global spaces / [edited by] Ana Corbalán and Ellen Mayock.
pages cm
Includes bibliographical references and index.
ISBN 978-1-61147-669-9 (cloth : alkaline paper)—ISBN 978-1-61147-670-5 (electronic)
1. City and town life--Spain. 2. Cultural pluralism—Spain. 3. Emigration and immigration—Social aspects--Spain. 4. Globalization—Social aspects—Spain. 5. Spain—Social conditions. 6. Cultural pluralism in literature. 7. Cultural pluralism in motion pictures. 8. City and town life in literature. 9. City and town life in motion pictures. 10. Spain—Intellectual life. I. Corbalán, Ana. II. Mayock, Ellen C. (Ellen Cecilia), 1965-
HT145.S6T69 2014
307.760946—dc23
2014022021

∞™ The paper used in this publication meets the minimum requirements of American National Standard for Information Sciences Permanence of Paper for Printed Library Materials, ANSI/NISO Z39.48-1992.

Printed in the United States of America

Contents

Acknowledgments

We are profoundly grateful to the seventeen collaborators who contributed their knowledge, ideas, and creativity to this volume. It has been a pleasure to work with this group due to their excellent work ethic and unique contributions to the volume. In addition, we would like to express our gratitude to all of those individuals who have supported this project, including colleagues, readers, family members, and editors. We would also like to thank most sincerely Harry Keyishian, director of Fairleigh Dickinson University Press, for recognizing the value of the research and Rowman and Littlefield editors Amie Brown and Brooke Bures for the careful editing work they did with us from start to finish. We are also grateful for the institutional support of the University of Alabama and Washington and Lee University (especially the Lenfest Summer Fellowship) for *Toward a Multicultural Configuration of Spain*. To Washington and Lee University student Jean Turlington goes our deepest gratitude for her eagle eye, keen organizational skills, and outstanding work ethic.

We would also like to thank the following directors and writers for their permission to include excerpts of their texts and films in this book: Lucía Sánchez, the director of *La guerra del Golf*; María Cristina Carrillo Espinosa to quote her documentary *La Churona: Historia de una Virgen Migrante*; Esther García Llovet for her comments on "La M-30, gran velada"; and Victoria López for her explanations about "Puerta bonita. La forja del barro."

We appreciate Sene Corbalán Vélez's willingness to help us design a relevant and beautiful cover for the book. Ana would also like to thank her parents and brothers for their inspiration as well as Sophie and Alicia for their patience while she worked on this and other projects. Ellen Mayock also thanks her family (Patrick Bradley, Charlie Mayock-Bradley, and Susanne Mayock-Bradley) for their smarts, humor, and love.

We sincerely hope that this book will open a productive and ongoing dialogue about and between the local and the global. Furthermore, we are grateful for the many people who are embracing a new multicultural configuration of Spain.

Introduction

Spain's Local Cities and Global Spaces

Ellen Mayock and Ana Corbalán

Schizophrenic headlines about Spain range from "Vamos a menos. España afronta a una tormenta demográfica perfecta: emigración, envejecimiento y baja natalidad. A partir de 2018, se registrarán más muertes que nacimientos" [We are becoming fewer. Spain faces the perfect demographic storm: emigration, aging, and low birth rates] (Nogueira) to "As Africans Surge to Europe's Door, Spain Locks Down" (Dailey). Is it possible that the first two decades of the new millennium have brought with them a curious blip on the demographic canvas of Spain, or will the country continue to absorb more and more migrants from Latin America, Eastern Europe, and Africa? Certainly these competing headlines demonstrate that Spain continues to be a desirable destination for many migrants *and* that Spain's already depopulated areas will continue to lose residents, to the big cities and to the aging and dying population.

In 2012, *El País* reported that, since 2007, unemployment rates in Spain have encouraged fewer immigrants to choose to settle in Spain and have also pushed more residents to leave Spain. In fact, the National Statistics Institute of Spain projects that "en los próximos 40 años saldrán de España 18,1 millones de personas y llegarán 16,7. Procederán sobre todo de la Unión Europea (4,9 millones), Sudamérica (3,7) y África (3,5)" [over the next 40 years, 18.1 million people will leave Spain, while 16.7 million will arrive. They will come mostly from the European Union (4.9 million), South America (3.7 million), and Africa (3.5 million)] These figures reveal not only the multiple changes in Spanish demographics since the turn of the millennium, but also a certain anxiety about who stays, who goes, and who is "Spanish." Nathan Richardson states that, "whereas in 1995, immigrants, principally

Latin American, Eastern European, and African, comprised less than 1 percent of the total population of Spain, by the end of 2005, estimates situate that number right around 8.5 percent" (3). While Francoism had us talking about what Gonzalo Navajas calls "the importance of Madrid as organizing national force" (174–75) and the tension between and among the "autonomías" in terms of national and "micronational" identities, globalization raises more extramural questions about national identities, access to public space and to the "marketplace" of health, education, and welfare.

Toward a Multicultural Configuration of Spain: Local Cities, Global Spaces explores the interaction between the local and the global and the effects of multiculturalism in the geography of Spain. A glance at Marc Augé's introduction to the 2008 translation of his seminal work, *Non-Places*, establishes the contours of the local-global question. Augé mentions potential utopian ideals of globalization but then quickly probes the ways in which the global city "absorbs and divides the world in all its diverseness and inequality" (xiii). His point that even the most iconic of "first world" cities have swaths of underdevelopment that are akin to many of the cities in the "third world" (term used by Augé) (xiii) signals the numerous geographic and social phenomena shared from place to place and from space to space, no matter our preconceived notions about "first" and "third" worlds. Furthermore, Augé posits that frontiers, architecture, and "the here and the elsewhere" (the local-global) all constitute potentially liberating but also constricting aspects of globalization. As will be shown, this encounter between the local and the global is extensively treated in the chapters that comprise this volume.

We must keep very much in mind that real human beings populate these globalizing landscapes, which are thereby influenced by the social identifications and interactions that comprise the concept of habitus. In their introduction to *Culture/Power/History*, Dirks, Shelly, and Ortner say that Pierre Bourdieu:

> argu[es] that the parameters of personal identity—especially of one's "place" within a system of social differences and inequalities—are structured into the objective environment. . . . The organization of space (in houses, in villages and cities) and time (the rhythms of work, leisure, holidays) embody [*sic*] the assumptions of gender, age, and social hierarchy upon which a particular life is built. As the actor grows up, and lives everyday life within these spatial and temporal forms, s/he comes to embody those assumptions, literally and figuratively. The effect is one of near-total naturalization of the social order, the forging of homologies between personal identity and social classification. (13)

In this sense, we can connect migrant human beings to new and different places, but their "habitus" in many ways is also portable. Nomadic people settling in a new place will bring with them ("embodied," to use Bourdieu's term) their own assumptions about identity and social order, thus layering these assumptions onto those embodied in the people already occupying this different space. In a phrase, this mosaic of social assumptions is constantly renegotiated through the reality of migration and the imposing force of globalization.

Given the competing notions and realities of globalization as both liberating and restricting, the role of art is crucial. In an artistic, literary context, Gilles Deleuze captures these notions of the transportable local and its influences on social identifications and assumptions made in a given space:

> The more our daily life appears standardized, stereotyped and subject to an accelerated reproduction of objects of consumption, the more art must be injected into it in order to extract from it that little difference which plays simultaneously between other levels of repetition, and even in order to make the two extremes resonate—namely, the habitual series of consumption and the instinctual series of destruction and death. . . . Each art has its interrelated techniques or repetitions, the critical and revolutionary power of which may attain the highest degree and lead us from the sad repetitions of habit to the profound repetitions of memory, and then to the ultimate repetitions of death in which our freedom is played out. (293)

In a multicultural space, then, repetitions of habit (the local) will encounter repetitions of memory (the translocal, and or the temporal layers of the local)—both in daily life and in their representation in art.

Five major issues arise from questions of multicultural configuration in these local and trans-local spaces. First, we must understand the ways in which we designate places and spaces as local, global, "glocal," and trans-local. If a local space is defined by its people, architecture, public art, sights, smells, sounds, and formal and informal marketplaces, is it still "local" when many of these elements can be found elsewhere—the corner Starbuck's, the Guggenheim museum, the smell of olive oil and kebabs? And when a global space, a space that seemingly can exist anywhere, is marked by "local color," does it gain back something of its regional or local independence? Or is it remarked as something different, or more individual and unique in its "glocal" nature? Finally, given the many ways in which we all can stay in touch with whatever it is we define as "home"—technological access to real-time conversations across the world, distribution of newspapers from around the world, moneygrams, movement of friends and relatives—might the "translocal" become the dominant mode of existing in the world?

The second major issue lies at the intersection between and among the rural, the urban, and the suburban. As Julio Llamazares so poignantly described the last inhabitants of a small town in the Pyrenees in *La lluvia amarilla*, we are mourning the depopulation of rural areas. Nevertheless, at the same time, we witness, for example, the *indignados'* reclamation of green spaces in urban locations as a means of celebrating the rural, honoring the earth, and feeding the hungry. The interplay among these three human-made spaces allows us to understand the movements of peoples predicated on access to food, water, employment, and each other. Even the many *urbaniza-ciones* (an interesting term in and of itself, given its semantics of urban planning) that have mushroomed around Spain's big cities seem to replicate in some ways the desire for connection that we observe so easily in city life—the corner bar, the park bench, and the small plaza.

Postmodern considerations of center and periphery comprise the third major issue of multicultural configuration. Of course, we tend to think of these words in geographical terms—the centralized nature of the city versus its radial peripheries in the suburbs and its ever-more distant connections to the outlying rural areas. Nevertheless, the city itself clearly establishes its own "in" groups and its "out" groups; it includes and excludes, assumes some identities, and "others" others. Given the overwhelmingly forceful pull of the city for immigrant arrivals in Spain, this center/periphery dichotomy is of fundamental importance because it can dangerously reinforce 1970s' US television character Archie Bunker's words that "we need to keep the sames with the sames and the differents with the differents." Labrador Méndez sees this dichotomy as manifested in "Aznarismo" (a centralized, *castizo* view of "Spanishness") versus "the Spain of others" (270) that emerges from the demographic sea change that takes place between 2000 and the present day. As several of the chapters in this volume attest, some of this tendency to create multicultural mosaics—with groups from similar regions establishing themselves in the same parts of the cities—stems from public corralling of immigrants and their access to public spaces and resources, while the tenden-cy also naturally foments itself through the need for social networks, linguis-tic commonality, and shared access to public goods.

Many who research space and place cite Marc Augé's notion of "non-places," that is, physical spaces of mass transit—highways, airports, malls—places through which people move en masse without capturing a certain essence of the space, and, similarly, without leaving any particular mark or evidence of their having passed through that space. This phenomenon of places, spaces, and non-places represents the fourth principal theme of multi-cultural configuration. The globalizing effects of the ever-increasing num-bers of these "non-places" can make Barajas feel like JFK and like the Jorge Chávez Airport in Lima. More importantly, the proliferation of these non-places cements humans' position as consumers, cogs in the world market-place, seekers of global, recognizable pleasures and of local "colors."

Finally, the fifth major issue of multicultural configuration points to defi-nitions of nationalism, micronationalisms, and power. Since Francisco Fran-co's death in 1975, numerous researchers have sought to understand the influence of Spain's participation in the European Union on the access to power of each of its seventeen "autonomies." The cultural boards, and, in many cases, the political bodies of the regions have sought to solidify and to foment manifestations of regional and local existence—through the exportation of specific products, the popularization of tourist attractions, the success of autochthonous sports teams, events, and so on. In other words, central Madrid has had its competition for international attention from the regions it had previously deigned to govern. These regional and national impulses to reset and to redefine what makes a certain place unique, or special, has intertwined with the unprecedented arrival of new residents and inhabitants from Africa, Eastern Europe, and Latin America, thus calling into question the move toward both regional and national redefinitions of patriotism.

Toward a Multicultural Configuration of Spain: Local Cities, Global Spaces examines how the converging of cultures has become a global reality and how emerging intercultural encounters define new patterns of community organization based on the mobility of people and capital. The interstices between the local and the global in the geographical spaces of Spain create contact zones that redefine national, ethnic, religious, social, and gender identities. According to Doreen Massey, "The uniqueness of a place, or a locality, in other words, is constructed out of particular interactions and mutual articulations of social relations, social processes, experiences and understandings, in a situation of co-presence" ("Power-geometry" 66). A number of points arise from this assertion: the nation-state is not a homogeneous entity; there is not a clear distinction of boundaries between the center and the periphery; and contact zones are key factors in redefining identities in a multicultural space.

The narratives analyzed in the following fifteen chapters offer insightful representations of the encounter with the "other." As a result, they imagine the experience of being displaced as well as the productive dialogue between two or more cultures. Nevertheless, according to Daniela Flesler, "Although Spanish national identity appears today as irreversibly variegated, heterogeneous, and decentered, . . . the idea of Spain as an ethnically and culturally homogeneous nation is far from having disappeared. In fact, it still permeates the staging of a defensive reaction toward the foreign: its perceived thread is answered with a return to old discourses of 'Spanishness' and centralist nationalism" (38). We argue that Spain has never been a homogenous nation, although many discourses tend to highlight this supposed standardized, but unique, Spanish identity. Such Spanishness does not exist (except, perhaps, in the artful recreations of the Spanish tourist industry), since the nation is being increasingly integrated into a system of transnational encounters which build connections and emotional bonds inside Iberian borders. In fact, these problematic encounters are depicted in many of the works that are analyzed in this volume.

Susan Martin-Márquez suggests that "the increasing presence of immigrants in Spanish life and cultural production is leading to a new form of 'disorientation,' as communities in Spain are forced to confront the realities of a modern-day convivencia" (355). This "disorientation" is what this volume proposes to examine, as it analyzes contemporary reactions to the multiple changes in the topography of Spain. At this point in Spain's history, intercultural dialogues can be problematic as not all longer-term local inhabitants are receptive to "others," nor do they all accept that Spain has become a pluralistic society in which different cultures are articulated in and around one another. According to Homi Bhabha, these interstitial locations are the places where "the intersubjective and collective experiences of *nationness*, community interest, or cultural value are negotiated" (2). Understood in this way, to be "in between" cultures, languages, and nations means that the articulation of cultural identity is negotiated in these dialogic spaces.

As Avtar Brah states, "The concepts of diaspora, border, and politics of location together offer a conceptual grid for historicised analyses of contemporary trans/national movements of people, information, cultures, commodities and capital" (181). These transnational communities have crossed geopolitical borders and now contribute to the cultural and economic strengths of globalization while concurrently transforming the imaginary of national identity. This practice moves progressively away from the boundaries that originated in the underlying preconceptions of an exclusively national paradigm within Spain. Nevertheless, in spite of this multinational shift, there is an interstice between the local and the global, in which the nation-state continues to have ethnic, linguistic, and cultural tensions.

Regarding the aspects that define globalization, Arjun Appadurai wrote a compelling piece in which he defined cultural identity in terms of movement in the complexity of the new global cultural economy. He rejected the world order that had been traditionally understood in terms of a reductive model of center versus periphery, and highlighted a new global economy based on a series of networks that crossed the borders of the nation-state. Thus, Appadurai coins five dimensions of the global cultural flow: ethnoscapes; mediascapes; technoscapes; financescapes; and ideoscapes. He argues that the global flows occur in and through the disjunctures caused by these conditions. For this book we are mostly interested in ethnoscapes, defined by him as "the landscape of persons who constitute the shifting world in which we live: tourists, immigrants, refugees, exiles, guestworkers, and other moving groups and persons constitute an essential feature of the world and appear to affect the politics of (and between) nations to a hitherto unprecedented degree." (32)

Henri Lefebvre asserts in *The Production of Space* that, "(Social) space is not a thing among other things, nor a product among other products: rather, it subsumes things produced, and encompasses their interrelationships in their coexistence and simultaneity—their (relative) order and/or (relative) disorder" (73). Likewise, Edward Soja notes, "Socially-produced space is a created structure comparable to other social constructions resulting from the transformation of given conditions inherent to being alive, in much the same way that human history represents a social transformation of time" (80).

The authors in this volume explore from a variety of perspectives the interstices between local and global encounters in Spain. Although they overlap in some ways, for the purpose of clarity, we have clustered the chapters into three groups: those that examine literary representations of the local and the global, those that explore migration, space, and tourism in documentary films, and those that analyze cinematic depictions of multicultural encounters in local spaces.

The first part, "Literary Representations of the Local and the Global" is divided into five chapters which explore the interaction between local and global through a literary lens.

Victoria L. Ketz studies the attempts of Rosa Montero to recreate the modern city with its chaos and disjunction as a place of community. She discusses the current phenomena occurring in large urban centers which promote alienation from and disillusionment with contemporary society. She also analyzes the stereotypical representations of the distinct ethnic groups, scrutinizing the mechanism in place that leads humans to seek out companionship, form communities, and create a "familial unit."

Hayley Rabanal examines the representation of the aversion of multiculturalism as depicted in Lucía Etxebarria's *Cosmofobia*. Her chapter scrutinizes the narrative's ambivalent attitude toward community and *convivencia*. Linking the absence of genuine intimacy to the wider lack of solidarity in Extebarría's fictional version of multicultural Lavapiés, her chapter incorporates insights from current debates concerning the viability of reconfiguring cosmopolitan thinking as a means of negotiating cultural difference and achieving solidarity.

Carmen Alfonso delves into ways in which female protagonists interact with certain places or Madrid neighborhoods with particular socioeconomic or cultural connotations. Her chapter shows how the mutual transformative influence between the metropolis and its peoples is articulated through the "sum of all"; that is, the stories and women that emerge in the urban space.

Pilar Martínez-Quiroga travels to Galicia. She analyzes how the role of the city in *O club da calceta* transgresses traditional nationalist discourse. As she notes, Galician nationalism has been based on the opposition "rural/urban," in which rural lifestyles have been used to represent authentic Galician identity. Author Reimóndez suppresses this dichotomy by showing a city that is not monolithic , but rather is stratified in different neighborhoods and is shaped by the onset of female immigration from the countryside.

This spatial trajectory moves then to Catalunya, where Raquel Vega-Durán explores a graphic novel in which the local space of North Street is considered a global contact zone, a space of encounters in which people who are separated by history and space meet and realize they are not as different from each other as they had thought. Bergés and Cazares's graphic novel thus proposes that we rescue a hidden history from oblivion to understand the present.

The second part of this book, "Migration, Space, and Tourism in Documentary Films," focuses on the function of documentary films in depicting cultural encounters and changes in geographical spaces in Spain. Megan Saltzman and Javier Entrambasaguas highlight the contentious and interconnected relationships in Spain between globalizing public space, immigration, and the struggle for what Henri Lefebvre has called "the right to the city." They approach these relationships through two documentaries which represent diverse narratives of immigrants in Madrid and Barcelona. They demonstrate how the content and the cinematographic techniques in these documentaries contribute to redefining our everyday communities and public spaces in a global era by reinvigorating political debates on inclusion, citizenship, and participatory democracy.

Alicia Castillo analyzes how Madrid is being transformed by immigration. According to Castillo, urban space is consequently a physical, social, and discursive space. As a result it can be said that immigration is a major factor in urban restructuring from a demographic point of view that encompasses both the population and diversity of nationalities in the neighborhoods. This also therefore begs the question of how space is transformed through immigration processes.

Maryanne Leone also explores another case study of immigration in Madrid. Her chapter focuses on the migration of Ecuadorians to Spain and the contiguous immigration of spiritual practices that redefine public and religious space in that city. Through an analysis of the film *La Churona*, she discusses Spanish resistance and acceptance of Ecuadorian immigrants in Madrid, Ecuadorians' active role in creating and asserting a place for themselves in twenty-first-century multicultural Spain, and the impact of global migration on urban spaces, religious practices, and local and national identities.

Sohyun Lee moves from the big city to the rural space. She shows how globalization is not a process exclusive to big cosmopolitan cities. Her chapter discusses the process of repopulation and the formulation of a "global village" in rural Spain as (re)presented in the documentary *Aguaviva*. The textual analysis of the film examines the treatment of social, cultural, and ethnic differences and/or affinities that come into play in the (re)configuration of Aguaviva as a local global space.

Thomas Deveny examines British tourism in Murcia, representing an extreme case of what is happening in all of Spain. Questions about water usage, over-construction of housing, foreign tourism, corruption, the economic crisis, and broken dreams are all themes in the documentary *La guerra del golf*, which makes audiences consider what type of future they want for Murcia and for Spain.

The third part, "Multicultural Encounters in Local Spaces: Cinematic Depictions" analyzes these same topics of the interaction of the local and the global as depicted through the cinematic lens. Donna Gillespie explores the spaces occupied by migrant "outcasts" and the subcommunities they form as they negotiate between *inside* and *outside* positions in contemporary Spanish society. Her chapter first explores the physical spaces occupied by women immigrants within the narratives and subsequently discusses the metaphorical spaces they inhabit, drawing on concepts developed by Dolores Juliano, Josefina Ludmer, and Zygmunt Bauman, among others. In discussing physical spaces, she presents metaphorical spaces designated as "islas urbanas" by Ludmer to demonstrate a new sense of "sub"-community among the immigrants. The films selected show a change in "spatiality" as women immigrants acquire new agency and new relations in their shift from peripheral to central spaces, both literal and metaphorical, between earlier and more recent texts.

María R. Matz and Carole Salmon also use Madrid as one of the most visible examples of globalization in Spain, where *local* and *global* intertwine at the political, economic and personal levels, creating a *glocal* place. They follow Pedro Almodóvar's film trajectory, which is centered on this capital city. Their article demonstrates how Madrid has evolved throughout the years and how new waves of Latin American immigration are feeding the *glocal* in Almodóvar's films, thus contributing to the multicultural reconfiguration of Spain.

William Nichols moves to another tourist city. A commodified "non-place," Torremolinos is emblematic of the early years of Spain's tourism industry. Nichols's essay examines the critique of the "narrative of development" in Spain by looking at cinematic representations of Torremolinos. By juxtaposing images from films from the era of "desarrollismo" ("development-ism") in the late Franco years to recent depictions of development along the Costa del Sol, Nichols explores an arc of modernization in Spain.

Diana Norton asks us to question the existence of a multicultural configuration of Spain by presenting the country as a fractured borderland between Europe, Latin America, and Africa, as portrayed in the film *No habrá paz para los malvados*. Her chapter shows that despite the contemporary image of multiculturalism prevalent in Spain and Europe, the resistance to hybridity in this film illustrates a continued attachment to the idea of a hegemonic national identity as defined by racial attributes. Norton highlights that, although there is an influx of immigrants to Spain in the 1990s to 2000s, migrant and nationalized Spanish citizens continue to remain separate and suspect, prompting us to redefine the parameters of multiculturalism.

Regarding this discussion of multiculturalism, Roberto Robles-Valencia emphasizes the tensions created by this new coexistence of diverse cultures, stressing the problematic nature of the concept of "multiculturalism." He argues that, in many films, immigrants and Spaniards share spaces but he questions to what extent there is a hybrid, common and lived-together (imagined-together) space. The problematic coexistence reveals, at the same time, the invisible but existing Spanish national "mark" which carries along its traditional aggressive outlook and its concept of the "other." Through the geographical concept of "landscape" and its inherent tensions, he underscores the intrinsic tensions of "multiculturalism" and focus on its origins: the economic globalization and the parallel process pointed out by Žižek: "the unprecedented homogenization of the contemporary world" (46). The question to address is then: is Spain a landscape of unproblematic multicultural coexistence or a stage for tragic tensions (minorities-nationalism) against the background of an invisible but unstoppable process of homogenization?

In conclusion, this collection contributes to the critical discussion regarding the interaction between local cities and global spaces in an era defined by global movements of people, places, and things. After reading these fifteen insightful examinations of the literary and audiovisual depiction of this topic, we must ask ourselves whether or not Spain is truly prepared to be defined or to identify itself as a multicultural, inclusive, global space.

WORKS CITED

Appadurai, Arjun. *Modernity at Large: Cultural Dimensions of Globalization*. Minneapolis: University of Minnesota Press, 1996.

Augé, Marc. *Non-Places. An Introduction to Supermodernity*. Trans. John Howe. London: Verso, 2008

Bhabha, Homi. *The Location of Culture*. London: Routledge, 1994.

Brah, Avtar. *Cartographies of Diaspora: Contesting Identities*. New York: Routledge, 1996.

Dailey, Suzanne. "As Africa Surges to Europe's Door, Spain Locks Down." *New York Times*, February 27, 2014. Accessed February 27, 2014.

Deleuze, Gilles. *Difference and Repetition*. Trans. Paul Patton. New York: Columbia University Press, 1994.

Dirks, Nicholas B., Geoff Eley, and Sherry B. Ortner, eds. *Culture/Power/History: A Reader in Contemporary Social Theory*. Princeton, NJ: Princeton University Press, 1994, (Introduction).

Flesler, Daniela. *The Return of the Moor: Spanish Responses to Contemporary Moroccan Immigration*. West Lafayette, IN: Purdue University Press, 2008.

Labrador Méndez, Germán. "Regarding the Spain of Others: Sociopolitical Framing of New Literatures/Cultures in Democratic Spain." Trans. Jeff Lawrence. *New Spains, New Literatures*. Eds. Luis Martín-Estudillo and Nicholas Spadaccini. Nashville, TN: Vanderbilt University Press, 2010, 261–76.

Lefebvre, Henri. *The Production of Space*. Trans. Donald Nicholson-Smith. Oxford: Black-well, |1974| 2000.

Martin-Márquez, Susan. *Disorientations: Spanish Colonialism in Africa and the Performance of Identity*. New Haven, CT: Yale University Press, 2008.

Massey, Doreen. "Power-Geometry and a Progressive Sense of Place." *Mapping the Futures: Local Cultures, Global Change*. Ed. Jon Bird, et al. New York: London: Routledge, 1992, 59–69.

Navajas, Gonzalo. "The Curse of the Nation: Institutionalized History and Literature in Global Spain." *New Spains, New Literatures*. Eds. Luis Martín-Estudillo and Nicholas Spadaccini. Nashville, TN: Vanderbilt University Press, 2010, 165–81.

Nogueira, Charo. "Vamos a menos. *El País*. November 19, 2012. Accessed February 27, 2014.

Richardson, Nathan. *Constructing Spain. The Re-imagination of Space and Place in Fiction and Film, 1953–2003*. Lewisburg, PA: Bucknell University Press, 2012.

Soja, Edward. *Postmodern Geographies: The Reassertion of Space in Critical Social Theory*. London: Verso, 1989.

Žižek, Slavoj. "Multiculturalism, or the Cultural Logic of Multinational Capitalism." *New Left Review* 225 (1997): 28–51.

I

Literary Representations of the Local and the Global

Chapter One

Urban Peripheries: Toward a New Vision of a Multicultural Community in Rosa Montero's *Instrucciones para salvar el mundo*

Victoria L. Ketz

The city has been conceptualized by different schools of thought since its inception. More recently, at the turn of the twentieth century, the Chicago School developed an urban ecological perspective of the city in which the human groups that collected within the metropolitan confines were united by class, occupation, or worldview. This gave way to the mid-century conceptualization of the city as communities based on extended kinship networks. This vision then transitioned in the 1980s to the anthropological approach toward the city based on political economy in which the social effects of industrial capitalism on the community were examined as they promoted confusion, inequality, and alienation, thus creating a new urban paradigm (Low 386). Many define a city by its geographic boundaries, historic monuments, or unique physical qualities. Located on a map, there is readily accessible data of a city's demographics, per capita income, and population density. Yet there are those such as James Donald, who goes so far as to negate the existence of cities: "There is no such thing as a city. Rather, the city designates the space produced by the interaction of historically and geographically specific institutions, social relations of production and reproduction, practices of government, forms and media of communication and so forth. The city, then, is above all a representation" (422). Whether imagined or real, the city is much more than buildings and boundaries; it is a place where people congregate to form a community.

This sense of community within the boundaries of an urban center manifests itself in Montero's *Instrucciones para salvar el mundo*. Rosa Montero, one of Spain's most prolific contemporary authors, has written in seemingly every genre: novels, children's works, essays, biography, autobiography, theater, television scripts, journalistic writings, and short stories. Yet her literary trajectory, initiated during the Spanish transition to democracy, has maintained its focus on feminist and social issues. In *Instrucciones para salvar el mundo* (2008), Montero critically represents the contemporary urban metropolis of Madrid, with its multicultural demographic constituency and many social problems. In this novel, Matías, a grieving widowed Spanish taxi driver; Daniel, a disenchanted doctor; Fatma, a Sierra Leonese prostitute; Draco, a violent drug lord; Cerebro, a failed alcoholic scientist; and Rashid, a vengeful young Muslim boy, are united by their feelings of alienation, disillusionment, and loneliness, as well as a lack of communication. Yet all of them forge bonds through brief interactions and create a small community in which they monitor and guard each other's well-being.

This chapter studies Montero's recreation of the modern city's chaos and disjunction. Here, I utilize a variety of theories on the construction of urban centers to analyze how Madrid is conceptualized as a global city. As such, there are socioeconomic boundaries established in the urban space which stratify the different social classes. The wealthy inhabit the center of the city controlling the institutions to maintain the status quo. Whereas, the disenfranchised live on the outskirts struggling to survive, lured by the corrupting forces of drugs and criminality. However, in *Instrucciones para salvar el mundo*, a liminal space is created in the peripheries of the urban centers. The community formed in this interstitial space does not correspond to the homogenous conceptualization of the city that is promoted by the oligarchy. It is in this space that the novel suggests a new concept of city will arise by negotiating interactions between different ethnicities and by sharing the many problems faced by the global city including immigration, violence, prostitution, and climatic changes. Finally, this essay will examine the solution to the urban problems presented in the text.

In her article "The Anthropology of Cities: Imagining and Theorizing the City," Setha Low has described the way in which contemporary literature represents the city through different foci including social relationships, economics, urban planning, and architecture, as well as religion and culture. Of the urban spaces that are represented in literature, *Instrucciones para salvar el mundo* is most closely associated with the concept of the global city. According to Low, the preeminent global cities have allowed technology and finances to reorganize the economic base, spatial organization, and social structure of the city, culminating in the "polarization of the city and economy, the internationalization and 'casualization' of labor, and deterritorialization of the social organization of work and community . . . that have reshaped the deindustrialized city" (393). [1] This gives rise to a dichotomous society in which the two extremes of the spectrum exist. At one end, the upper class pursues its own interests, diverging from those who live in pluralistic neighborhoods at the other end. This is represented in *Instrucciones para salvar el mundo* through the distinction that is established between the different neighborhoods of the capital. When Matías looks into his rear view mirror he sees the demarcation of the city:

> Pero antes de llegar a ese reino de poder y riqueza, a esa ostentación de acero y kilovatios, estaba la mancha oscura de los desmontes suburbiales [. . .] campos áridos que siglos atrás debieron de ser de labranza, pero que ahora no eran más que sucios baldíos invadidos por una horda de drogadictos y miserables. [2] [But before arriving at that kingdom of power and wealth, to that ostentation of steel and kilowatts, was the dark stain of the suburban clearings . . . arid fields that centuries before had been for farming, but that now were not more than dirty wastelands invaded by a horde of drug addicts and the wretched.] (51–52) [3]

In this description a series of oppositions are formed between the city and the suburbs, that of power/powerlessness, wealth/poverty, waste/need, light/darkness, productivity/uselessness, acceptability/marginalization. It also highlights the fact that the agrarian economy has been supplanted in the space by a capitalist agenda which has caused a change in how the city is configured. In the novel, the center of town is always portrayed in the distance with glimmering lights, almost as if it were the unattainable dream, far from where the majority of the action takes place (54). Only once is this inner sanctum breeched, when Daniel, the disenchanted doctor, goes to spend Christmas Eve with his girlfriend Marina's brother. The apartment possesses all of the modern commodities: pistachio colored Italian sofas, intelligent climate control, remote controlled appliances, solar panels, instant piston elevators, and floor to ceiling windows (90–98). In this novel, the social stratification concentrates the wealthy at the center of Madrid while the less affluent are marginalized at the peripheries of the urban center dividing it into two.

Counterposing the wealth of the inner city is the appearance of another neighborhood, that of the *Poblado*. This squatter's settlement, located on the outskirts of Madrid, serves as home to the poorest segment of the population. The novel does not specify if it refers to *Cañada Real* or one of the other thirteen *poblados* that currently exist in Madrid. The first time Matías has to take a passenger there, it is described as a, "otro lugar aún más terrible. Era el Poblado, la barriada más peligrosa de Madrid; estaba rodeada por una franja de hogueras y de carcasas de coches calcinados que formaba una especie de cinturón de exclusión, una muralla defensiva que nadie se atrevía a cruzar. De modo que hasta el infierno tenía sus arrabales" [an even more terrible

place. It was the Poblado, the most dangerous slum of Madrid; it was surrounded by a border of bonfires and blackened carcasses of cars that formed
a type of belt of exclusion, a defensive wall that no one dared to cross. So
that even hell had its suburbs] (53). The fact that this area is delimited by
trash to form a wall to separate the two populations is telling. Draco, the drug
lord and flesh trader, makes his home in this neighborhood which is likened
to hell.[4] This community originally had been established as an Unidad Veci-
nal de Absorción (UVA), whose primary function was to provide temporary
housing for people until decent lodging could be found. The disenfranchised
are relegated to inhabit the uninhabitable where no one dares enter (289). The
depiction of this neighborhood with litter, broken windows, damaged appliances, and naked children playing in the street signals the deplorable conditions that exist in one of the wealthiest cities in the world. This problem of
socioeconomic inequities in society faces all major urban centers today.

   In between this heaven and hell, a liminal space is created at the periphery
of the city. The concept of liminality, as defined by van Gennep, denotes the
condition of being on a "threshold" where transit between two spaces is
possible. These liminal spaces existent in an urban setting serve as a place to
reconstruct a "desired city" with the preferred attributes since there is ambivalence, indeterminacy, and openness. It is in this interstitial space that there is
the opportunity to regenerate or create a new social order.[5] According to
Stefan Brandt, the characters of modern texts tend to gravitate toward these
intermediate zones which lie between the public and private sphere (556). It
is in this liminal space that the majority of the novel's action takes place:
Matías's house is in the desolate encampment of a neighborhood under construction, Matías's taxi route follows the outer belt of the M 40; even the bar,
the Oasis, and the brothel, El Cachito, are located on the highway to La
Coruña (N-VI). The several dwellings described in this interstitial setting
highlight the transitory nature of this zone. It is in the peripheries of the city
that Rashid, the Moroccan boy, lives in a "casucha de construcción miserable
y destartalada, casi una chabola." [shack of poor and dilapidated construction, almost a hovel.] (36). The make shift construction of this dwelling
emphasizes one of the immigrant problems that Kitty Calavita has highlighted in her work: that of inadequate housing. The social reality of crowd-
ing, lack of sanitation, and ghettoization face many of the disenfranchised
(Calavita 554). Also located in this transitional zone is Cerebro's home,
which was once a palatial estate, but now lays in the same decay as the social
class that once inhabited it:

> Su casa era un enorme palacete de piedra, una de las antiguas villas señoriales
> que antaño jalonaban la salida noroeste de Madrid. A medida que la autopista
> fue ensanchando, el asfalto se había ido comiendo los jardines. . . . Los acauda-
> lados dueños originales hacía tiempo que habían vendido sus propiedades y

ahora los pocos palacetes que quedaban, . . . habían sido reconvertidos en oficinas, tiendas o discotecas. [Her house was an enormous stone palace, one of the old stately villas that marked the Northwest exit of Madrid. As the freeway was widened, the asphalt had eaten the yards. . . . The affluent original owners had long ago sold their properties and now the few palaces that were left, . . . had been converted into offices, stores, or discotheques.] (187)

In this case, the city has responded to the needs of modernization symbolized by the ever-widening freeways that devour the private space. As a consequence, the oligarchy divested their properties which were then repurposed to meet the consumptive needs of the new society. Both of these dwellings mark the impermanence of this peripheral zone. By placing the characters in a liminal space, they can create a society in transition which is endowed with the idealized attributes of their desires.

In this liminal space, the characters of the novel congregate at different localities including the hospital, the brothel, and the bar which form a microcosm of this cross section of the population. In the hospital, social class disappears as all of humanity is reduced to a basic biological machine, in pain and suffering. The brothel is another place that different sectors of the population can meet. As Mayock notes this space overcomes any alienation felt by the individuals, "This connection of all four characters to el Cachito suggests that there exists a club of outsiders, and that by the mere existence of this 'club', those who considered themselves other or who were considered other have found a place of community" (169). The Oasis constitutes a zone of neutrality where characters can meet regardless of their social class. In the bar, the patrons stop in to gain respite from their weary work, to find consolation, and to have their biological needs sated with food and drink. The bar holds different significance for each of the characters in the novel: for Daniel it is a shelter (149); for Matías, part of his daily activity (219); and for Cerebro, a place to forget the past (248). During their time at the bar, stories exchanged among the clientele deepen their bonds of friendship and allow a small community to be formed, "Era un bar de ambiente familiar, aunque se tratara de una familia un poco triste de desarraigados y noctámbulos" [It was a bar with a family atmosphere, even though it was a sad family of the marginalized and sleepwalkers] (56). As is expected, families of any type protect each other. This is why Luzbella cares for Matías, since she knows he is recently widowed; he in turn takes care of Cerebro until her dying day. Also Fatma seeks assistance from Matías and Daniel when she realizes that she is pregnant and that her pimp will make her abort her unborn child. Thus, in a place such as the Oasis, the angst and the despair harbored in each individual becomes a collective anguish as the community shares and understands the misapprehensions of contemporary society.

In the modern city, liminal space is also allocated to the composition of an alternative reality, located in hyperspace. Douglas Kelbaugh describes a series of alternative "urbanisms" which are dependent on the technological innovations in globalized society, including the simulated lives found in Internet gaming. In *Instrucciones*, Daniel delves into this alternative world when Marina gives him the game of Second Life as a birthday gift. His integration into the simulated world in hyperspace responds to the fact that his life in Madrid is meaningless to him. Prior to becoming a regular on Second Life, Daniel's ambition disappears leaving the disillusionment of Christmas tree lights in January and he lives his life aimlessly like a cork bobbing in the water (41). Upon reflection, he concludes "Su existencia, en fin, había ido encogiendo como un jersey barato" [His existence, in the end, had been shrinking like a cheap sweater] (42). All of these similes point to Daniel's inability to communicate directly the malaise and alienation that he feels. Edward Soja has illustrated that the postmodern city is organized through strategies of fragmentation and dislocation, which lead the inhabitants to reflect these feelings of confusion and "bottomlessness." Daniel's foray into the simulated world allows him to become part of another community of individuals that were as "patético[s] como el que más y unido a los otros menesterosos afectivos, a la vasta y oscura red de solitarios, por el hilo umbilical de Second Life" [pathetic as any other and joined the affective needy, to the vast and dark network of the lonely, by the umbilical cord of Second Life] (96). In SIMS, Daniel reinvents himself by creating images such as his avatar and partaking in new experiences. The construction of a simulated world illustrates the growing tension that exists between globalization and individualization (Castells 34).

The city's massive size often leaves the inhabitants decentered and disoriented, thus creating sentiments of alienation and fragmentation. To negotiate this, there is a need by humans to feel that they can control the city in which they live. One of the ways humans conquer this alienation is through the motif of traveling. According to Edward Soja, urban settings have an influence on people, "our mental or cognitive mapping of urban reality and the interpretive grids through which we think about, experience, evaluate, and decide to act in the places, spaces, and communities in which we live" (324). The displacement through urban locales allows people to reconfigure and renegotiate their concept of a city. The characters traverse the labyrinthine metropolis by forging their own paths and exerting some control over the environment. In this novel, travel is represented through the metaphor of driving, where the city is staged as a space in which transit is possible. Faced with living alone without Rita, Matías uses driving as a way to find normalcy (12–13). Matías's need to drive his taxi is an attempt to come to terms with his present situation. It is interesting that in the novel Matías is often portrayed as traveling away from the city, accentuating his own feelings of alienation. Negotiating the complexity of the city by exercising different options at distinct junctures allows the characters the ability to overcome their sense of disorientation. This strategy, in which exploration of the city occurs, allows the surveyor to become a creator of the city space by establishing boundaries and limiting the environment.

In a metropolis, there are multiple identities coexisting in the same space, vying for dominance, creating interesting cultural cartographies. The city thus provides a fluid space where identities can be formed, expressed, and reinforced:

> Thus, conceived, cities, as adequate manifestations of cultural experience, epitomize the multimodal and sometimes paradoxical structure of identity formation in the modern and postmodern eras. Since the urban experience encompasses a wide range of conditions and contexts born out of the situations such as mass immigration, ethnic miscegenation, and political emancipation, it opens up the space for concepts such as transnational urbanism and ethnic and gender diversity. (Brandt 556)

The homogeneous concept of a national identity used by hegemony caused there to be an erasure of the differences distinguishing individuals within the country (Reid 426). Yet, the design of cities integrates disparate classes and ethnicities of the social structure. Susan Fainstein has noted that large cities develop in a very progressive fashion, "This built environment forms contours which structure social relations, causing commonalities of gender, sexual orientation, race, ethnicity, and class to assume spatial identities. Social groups, in turn, imprint themselves physically on the urban structure through the formation of communities, competition from territory, and segregation—in other words, through clustering, the erection of boundaries, and establishing distance." (1) Therefore, the current concept of national identities is in a state of dissolution since the concept of nationality does not address the multiculturality that exists in the population.

Rosa Montero, by using a marginal space to formulate a social or community identity, rejects the worldview of the hegemony. To create this new national identity, the different groups of immigrants present in the text must be integrated into the society. This novel cleverly presents what national discourse has done to the immigrants, relegated them to invisibility. Luzbella, the middle-aged Colombian immigrant who works as a waitress at the Oasis, is a prime example of this treatment. Although she has frequent interaction with the Spaniards at various times in the narration, she fades into inconspicuousness, existing, but not calling attention to herself. As Alejandra Aquino Moreschi notes, "en todos los países industrializados que reciben flujos migratorios del sur, los migrantes indocumentados son orillados con la ayuda de políticas migratorias estigmatizantes . . . que provocan su invisibilidad y exclusión del espacio público" [in all of the industrialized countries that receive a migratory flux from the south, the undocumented migrants are waterlogged with the help of stigmatizing migration politics . . . that provoke their invisibility and exclusion from public space] (65). Her importance is not noted until the end of the novel when she emerges from the shadows to become Matías's love interest. This then suggests the importance that immigrants have in the new conceptualization of the society. If once they were ignored, they now become relevant and they incorporate themselves into the community.

Another impediment to integration that is faced by the immigrants in the novel is isolation. According to Ybelice Briceño Linares, alienation is created through four discourse strategies found in the dominant culture, typically associated with immigrants: culturalization, racialization, criminalization, and victimization (206). The encounters that immigrants have with the natives of the host country in *Instrucciones* are of two types: passive indifference or aggressive hostility. The first meetings are brief and pass almost unperceived by the reader, but have as much significance as more hostile ones. Ahmed and his wife, who own the bar across from Daniel's apartment, are Lebanese immigrants. Although they appear to be friendly, they are characterized by Marina as the biggest busybodies of the neighborhood (152). By typifying these Lebanese immigrants as "gossips," Marina uses the discourse of culturalization, which occurs when one facet of the immigrant population is highlighted and this, is then in turn applied to all of those of that nationality. Racialization of the immigrant occurs when Rashid, Matías's Muslim neighbor, is discriminated against for his cultural heritage. In his article, "Is There a 'Neo-Racism'?", Etienne Balibar examines racism in the age of decolonization. He finds that differential treatments and effective segregation of the marginalized are defended by the hegemony as a way to maintain cultural differences (22). The treatment Rashid receives from the Spaniards responds to the discrimination faced by, "colectivos de religión musulmana, cuyas prácticas son subrayadas y dramatizadas, entre otros, por el tratamiento sensacionalista que les dan los medios de comunicación. . . . Esta modalidad discursiva sirve para legitimizar formas de rechazo social que puede ir de las prácticas de descalificación más sutiles a la violencia física y verbal" [collectives from the Muslim religion, whose practices are underscored and dramatized, among others, by the sensational treatment that they receive by the media. . . . This discursive modality serves to legitimize forms of social rejection that can go from the most subtle disqualifying practices to physical and verbal violence] (Briceño Linares 210). Matías, who physically attacks Rashid fearing he is an assassin, realizes that he has made a mistake and guiltily tries to make amends for his prior interaction. Draco,[6] the owner of the *Cachito*, responds to the discourse of criminalization, as his values do not align with those of the hegemony. By making money from the drug and sex trade, Draco finds himself ostracized by society. He is unable to integrate himself into the mainstream due to his own perceived deficiencies, "era en efecto rico, y desde luego podría vivir en un chalé de lujo en la zona más elegante de Madrid; pero había nacido y crecido en el Poblado, y . . . escondía dentro de sí un complejo de inferioridad social que le hacía preferir ser cabeza de ratón que cola de león" [He was in effect rich and certainly could live in a luxurious house in the most elegant area of Madrid; but he had been born and raised in the *Poblado,* and . . . he hid inside himself a social inferiority complex that made him prefer to be the head of a mouse than the tail of the lion] (292). All of his interactions with others involve violence, intimidation, and bribery to ensure obedience (288). The portrayal of the victimized immigrant is represented with the figure of Fatma, the prostitute, who migrates to escape being the sex slave of the Kamjor guerillas (166–67). She does not mind the wounds inflicted, the beatings, verbal abuse, and other forms of mistreatment because it is better than the mutilations and killings she witnessed. Fatma is triply marginalized due to her condition as immigrant, prostitute, and woman, and will find integration into society more difficult (Agrela 18–19). This discourse on the multiculturality in liminal space initiates a discussion on issues of race, class, ethnicity, and nationalization which are all concerns of the global city.

The consequences of globalization examined in the text introduce topics that are pertinent to urban centers. These concerns have become fixtures of the modern landscape such as the abandonment of pets (14), the rise of fast food consumption (14), the addiction to video (20) and drugs (52), the abuse of the elderly (37), the litter on the streets (82), the capture of aggressive acts on cell phones (262), and the dwindling resources of the social security system leading to errors in patient care (272). In conjunction with these social concerns are environmental ones. Society is portrayed as situated in a wider environmental community that has obligations and responsibilities. The social space of a city forms part of a larger web that relates to the environment. Several of the social and environmental problems faced in the urban centers gain prominence in the text. Highlighting the themes of random acts of violence, prostitution, and global warming creates a common focus for the characters in the text. By sharing their points of view on these topics, they bond together as a community, conscientious of these issues.

The title of the novel, *Instrucciones para salvar el mundo,* evokes the need to address these social and environmental concerns. To save our current global community, many of the societal problems portrayed need to be overcome and, if ignored, will lead to ruin. The text does not directly offer any solutions to the problems, but instead provides clues for the salvation. These indications are found in the various discussions Cerebro has with Matías in the bar. In her talks, Cerebro presents relevant scientific theories to Matías including Paul Kammerer's Law of Seriality (66), James Lovelock's Gaia Hypothesis (107), Antoine Lavoisier's Law of Conservation of Mass (184),

Aaron Fieldman's Lot Effect (224), and Rupert Sheldrake's Theory of Human Interconnectivity (228). Thus, Montero's solution to the problems facing humanity lies within these theories. All point to the need for the universe to have order and for humans to follow the golden rule because, as Fieldman found, "Si cometemos actos malignos, malignizamos el mundo. Y si hacemos algo bueno, contribuimos a mejorarlo y a redimirlo . . . cada individuo influye en la totalidad" [If we commit a malignant act, we make the world a bad place. And if we do something good, we contribute to make it better and to redeem it . . . each individual influences in the totality] (227). Here the author advocates for humans to bond together, because everything we do affects others and not always in a positive fashion. The community formed must assist one another so that the strong watch over the weak, and the wise protect the ignorant (172). For there to be any chance of survival, people with knowledge, like Cerebro, will have to unite with people of action, like Matías, to be successful in saving the world from destruction.

As is seen in *Instrucciones para salvar el mundo*, the localized problems are easily translatable to the global city. Through Montero's careful construction of the modern metropolis of Madrid she makes several things apparent. The current structure that is in place in urban centers which stratifies the society due to social class is a defunct practice. A new global order then must arise from the liminal spaces where there is the possibility to create a society which is multiracial and multiethnic. These newer cities will liken themselves to the mythical Babel where there exists a place of multilingual and multicultural coexistence. However, before this can occur, the global reality must address some transnational problems such as migration, shifting national identities, violence, prostitution, and environmental concerns. These problems will not solve themselves, but need participation from all to arrive at a viable solution. Our local identities can no longer be constituted by a homogeneous term which erases the differences between individuals, but need to be nationalities composed of a multicultural mosaic, as is represented in the novel.

NOTES

1. Jonathan Friedman believes that the major cities respond to an allegiance of a world system that overshadows national boundaries. These "world cities," that he classifies, share common aspects such as perceiving their local economies in a global way, allow for private accumulation of capital, serve as centers for intense economic and social interaction, have a hierarchical arrangement, and allow for capitalist class system.

2. All translations in this text are mine.

3. Unless otherwise indicated, the primary text, *Instrucciones para salvar el mundo* will simply be cited with parenthesis.

4. This representation highlights a perverted version of the myth of Orpheus and Eurydice which occurs when Daniel and Matías go to visit Draco at his home to procure Fatma's

freedom. Of course in this modern day myth, her release from the hands of this evil lord of the underworld is bartered by cold hard cash instead of a song (288–91).

5. Due to the brevity of this article, this idea was not developed, but it is easy to posit that in the interzone the historical past of Spain can be forgotten leading to an emphasis of the present and the future.

6. Draco is a Greek name meaning Dragon. This name was also made famous by the first law scribe of ancient Athens. He transcribed the stringent laws in 621 BCE which called for death for minor offenses and slavery for debt. This gave rise to the adjective "draconian" to describe harsh treatments, which in this case is applicable as the pimp routinely marks and beats his "girls."

WORKS CITED

Aquino Moreschi, Alejandra. "De la indignación moral a las protestas colectivas: la participación de los migrantes zapotecos en las marchas de migrantes de 2006." *Norteamérica* 5, 1 (2010): 63–90.

Agrela Romero, Belén. "De los significados de género e inmigración (re)producidos en las políticas sociales y sus consecuencias para la acción e integración social." *Migrations and Social Policies in Europe*. June 8–9, 2006. Sesión de Trabajo. Pamplona: Universidad Pública de Navarra, 2006. 1–20.

Balibar, Etienne. "Is There a 'Neo-Racism'?" *Race, Nation, Class: Ambiguous Identities*. Ed. Etienne Balibar and Immanuel Wallerstein. London: Verso, 1991, 17–28.

Brandt, Stefan L. "The City as Liminal Space: Urban Visuality and Aesthetic Experience in Postmodern U.S. Literature and Cinema." *American Studies* 54(4) (2009): 553–81.

Briceño Linares, Ybelice. "Inmigración, exclusión y construcción de la alteridad: La figura del inmigrante en el contexto español." Coord. Daniel Mato. *Políticas de ciudadanía y sociedad civil en tiempos de globalización.* Caracas: FACES, Universidad Central de Venezuela: 2004. 201–19.

Calavita, Kitty. "Immigration, Law and Marginalization in a Global Economy: Notes from Spain." *Law and Society Review* 32(2) (1998): 529–66.

Castells, Manuel. "The Net and the Self: Working Notes for a Critical Theory of the Informational Society." *Critical Anthropology* 16(1) (1996): 9–38.

Donald, James. "Metropolis: The City as Text." *Social and Cultural Forms of Modernity*. Eds. Robert Bobcock and Kenneth Thompson. Cambridge: Open University, 1992, 417–71.

Fainstein, Susan S. *City Builders: Property, Politics and Planning in London and New York*. Oxford: Blackwell Press, 1994.

Friedman, Jonathan. "Where We Stand: A Decade of World City Research." *World Cities in a World System*. Eds. P. L. Knox and P. J. Taylor. Cambridge: Cambridge University Press, 1995, 21–47.

Gennep, Arnold van. *The Rites of Passage*. Trans. Monika B. Vizedom and Gabrielle L. Caffee. Chicago: University of Chicago Press, 1960.

Kelbaugh, Douglas S. *Repairing the American Metropolis*. Seattle: University of Washington Press, 2002.

Low, Setha M. "The Anthropology of Cities: Imagining and Theorizing the City." *Annual Review of Anthropology* 25 (1996): 383–409.

Mayock, Ellen. "West Meets East in Rosa Montero's *Instrucciones para salvar el mundo*." *Cuaderno Internacional de estudios humanísticos y literatura* 6 (2011): 162–71.

Montero, Rosa. *Instrucciones para salvar el mundo*. Madrid: Santillana, 2008.

Reid, Michelle. "Urban Spaces and Canadian Identity in Charles de Lint's 'Svaha.'" *Science Fiction Studies* 33 (3) (2006): 421–37.

Soja, Edward W. *Postmetropolis: Critical Studies of Cities and Regions*. Malden: Blackwell Press, 2000.

Chapter Two

"Una mezcla de amor profundo y asco": A/Version of Multiculturalism in Lucía Etxebarria's *Cosmofobia*

Hayley Rabanal

Lucía Etxebarria's 2007 novel, *Cosmofobia*, contemporaneously set in Madrid's multicultural *barrio* of Lavapiés, closes on a powerful image of childbirth in which the narrator recollects her first glimpse of her newborn daughter and the ambivalent feelings this elicited in her:

> Veía un bulto que se movía, completamente cubierto de sangre y de una baba viscosa que, supongo, eran restos de placenta adheridos a la piel del bebé: la vida, que desde el principio mismo, causa una emoción que hace llorar, una mezcla de amor profundo y asco. [I saw a wriggling form, completely covered in blood and a gooey substance that must have been the remains of the placenta sticking to the baby's skin: life, right from the beginning it provokes an emotional reaction that makes you cry; a mixture of profound love and disgust.] (366)

These charged words follow evocations of the fictional Lavapiés as a site of embattlement, struggle, an abyss (363, 365, 366). It is as if the emergence of new life and, with it, love, in this concluding passage seeks to mitigate the largely negative impression of coexistence there by offering a final message of optimism and hope. Structurally, this seems necessary for two reasons: first, the stark criminal revelations regarding one of the novel's pivotal immigrant characters, which are also part of the denouement; and, second, Etxebarria's extra-literary assertions about her aims. She has stated that the novel promotes the idea of dialogue over confrontation ("Etxebarria retrata"), a matter of urgency in a context in which she observes that levels of xenophobia are rising ("La escritora"). Etxebarria's arresting image of abjection—

intertwining love and disgust—is highly suggestive for the subject matter explored in the novel and crystallizes the ambivalence I argue characterizes the novel's stance toward the immigrant others depicted in the fictionalized multicultural space of Lavapiés.

As influentially theorized by Julia Kristeva, abjection is the process by which the borders of the self are constituted and maintained, originating in the first separation from the mother. Yet these borders are not solid and fixed: although the abject, "the jettisoned object" (*Powers* 2), opposed to the "I" of subjectivity, is "radically excluded," it lingers on the edge of consciousness "challenging its master" (2) and "simultaneously beseeches and pulverizes the subject" (5). Ambiguity is a critical feature, since the opposition between self and other, inside and outside is "vigorous but pervious, violent but uncertain" (7). In this way, the abject both establishes and menaces selfhood and, consequently, signifies "a deep anxiety over the possibility of losing one's subjectivity" (McAfee 49). Embarking on motherhood, perhaps the most intimate relation with an other, is likely to be one circumstance in which such anxiety might arise, for Kristeva argues that abjection is experienced as particularly intense when the subject is faced with her own otherness or strangeness: "when it finds that the impossible constitutes its very *being*, that it *is* none other than abject" (5, original emphasis).

It is significant that Etxebarria highlights abjection following childbirth apparently as a distillation of the novel's problematization toward otherness. Not the subject's original abjection of the mother to forge the boundaries of subjectivity but, rather, the mother's feelings of abjection toward what her own body has generated; what was once inside, blurring the distinction between self and other in a relation that can be thought of as "the very embodiment of alterity-within" (Oliver 4). The traces of these unstable borders contained within the maternal body, which render both the subject and the other's identity questionable, remain discernible in the remnants of the placenta clinging to the infant's skin.[1] In choosing to depict a mother's partial disgust toward these "restos," the narrator exhibits a foundational abjection, a "casting out" or rejection of the other, that in the context of a novel about multiculturalism has clear implications for attitudes toward immigrant others.

Etxebarria's image is reminiscent of Kristeva's deployment of the radical expression of "otherness within" encapsulated in pregnancy and birth as a potential model for an ethics of engagement with the other that does not resort to the idea of the self-same as the grounds for ethical obligations (Oliver 4–7). This model is pertinent for conceptualizing interrelationship with those with whom blood ties or salient similarities may not be shared, or where relying on similarities to conceive of the other may involve reduction to a version of the same in a tyrannical relation. In the case of Spain and the reception of Moroccan Muslim immigrants specifically—a central issue in

Cosmofobia—there is a seemingly paradoxical situation which captures this well. Daniela Flesler persuasively argues that of all immigrant groups they face the most hostility (2): on the one hand, they are viewed as less assimilable because of the perception that they are culturally very different; while on the other, the historical ties between Spain and Morocco, entailing mutual invasion and conquest, and the disquieting figure of the *Morisco* for a homogenous Spanish identity, mean that they are threateningly similar (3–10).[2]

It is precisely this combination of the familiar and the alien that Kristeva emphasizes as disturbing for identity. In *Strangers to Ourselves*, she directly addresses the challenges posed by immigration by invoking another model of "alterity within"—the existence of the unconscious as implying an already heterogeneous and divided self in its composite "incoherences" and "strangenesses" (2)—to contemplate how the subject might strive consciously to overcome an instinctual aversion to be "able to live with the others, to live *as others*, without ostracism but also without leveling" (2). If, as noted, abjection is heightened in conditions where an impression of internal otherness is more acute, then confrontation with those who deeply unsettle self-identity would seem especially prone to produce those conditions. As Kristeva summarizes, "the weight of foreigners . . . is also determined by the consciousness of being somewhat foreign as well" (19).

The term "cosmofobia," defined by the *Urban Dictionary* as "Morbid dread of the cosmos and realising ones [*sic*] true place in it" in one of *Cosmofobia*'s two epigraphs, evokes this unsettling and the fear of alterity which might be occasioned by multiculturalism. In signaling the tenuousness of the borders between self and other in a moment of abjection/self-abjection, *Cosmofobia* appears implicitly to advocate a Kristevan ethics. This chapter investigates how the novel in fact mostly undercuts such a model by focusing on the character Yamal Benani and the attendant sustained critique of multiculturalism. An Arab Muslim immigrant from Morocco, Yamal arguably provides an archetypal model of otherness for an exploration of the multicultural in Spain.[3] Further, he is configured as a confoundingly ambiguous body whose ambiguity is rather satisfyingly unraveled for the reader by a fictional version of the author herself in the concluding chapter. I am not primarily concerned here with Etxebarria as an individual—although ambivalence and contradiction can be considered hallmarks of her fiction (Bermúdez 100)—but instead with how her novel resonates with attitudes in Spain and Europe at large toward immigration and multiculturalism in an international political climate in which Arab Muslims are a stigmatized population, a reality bolstered by the circulation of negative stereotypes in contemporary Western media and cultural production.[4]

Nevertheless, given Etxebarria's framing of her novel with progressive intentions and her authorial presence in the narrative, the reader is naturally

invited to associate her closely with its principal discourse. In spite, or perhaps because, of this she issues what reads like a statement of disavowal in
regard to its content: a second epigraph cites artist Alfredo Álvarez Plágaro
averring that his work is by and large "accidental" and "casi siempre estoy en
desacuerdo de por dónde va" [I'm almost always at odds with where it's
going] (6).[5] Additional disavowals mark the text, suggesting that the author
is attuned to the thorny nature of the topic and seeking to dissociate herself
from any borderline racist or xenophobic views within it—there are places
where these are obvious, such as the reporting of racist insults or xenophobic
attitudes (e.g., 16, 28, 47–48, 70, 87). When it is clearly the narrator's perspective, Moroccans are referred to as "árabes" rather than the pejorative
term "moro" applied elsewhere (e.g., 87, 97, 196, 345). Furthermore, a dis-
claimer explains that some of the characters are real people and certain
events inspired by testimonials collected by the author, thus also intimating a
limited responsibility for what follows (8).[6]

   As stated, it is important to situate *Cosmofobia* in the broader context of
debates concerning multiculturalism. Written and published prior to the global financial crisis, Etxebarria's aims reported earlier are consistent with the
largely positive stance of the Partido Socialista Obrero Español government
on immigration at the time (Kennedy 196). More broadly, they echo then
Prime Minister José Luis Rodríguez Zapatero's "Alliance of Civilizations
between the Western and the Arab and Muslim worlds" (5), which he had
proposed at the UN in September 2004 following the Madrid train bombings—perpetrated by terrorists affiliated with al-Qaeda, several of whom
were of Moroccan origin—and whose formulation implied a contestatory
response to Samuel Huntington's influential "clash of civilizations" thesis.[7]
Etxebarria's desire to promote dialogue in the face of confrontation carries
with it the assumption of conflict within a multicultural space. Contrary to
her solidary intentions, this pessimistic outlook tends to be embedded in the
novel, ultimately concurring with a Huntingtonian paradigm of inherent in-
compatibility and inevitable antagonism between Islam and the West.

   One notable way in which the novel underwrites this paradigm is through
the opposition of the concepts of multiculturalism and interculturalism.
Multiculturalism is a polysemic and sometimes contested term (Meer and
Modood 179), so for the purposes of this chapter, I draw on Tariq Modood
and Nasar Meer's review of theorizations of both terms to probe the rather
narrow understandings offered by Etxebarria intra- and extra-diegetically. In
their efforts to ascertain whether interculturalism differs significantly from
multiculturalism and/or constitutes an updated elaboration of it, Meer and
Modood identify four key traits: that interculturalism is more concerned with
promoting dialogue and communication; facilitates an interactive and vibrant
cultural "exchange"; fosters social cohesion and national citizenship; and is
less relativistic than multiculturalism and therefore more able to be critical of

illiberal cultural practices (177). Overall, they conclude that the qualities associated with interculturalism are integral to versions of multiculturalism, arguing that the latter has not yet been intellectually superseded (192). Even so, Modood recognizes elsewhere that multiculturalism is in crisis and it is specifically Muslims who are targeted in the critique of multiculturalism that typifies dominant political discourses in Western Europe (Modood 158).

Etxebarria tends to reflect this widespread "disaffection with multiculturalism" (Modood 158). She maintains that while *Cosmofobia* is set in Lavapiés, it could represent any multicultural district in Spain, for in such places, as she sees it, the inhabitants "conviven pero no se mezclan, y conforman por tanto una sociedad multicultural pero no intercultural" [live together but they don't mix, and therefore they make up a multicultural rather than an intercultural society] ("La escritora"). Her verdict is frequently reiterated in *Cosmofobia*; for example, Antón, a volunteer at a children's play center run by social services, shares social worker Claudia's observation that "el barrio es multicultural, no intercultural . . . ; las comunidades se toleran pero no se mezclan, los límites se respetan" [the neighborhood is multicultural, not intercultural . . . ; the communities tolerate one another, boundaries are respected] (27). Besides criticizing the existing state of affairs, the remarks here and elsewhere in the novel can be read as a general indictment of multiculturalism. The idea of separate spheres with little or no interaction or exchange between them, thus harboring the potential for antagonism, versus an intercultural ideal in which such segregation and mutual disengagement would be overcome, is congruent with the positive contrasting of interculturalism with multiculturalism by critics of the latter "in a manner," observe Meer and Modood, "that is not necessarily endorsed by wider advocates of interculturalism" (177). In other words, the negative verdict on multicultural Lavapiés and Etxebarria's rather reductive characterization of multiculturalism is reminiscent of what Meer and Modood identify as the appropriation of interculturalism in the critique of multiculturalism (177). Furthermore, Etxebarria inadvertently conforms to Spanish right-wing, anti-immigration discourse that impugns multiculturalism for social ills. [8]

Etxebarria's vision of multiculturalism is replicated in the novel's diegetical structure of multiple, interconnecting stories. These are conveyed in character-focused chapters, some of which rely on the conceit of recorded interviews while others use an omniscient third-person perspective, occasionally focalized through its key character, or have a first-person narration. The novel is introduced in the opening chapter by a first-person narrator who seeks to establish an intimate relationship with the reader, addressing her as "tú" and inviting her on a "guided tour" of the *barrio*. Though unnamed, the reader can easily identify this as a version of the author given the reference to her daughter (also one of the novel's dedicatees) and other details many readers will know about Etxebarria, given her very public persona. [9] In subsequent chapters, the narrator's presence recedes into the background (until the final installment, discussed next), but the reader is periodically reminded of her role in the construction of the narrative through characters' references to her as a writer (24, 250), or the process of recording their conversations (52). Attesting to the narrator's adeptness as a mediator across the separate spheres of Lavapiés, Amina (born in Algeciras to Moroccan parents) and a famous Spanish actress, Leonor, both insist that she is their preferred interlocutor (148, 249). Yet this trustworthiness is somewhat negated by the fact that the novel proceeds to reveal what the narrator promises to keep confidential. This also compromises the intention to enable the immigrant characters to speak for themselves, an intention which recalls one of the core tenets of multiculturalism (Modood 160). Ultimately, the effect in *Cosmofobia* is of an unproblematized appropriation of their voices, a technique employed by Etxebarria elsewhere.[10] Here the issue is elided via the immigrant characters' granting of the interviews, although the asymmetry of the relationship is underscored by their deferral to the narrator who is addressed as "usted."

The "insider perspective" claimed is also problematic for other reasons. Author and narrator both reside in Lavapiés amid a daunting diversity that is signaled in a far from neutral manner. The narrator observes that her daughter is often the only blonde child who plays in the park with children who are "casi siempre . . . morenos" [mostly dark-skinned] (12), thus flagging her "tolerant" and "progressive" attitude while aligning herself with a perspective of Spanish identity as homogenously "white" and European. The intricacy of the interweaving narrative strands structurally evokes the complexity and plurality of the community—there is a cast of more than one hundred characters listed in an appendix, accompanied by brief biographies, presumably to help the reader keep track. But the impression is that such pluralism is overwhelming and indicative of a fragmented community under pressure. The very title "Cosmofobia" expresses an intractable vastness and disorientation akin to what Ulrich Beck describes in his eloquent evaluation of cosmopolitanism as "[g]lobal sense, a sense of boundarylessness" that contains both "the 'anguish' but also the possibility of shaping one's life and social relations under conditions of cultural mixture" (3). It is the negative side of this ambivalent awareness of "boundarylessness" that prevails via the representation of Lavapiés as a mainly dysfunctional space in which drugs and violence predominate. There are repeated assertions of the dangerousness of the *barrio*, which after dark becomes a no-go area for taxi drivers (30, 97, 127) and in which police suspect the existence of terrorist cells (101).

Domestic violence is also prevalent and can occur with impunity, partly owing to the perceived relativism of multiculturalism: "Maltrato psicológico, lo llaman unos. Diferente cultura, lo llaman otros. Un hijo de puta, le llamo yo" [Some call it psychological abuse, others call it cultural difference. A son of a bitch is the name I'd give it] (141), proclaims Esther in relation to the story of Amina, previously entrapped in an abusive relationship with Karim and, despite being born and raised in Spain, remains subject to restrictive Moroccan cultural norms regarding gender (147). Conversely, some of the Spanish characters, who happily form part of the hegemonic culture, reap the benefits of an advanced modern society and are to a degree protected from patriarchal violence. Thanks to the provisions of the 2004 *Ley contra la Violencia de Género*, for example, Sonia's father has been prosecuted for violence, and the threat of further action suffices to keep his aggressive impulses in check (46–48).[11] There is evidently a self-congratulatory element to these observations in that they highlight Spain's modernity in contradistinction with the "backwardness" of cultures founded on values portrayed as intrinsically irreconcilable with European ones. Unsurprisingly, intercultural relationships are on the whole precluded (26–27, 66, 142, 147). The sole real exception is Alba and Aziz, a couple which it is made plain only functions because he is a "calzonazos" [a wimp] (48), that is, effectively emasculated. In this way, *Cosmofobia* confirms the impossible nature of intercultural romance recurrent in Spanish literature and film about immigration.[12] None of the other love relationships featured fares much better, but in short it is difficult not to connect the catalogue of problems that beset the fictional Lavapiés to the immigrant presence. Other than the narrator, the only character able to navigate this bewildering multiculturality is Yamal Benani.

Despite the foregrounding of the intercultural as an ideal, or refined version of multiculturalism, the novel is ambivalent and even displays aversion toward multiculturalism in any form. Yamal Benani exemplifies this uneasiness and as a Lebanese-Moroccan Muslim Arab, serves as a placeholder for all Muslim Arabs, not just those from North Africa who chiefly compose the immigrant population. The final chapter divulges that not only is he the distributor in Spain for a major Moroccan drug network, he is also a plagiarist who has achieved his current wealth and artistic renown through stealing others' ideas, purchasing his own paintings with the profits of drug trafficking and is probably responsible for the murder and dismemberment of a North American art curator, Michael Tarantine, whom he attempted to seduce in order to further his career.

Yamal, however, is a cosmopolitan, intercultural being, and a potential site for interculturality. All the characters are connected to him, via romance, business, or friendship. He is also cast in a confessor role similar to the narrator's, establishing him as a foil to her, particularly given their encounter in the final chapter. With his bar *La Taberna Encendida*, he has accomplished "lo imposible" (361), since it is frequented by inhabitants from the range of social classes and cultural groups that make up Lavapiés, acting as a nexus among them. Yamal himself is an amalgam of European and Eastern traits, having been raised in Paris and a graduate of the Sorbonne—he is sometimes referred to as French (87, 346). Unlike the other Moroccan Muslims, then, he straddles and is fully conversant with the *barrio*'s distinct worlds, consisting of the varied immigrant populations, the Spanish working class, and the affluent bohemian middle and upper-middle classes. Depending on his interlocutor, Yamal is religious or secular, drinks alcohol or abstains, is heterosexual, homosexual, or bisexual, holds forth on postmodernist theory or engages in black magic. His chameleonic character is conducive to facilitating intercultural interaction yet at the same time he embodies the perturbing ambiguity of the stranger, who in "multiplying masks and 'false selves'. . . is never completely true nor completely false" (Kristeva, *Strangers* 8). The depiction of Yamal as an ambiguous body is also replete with Orientalist clichés voiced by several characters: he is physically attractive and hypnotizing (88, 149–50, 196, 214), but a dark force (195) who is diabolical, irresistible (259) and pertains to the realm of the exotic, unknown and forbidden (260). Such tropes indulge and remobilize the association identified by Edward Said of the Orient and "Orientals" with "the freedom of licentious sex" (190) and as "synonymous with the exotic, the mysterious, the profound, the seminal" (Said 51). Yamal's enigmatic intervention with Moroccan magic even causes an apparently infertile couple, Isaac and Claudia, to conceive. Although not presented as the result of infidelity, stuck in a monotonous relationship which, moreover, is founded on an initial deception by Isaac, both characters harbor desires for "exotic" others; Amina in Isaac's case (203) and Yamal in Claudia's (195–96). Because these desires conform to the same Orientalist stereotypes, what might otherwise be interpreted as a gesture toward *mestizaje* as a potential solution to the stagnation and disillusionment of the Spanish characters' relationships is essentially textually foreclosed. In fact, *Cosmofobia* dwells disproportionately on the emotional dilemmas faced by the Spanish characters. Over half of the novel is exclusively occupied with them, ultimately suggesting a waning interest in the issue of multiculturalism which finally coalesces in the figure of Yamal.

The ambivalence toward Yamal is borne out by the revelations of the aptly titled concluding chapter "Le beau terrible," which also positions him as a placeholder for a suspect multiculturalism: the narrator admits that he is the object of her fascination because he represents "la esencia misma del barrio" [the very essence of the neighborhood], concealed "tras tantos disfraces distintos . . . todas estas gentes que viven juntas pero que no se conocen ni se reconocen" [behind so many different disguises . . . all these people who live together without knowing or recognizing one another] (363).[13] Significantly, here the narrator takes center stage and the correspondence between author and narrator is accentuated by having the latter, now explicitly, "Lucía Etxebarria" who is writing "esta novela" [this novel] (343, 361), reflect on her decade-long acquaintance with Yamal beginning in 1992. The symbolic significance of that year is emphasized with reference to the events Spain hosted (Barcelona Olympics, Madrid as Cultural Capital of

Europe, the World Exposition in Seville) which celebrated its status "as a modern, democratic, European nation-state" (Graham and Sánchez 406). And a critical meeting with Yamal occurs days before the *Día de la Hispanidad* (346), which in 1992 marked the quincentenary of Columbus's 1492 voyage to the New World, but also, of course, the culmination of the Reconquista and the ensuring purging of the Islamic element of Spanish identity (346).[14] An additional indicator of Spain's European credentials in 1992 came with its transformation into an attractive destination for immigration following European Union entry. It hardly seems coincidental that Yamal arrives at this conjunction: obliquely, 1992 initiated a dysfunctional present.

The narrator's emergemce in the foreground of the diegesis is not just an assertion of authority by assuming charge of the narrative, it also proffers a psychologically rather satisfying unmasking of Yamal, the only main character to whose thoughts the reader is denied access. His unfathomableness recalls Kristeva's conceptualization of the stranger as a "lost origin," and "[a]lways elsewhere" (*Strangers* 5, 7, 10), and is mirrored in the narrator's characterization of Yamal as "una presencia siempre ausente" [an always absent presence] (351). Insofar as she is able to glean information regarding his origins, she discovers that his father was a notorious government minister, responsible for the torture and incarceration of political prisoners (347), suggestive of a nefarious biological heredity that has broader historical implications.[15] In any case, the relation of power established by Etxebarria in the author/narrator-versus-character dichotomy and her detective role in a sense tells us all we need to know, giving the narrator mastery over her subject, much as Said reflects in a cognate context that asserting knowledge is an act of power (32).

Such a move runs contrary to the model of ethical relation with the other alluded to via the closing image of childbirth and abjection/self-abjection. It is possible now to return to the element of disgust registered there to consider its implications for the relationship between Yamal and the narrator. In Sara Ahmed's intriguing analysis of how emotions operate to align individual and collective bodies with orientations toward others, she scrutinizes disgust as a reaction to immigrant others and, specifically, Muslim Middle Easterners in the wake of the 9/11 attacks (82–100). In her account, she stresses the profoundly ambivalent nature of disgust which involves both desire/attraction and repulsion (84). The former is manifest in the seductive pull Yamal exerts on the narrator: "me arrastraba como un remolino" [he swept me away like a whirlwind] (353), leaving her physically craving his presence after a few days' absence. Crucially, though, in contrast to the other female—and male—characters in the novel, the narrator alone manages not to capitulate to her desires and consummate the relationship, and her resistance to his charms, her self-mastery, appears to be validated by what she later uncovers. According to Ahmed, while the "contradictory impulses" inherent in the disgust reaction may not resolve, they nevertheless always terminate in the recoiling of the subject faced with repulsion and, tellingly, Etxebarria's narrator does indeed pull away (84). In so doing, she reinstates the border between subject and object that Ahmed posits is simultaneously identified *and* generated through the sense of border transgression which is felt in disgust, and which stems from a perceived excessive proximity (87).

The question of borders which need to be policed, insinuated by Yamal's disruptive unclassifiability is further obliquely explored in reference to Gilles Deleuze's concepts of difference and repetition. Etxebarria also makes her text playfully performative of these concepts by including details about art exhibitions and characters which have verifiable, albeit slightly different, "real life" equivalents, just as her narrator has a "real life" counterpart. When Lucía-narrator re-encounters Yamal at the exhibition *Repetición/ Transformación*, he is trying to impress art curator, Michael Tarantine, and she realizes that he is plagiarizing her friend Álvarez Plágaro's *Cuadros Iguales*. These are sets of seemingly identical paintings whose small discrepancies are intended to illustrate Deleuze's notion that difference inhabits repetition (Deleuze 76). The key point made in Yamal's rendering of Deleuze is that difference is always represented in relation to a preexisting identity envisaged within a hierarchical binary (350). However, the fact that he is plagiarizing these ideas obstructs a possible reading of Deleuze's critique of identity as being deployed in Yamal's favor. In the Deleuzian scheme, the concept of plagiarism would be open to interrogation, just as the paintings by Plágaro (whose very name references the practice), purposefully have no original.[16] Yet in a reversion to the conventional idea of the defective copy, the narrator condemns Yamal's lack of originality and cites his plagiarism as evidence of his fanaticism: his boundless ambition reveals a "pathological" (358) character.[17]

The revelation that Yamal is a plagiarist also recasts the act of plagiarism as a metaphor for his threatening similarity—a repetition that is perilously transgressive (Deleuze 3). Foreshadowing Tarantine's murder, the chapter opens with the narrator studying the sinister quality of the (as we later learn) plagiarized *Cuadros Gemelos* he has given her. Over time, she notices that two wine-colored areas seem to be growing darker, evoking blood stains. Can all this be understood as a postmodern, ironic twist to a novel inexplicably turned *novela negra*? The closing words introduce another repetition, the cycle of life, which as suggested, seems to advocate the embrace of the other. The ambivalence encompassed in the narrator's feelings of abjection/ self-abjection perhaps even hints at the fact that the author whom she closely resembles[18] and who has laudable social intentions is herself inevitably unconsciously susceptible to hostility toward the immigrant others in her midst—in other words, it is another strategy of disavowal. But this double game is unconvincing. Even earlier than "Le beau terrible," we learn that there are other stereotypes that Yamal neatly fits, such as his abysmal treatment of Miriam, his Spanish girlfriend, which leads her to attempt suicide, thus fulfilling all her mother's expectations about how a "moro" behaves toward women (87–92).

In conclusion, it can be argued that the novel operates to institute a more basic repetition: that of prevalent negative cultural stereotypes. If, as Etxebarria claims, the novel was written to combat the widespread "fear of the unknown," which she censures the mainstream media for fomenting ("Etxebarria retrata"), then the character of Yamal, and the multiculturalism he represents, belie these conciliatory motivations. Through him, immigration and multiculturalism are connected with illegal—indeed murderous—activities and other dangers that evoke the threat of terrorism, metonymically prefigured in one tongue-in-cheek reference to him by Sonia as "un arma de seducción masiva" [a weapon of mass seduction] (126). These are the dangers intrinsic to the divided loyalties underlined in the narrator's wary description of the mainly Muslim immigrant inhabitants of Lavapiés as "adscritos a una patria, pero emocionalmente fieles a otra" [administratively attached to one country, but emotionally loyal to another] (363). Lamentably, it is a view which buttresses the habitual portrayal of Muslims in the West as "unenlightened outsiders" who, alarmingly, "still have an allegiance to values different from those recognized in Europe and North America" (Morey and Yaqin 145). The text thus registers intense disquiet about any kind of improved version of multiculturalism in interculturalism. Yamal is somewhat of a Trojan Horse: he is homegrown, European-grown, and it is partly his uncanny ability to integrate by knowing what to say and how to behave in every situation (358) that constructs him as a risk. Notwithstanding that the novel's ambivalence verging on aversion is conveyed through what can be construed an inherently unreliable narrator, but this slippery device also refuses the reader a coherent critical position from which to read the narrative. Furthermore, to keep reproducing negative stereotypes in a context already saturated with them, without, for example, putting the reader in the position of the foreigner who makes "[the truth] and himself relative," is insidiously counterproductive (Kristeva, *Strangers* 7).[19] On a social reading, then, the novel largely fails, especially in light of its ending, which has to be interpreted as either so ironic and ludic as to nullify the author's stated aims, or as (an albeit inadvertent) vindication of current fears and suspicion directed toward (notably Arab Muslim) immigrant others that contributes to their continued stigmatization. Neither conclusion is satisfactory. Moreover, the author's intimations that the novel has a basis in fact cements ideas of criminality and fanaticism, which Yamal Benani ultimately emblemizes, as the worrying potential underside of multiculturalism in Spain.

NOTES

1. As Kelly Oliver elucidates, the other is contained within the maternal body without this resulting in the disintegration of the mother's identity. It is this ambiguity surrounding subject and object positions, and the ensuing destabilizing of notions of identity and difference, that gives rise to Kristeva's "herethics," a reconceptualization of the ethical relation to the other founded on the idea of "otherness within" (4–5).

2. It is worth noting in this connection that a framework of underlying commonality was strategically deployed by Spain from the mid-nineteenth century through the Franco regime to justify colonial enterprises in Morocco (Martín-Márquez 50–63).

3. In his analysis of the Spanish colonial penetration of Morocco in the years preceding the Civil War, Sebastian Balfour discusses how the figure of the Moor/Moroccan was imagined as the 'archetypal Other of Spanish national identity' (194), a construction that was nevertheless riven with ambiguity and contradiction given its long history of formulation and reformulation and, during the Civil War, the ideological incoherence and pragmatism of the Nationalists (193–202, 280–87).

4. This issue is extensively explored in a special issue of *Interventions* 12(2) (2010): "Muslims in the Frame."

5. As discussed later, the artist is also a character in the novel, who is plagiarized by Yamal.

6. It is beyond the scope of this short essay to incorporate discussion of other Spanish novels on this subject, hence it functions as a kind of discrete case study with the corresponding limitations this presupposes. See, for example, Tabea Alexa Linhard (2007) for an overview of immigration literature.

7. Huntington contends, in his 1993 article, that future sources of conflict will be of a cultural nature and take place between a number of "civilizations," with Arabs posited as a subdivision of an Islamic "civilization" inherently antagonistic to the West.

8. Responding to the success of Jean Marie le Pen, leader of the French racist party, the Front National, in the first round of the 2002 presidential election, José María Aznar, then Prime Minister of the right-wing Partido Popular government, saw this as symptomatic of European center-left policies, declaring that "Multiculturalism divides society: it is not living together, it is not integration" (quoted in Encarnación 185). More controversially, Mikel Azurmendi, president of the Foro para la Integrácion Social de la Immigrantes during the PP goverment (2000-2004), once reviled multiculturalism in parliament as an "authéntica gangrena de nuestro sistema democràtico (Azurmendi 103 n.1)"

9. Francisca López notes her "preponderant position" and cultivation of an "outspoken and often controversial" public image (2).

10. See Linhard's critique of her "seamless appropria[tion] of the voice" of a young Saharawi woman (410–11) in the 2005 short story "Sintierra."

11. Whist also registering some of the tensions and contradictions in Etxebarria's endeavors to attentuate and problematize narrational authority, Maryanne Leone's gender-inflected analysis of *Cosmofobia* ("Narrating Immigration") offers a more positive reading of her construction of the immigrant experience by concentrating on the common struggles faced by the diverse female characters and the potential therein for transnational feminist solidarity.

12. See Flesler "New Racism, Intercultural Romance" and *Return of the Moor*, chapter 4.

13. "Reconocer" means to recognize in the sense of "to accept" as well as simply "to identify." This play of meanings, germane to the issues at stake, is less prominent in the English.

14. The failure to engage adequately with the past in the 1992 public events is criticized by Graham and Sánchez (406, 408).

15. Namely, the brutality of the Moorish/Moroccan other which can be seen as stemming from the racism and historical "myth-making" noted by Balfour (195).

16. Anecdotally, it is noteworthy that Etxebarria has twice faced allegations—refuted in both cases—of plagiarism (Aparicio).

17. Yamal's "mimicking" of a Spanish artist could also be read as symbolic of the perceived risks to Spanish identity of immigration which are enmeshed in longstanding anxieties over Spain's Islamic past and how that legacy continues to "disrupt" the present (Aidi).

18. Etxebarria herself has specified that "la Lucía personaje no es exactamente la Lucía real, por supuesto, sino un alter ego" [the Lucía character is not exactly the same as the real Lucía, of course, it's an alter ego] ("La escritora").

19. Curiously, this broadly seems to have been Etxebarria's aim: she has explained that Yamal's principle "[n]o existe mi verdad o la del otro, sino mi verdad y la del otro" [there's no such thing as my truth or the other's; there's only my truth *and* the other's] (102) sums up the spirit of the novel ("Etxebarria retrata"), although this would surely be an example of the kind of relativism that she also seems to criticize as part and parcel of multiculturalism.

WORKS CITED

Ahmed, Sara. *The Cultural Politics of Emotion.* New York: Routledge, 2004.

Aidi, Hisham D. "The Interference of al-Andalus: Spain, Islam, and the West." *Social Text 87* 24(2) (2006): 67–85.

Aparicio, Sonia. "Lucía Etxebarria demandada por 'copiar'." *El Mundo,* September 12, 2006. Web. Accessed September 6, 2013.

Azurmendi, Mikel. "Diez tesis Sobre el Multiculturalismo." *Cuadernos de Pensamiento Politi-co* October/November (2005) 97–111.

Beck, Ulrich. *The Cosmopolitan Vision.* Cambridge: Polity Press, 2006.

Balfour, Sebastian. *Deadly Embrace: Morocco and the Road to the Spanish Civil War.* Oxford University Press, 2002.

Bermúdez, Silvia. "Here's Looking at You, Kid": Giving Birth and Authoring, or the Author as Mother and the Mother as Author." *Visions and Revisions: Women ' s Narrative in Twenti-eth-Century Spain.* Eds. Kathleen M. Glenn and Kathleen McNerney. Amsterdam and New York: Rodopi, 2008, 95–107.

Deleuze, Gilles. *Difference and Repetition.* Trans. Paul Patton. London: Continuum, 2004.

Encarnación, Omar. "The Politics of Immigration: Why Spain Is Different." *Mediterranean Quarterly* 15(4) (2004): 167–85.

Etxebarria, Lucía. *Cosmofobia.* Barcelona: Destino, 2007.

———. "Etxebarria retrata a gente de toda raza y condición en *Cosmofobia*." *El Confidencial* March 22, 2007. Web. Accessed May 31, 2013.

———."Lucía Etxebarria, la escritora del realismo se pasa a la literatura infantil." *Europa-press.es.* 15 May 2007. Web. 28 Aug. 2013.

Flesler, Daniela. "New Racism, Intercultural Romance, and the Immigration Question in Con-temporary Spanish Cinema." *Studies in Hispanic Cinema* 1.2 (2004): 103–18.

———. *The Return of the Moor: Spanish Responses to Contemporary Moroccan Immigration .* West Lafayette , IN : University of Purdue Press, 2008.

Graham, Helen , and Antonio Sánchez. " The Politics of 1992. " *Spanish Cultural Studies: An Introduction .* Eds. Helen Graham and Jo Labanyi. New York: Oxford University Press, 1995 , 406–18.

Huntington, Samuel P."The Clash of Civilizations?" *Foreign Affairs* 72(3) (1993): 22–49.

López, Francisca . " Female Subjects in Late Modernity: Lucía Etxebarria ' s *Amor, curiosidad, prozac y dudas .* " *Dissidences: Hispanic Journal of Theory and Criticism* 4.5 (2008): 1 – 23. Accessed August 1 4, 2013.

Kennedy, Paul. "Phoenix from the Ashes. The PSOE Government under Rodríguez Zapatero 2004–2007: A New Model for Social Democracy?" *International Journal of Iberian Studies* 20(3) (2007): 187–206.

Kristeva, Julia. *Powers of Horror: An Essay on Abjection.* Trans. Leon S. Roudiez. New York: Columbia University Press, 1982.

———. *Strangers to Ourselves.* Trans. Leon S. Roudiez. New York: Columbia University Press, 1991.

Leone, Maryanne L. "Narrating Immigration, Gendered Spaces, and Transnational Feminism in Lucia Etxebarria's *Cosmophobia* (2007) *Letras Hispanas* 9.1 (2013): 48–64.

Linhard, Tabea Alexa. "Between Hostility and Hospitality: Immigration in Contemporary Spain." *Modern Language Notes* 122(2) (2007): 400–22.

Martín-Márquez, Susan. *Disorientations: Spanish Colonialism in Africa and the Performance of Identity.* New Haven, CT: Yale University Press, 2008.

McAfee, Noëlle. *Julia Kristeva.* Abingdon: Routledge, 2004.

Meer, Nasar, and Tariq Modood. "How Does Interculturalism Contrast with Multiculturalism?" *Journal of Intercultural Studies* 33(2) (2011): 175–96.

Modood, Tariq. "Multicultural Citizenship and Muslim Identity Politics." *Interventions* 12(2) (2008): 157–70.

Morey, Peter, and Amina Yaqin. "Introduction: Muslims in the Frame." *Interventions* 12(2) (2010): 145–56.

Oliver, Kelly. "Introduction: Julia Kristeva's Outlaw Ethics." *Ethics, Politics and Difference in Julia Kristeva's Writing.* Ed. Kelly Oliver. London: Routledge, 1993, 1–22.

Rodríguez Zapatero, José Luis. "Statement by the President of the Spanish Government, Mr José Luis Rodriguez Zapatero." *United Nations*, September 21, 2004. Accessed May 14, 2013.

Said, Edward W. *Orientalism.* 1978. London: Penguin, 2003.

Chapter Three

The Sum of Us All: Alternative Images of Madrid in Short Stories by Contemporary Women Writers

María del Carmen Alfonso García

REPRESENTING CONTEMPORARY MADRID[1]

On October 6, 2013, under the headline "The Decadence of Madrid," the Sunday magazine of *El País*, one of the most influential newspapers in Spain, ran a lengthy cover story entitled "De Madrid al suelo" [From Madrid to the ground] (Méndez and De Cózar).[2] Its pages offered the image of a city impoverished and defeated by too many instances of bad management, perpetrated by permissive or inefficient members of its local council and the regional government. The dominant image was that of Madrid as a conglomerate, devoid of any specific profile,[3] marred by financial speculation, a city whose cultural life, formerly bordering on the mythical (during the creative years of *La Movida*), lay dying in the midst of general inertia. This grim picture was completed by data on the spectacular decrease in the number of tourists to the city, the highlighting of a sense of decay, both physical and moral (the destitute and homeless installed in their cardboard homes in the heart of the capital), and by reference to the city's future, which, following the failed bid for the 2020 Olympics, rested on its hope of hosting Eurovegas, facing its legal challenges (Méndez and De Cózar 2–5).[4]

Among the many comments composing this portrait of decline, I was particularly struck by the assertion that "Madrid no tiene . . . un relato que la haga conocida e interesante" [Madrid does not have a story . . . to make it well known or interesting] (Méndez and De Cózar 3). The following week, and from the pages of the same publication, writer Elvira Lindo reacted to such pessimism in the form of an article titled "Defensa de Madrid" [In

29

Defense of Madrid]. Expressing her surprise at this statement and, although acknowledging the reference as symbolic and identity-oriented rather than strictly literary, she countered with a homage to the capital city. In her view, no matter how affected by the shortsightedness of its politicians, ideologists, and urban planners, the city maintains its heartbeat through its residents, as "Madrid es resistente por naturaleza" [Madrid is resistant by nature] (Lindo 10).[5]

Madrid has attracted a multitude of literary approaches, which, from Ramón Mesonero Romanos to the present day, have aspired to address the peculiarities and problems of the city. In favor of the city, they show its reading as a national microcosm of critical and intelligent significance; when looking on its dark side, they weave a web of difficult-to-digest topics. Cela and *La Colmena* [The Beehive], like Galdós before him with his "contemporary novels" and Baroja, Valle Inclán or the realists of the mid-twentieth century after him, are essential to this chain of physical and affective cartography which, moving from the center to the suburbs, from wealth to absolute poverty, from the University and the Stock Exchange to the shanties and slums, suggests the multiple conflicts that only a rich network of spaces could produce.

One of the latest links in this long chain is *Madrid, con perdón* [Madrid, If You Don't Mind], a volume published in 2012 by Caballo de Troya and coordinated by Mercedes Cebrián. The collection includes fifteen texts in which the authors write about the capital of Spain in a manner both personal and, at times, unexpected or surprising. These texts share the coexistence of a present and a past, of what is (or might be) next to what has been (or may have been). Their narrative is mostly story, which reads at times as chronicle, at times as essay, and even captures the rhythm of autobiography.

This play between and among genres is disconcerting, as it breaks the pact with the reader in various dimensions and, in so doing, complicates our expectations. It is true that the postmodern paradigm has put us on the trail of what this blurring of boundaries may mean. It allows us to assume that in *Madrid, con perdón*, these genre cracks are indicative of a deeper fissure, one which, by different routes and with various implications, leads us to reflect on an essential splitting of the subject, an aspect I intend to examine in these pages, concentrating on four authors who contribute to this anthology, Esther García Llovet, Natalia Carrero, *Grace Morales* (pen name of Victoria López), and Elvira Navarro.[6]

The reason for the title, *Madrid, con perdón*, according to Mercedes Cebrián (7), relates to the inferiority complex that Madrid feels with respect to Barcelona (and which, I would argue, may be associated with the negative self-image mentioned earlier). However, and leaving aside the (ironic) indulgence which the cover solicits from us, the book offers a superb opportunity to meditate upon specific and crucial questions associated with urban theory.

Without seeking to be exhaustive, the texts prompt questions such as: What do we mean by the very term "city"? What is an urban community? How should we articulate the distance that separates the real and the imagined? How do we interact with spaces? Where do we set the limits between suburbs and city center, the public and the private?

The texts which I discuss here provide an occasion to apply the concept I earlier described as the essential splitting, whose profile is different in each case but always contains an estrangement born of uncertainty and dislocation. The issue of safety appears to be unresolved for Madrid and its inhabitants (or, more precisely, for a specific Madrid and a certain subset of its inhabitants). By this I do not mean only the security related to physical integrity, as discussed theoretically in terms of the "geography of fear," I am referring rather to the broader concept which integrates relationships and contact as guarantors of diversity, described by Jane Jacobs in 1961 (Jacobs 143–51), as an indispensible requirement for the regeneration of the cities.

It would therefore seem useful to adopt the notion explained by Alicia Lindón paraphrasing Francisca Márquez, that in today's city "en términos de orden y coherencia, más bien prevalecen las incongruencias" [in terms of order and coherence, it is mostly incongruity that prevails] ("La ciudad," 14). In this way we open the door to urban imaginaries and their logic of the nonsolid, since, as Néstor García Canclini has argued, cities are much more than the material:

> lo imaginario remite a un campo de imágenes diferenciadas de lo empíricamente observable. Los imaginarios corresponden a elaboraciones simbólicas de lo que observamos o nos atemoriza o desearíamos que existiera. . . . Lo imaginario viene a complementar, a dar un suplemento, a ocupar los huecos y las fracturas de lo que sí podemos conocer. [the imaginary suggests a field of images different from those empirically observable. Imaginaries constitute symbolic productions of what we observe or what we fear or desire to exist. . . . The imagined comes to complement, to supplement, to fill the spaces and fractures in what we are able to know firsthand] (in Lindón "Diálogo con Néstor García Canclini" 90).

These allusions to a cultural geography incorporate a number of theories I will address (De Certeau, Augé, and Bourdieu) and highlight the transcendence of the subject in a universe in tension; a subject who must establish a way of being in the world by engaging with the general values through a process of "refundación territorial" [territorial refounding] (Berdoulay 57). I take this stance to approach the texts as literary expressions of a personal attempt to understand the world in general and to understand ourselves from a specific geographic scale (scale is "the criteria of difference not so much between places as between different *kinds* of places," Smith 1993: 99).

CHRONICLE OF HIDDEN ITINERARIES

"La M–30, gran velada" ["The M–30, A Great Evening"] by Esther García Llovet, was inspired by *London Orbital* (2002), Iain Sinclair's novel on the M25, the highway which circles London. It presents interesting links to Michel de Certeau's iconic "Walking in the City"; in fact, their starting points are identical, as the philosopher and historian places himself on the 110th floor of the World Trade Center to observe Manhattan, while Alcázar, the engineer protagonist of Llovet's story, is on the 33rd floor of the Space Tower in Madrid, one of the four skyscrapers composing the "Cuatro Torres Business Center," which Madrid built, in its day, to compete in the arena of world verticality.

If the French theorist, from his privileged outlook, fantasizes about the possibility of knowledge/power through his reading of the distant lives below, Llovet's character observes the city, this "allá abajo, donde las cosas mortales" [down there, where mortal things are] (García Llovet 143), with a certain empowered air, maybe the result of looking from her unique watchtower, the Catholic chapel which claims to house the highest sacrarium in Spain and possibly in the world (www.capilla torreespacio.es). [7] From the outset the atmosphere is unnerving; only later do we learn that the engineer has attended a funeral mass (hence her being in the chapel) and is in charge of taking the car of the deceased to the funeral home on Madrid's earliest orbital highway, the M–30, and deliver it to a relative of the deceased.

The text, like de Certeau's piece (93), does not believe in the "theoretical simulacrum" of the "panorama-city" which comes from above and immobilizes and homogenizes the world. So Alcázar quickly descends to street level, to road level, and then during her journey, equating journey and discourse, she writes the story of a bewildering and foreboding drive. She moves us from a financial space, which enjoys a certain privilege on the global stage, to another which, along with the cemetery, is today one of the funerary environments par excellence. Hence the twist of the title (in Spanish, the semantic movement from "velada" [evening, celebration] to "velatorio" [wake]).

The itinerary is as much physical as metaphorical. Driving around the M–30, Alcázar enters a space whose coordinates end up being, for her, those of a non-place (Augé 77–78), where isolation and non-communication impose their own law (she has great difficulty finding a bar to have a drink, and she cannot communicate with the Japanese group she meets). At the same time, she moves into a territory of neglect and collapse, in terms of people and physical space: the former Mahou brewery is a ghost building, the rehousing complex of El Ruedo is perceived as a hotspot of danger while the Matadero (slaughterhouse) in Legazpi, the scene of past slaughter and butchering, has been converted into a state-of-the-art cultural center. The engineer protagonist thus crosses the border into a seemingly parallel world, which is almost incomprehensible to her (to the point of suspecting that the bouncers at the Puerta de Hierro Club "no [sean] de verdad" [[are] not real] (García Llovet 146).

From this perspective, the text articulates, along the same lines as de Certeau, an exercise in counter-power. If the city is given meaning by, and imposes its identity through, certain mechanisms of control (de Certeau 95, 98), the subject is able to transgress these margins. The subject's options increase; she or he is able to uncover what the dominant imaginaries wish to conceal and, in rhetorical terms (de Certeau 100), reveal a personal style. By doing so, she or he escapes unsettling cognitive gaps and gives voice to the desire to investigate (Lindón "La ciudad" 93). García Llovet confirms this desire to explore an alternative reality when she says: "Siempre me ha parecido que el extrarradio es más real que el centro, donde todo es autorreferente . . . , mientras que el extrarradio no pretende nada, no tiene ambición de nada" [it has always seemed to me that the suburbs are more real than the center, where everything is self-referencing . . . , while the outskirts do not seek anything, they have no ambition] (Peronal Email 2013).

In the end, late in the evening, nobody shows up to collect the car. Alcázar's three hours of waiting are also a time of solitude: she sits at a table with seven chairs which she slowly lets people take. She eventually leaves the car keys along with a note and, for the second time, in a kind of permanent escape, on the hunt for who knows what destination, she will depart: "al fin lo ve. La Salida de Emergencia. La señal universal del tipo corriendo escaleras arriba como si se lo llevaran todos los diablos" [she finally sees it. The Emergency Exit. The universal sign of the guy escaping, running up the stairs as if chased by the devil himself] (García Llovet 154). This seems a logical ending if we understand, like de Certeau, that "To walk is to lack a place. It is the indefinite process of being absent and in search of a proper" (103) ("proper" standing here for a place to belong, a closure).

In theoretical and literary terms, highlighting the importance of recomposing and redefining a space supposes an act of practical resistance. Alicia Lindón ("La construcción socioespacial de la ciudad" 10), following de Certeau and Denis Cosgrove, reminds us of the efficiency of "la descorporización y la desterritorialización del sujeto que observa" [the disembodiment and deterritorialization of the subject that observes] as a mechanism of domination in colonizing processes. In her own analysis, Lindón works in the opposite direction, with the object of recovering a spatially conceived subject, one that constructs the social with his/her body and emotions and within a dynamic of production/reproduction.

A perfect example of what Lindón postulates may be found in "Necesidad de doblar esquinas" [The need to turn corners], the story by Natalia Carrero. The title evokes Jane Jacobs and her book *The Death and Life of Great*

American Cities where corners are associated with small blocks and these in turn with the neighborhood, with the enriching stroll and, specifically, desirable urban contact and diversity (Jacobs 178–86). None of this, though, is retained in Carrero's text; the setting is that of Las Salesas, one of the most distinguished neighborhoods in Madrid, whose inhabitants match the expected homogenized profile of those living in "una zona consolidada como alternativa perfecta al barrio de Salamanca, de aires más desenfadados, donde abundan las tiendas multimarca" [an area long considered the perfect alternative to the Salamanca neighborhood, with a more casual and easy style, where multibrand shops abound] (www.esmadrid.com/es/salesas). Onto such a "distinguished" and renowned stage enters Lucy, the immigrant Latin American girl who, encouraged by her aunt, is to work as a nanny in the home of Olivia, the young businesswoman who has just had her second child and is trying to succeed with her business. The story can be read in postcolonial terms, showing a persistence of transatlantic hierarchies and revealing the less friendly face of the prefix *trans-*. It is useful to consider here what Pierre Bourdieu defines as symbolic capital (179–93), that which, although material (good taste, good manners, sartorial style, and elegant speech) is perceived as belonging to the sphere of the intangible and almost magical. It thus functions as an invisible element of categorization and hierarchy, thanks to socially instilled and uncritically assumed expectations. This allows the existence of wealthy people, like Olivia and her husband, who continue to believe themselves superior to those less fortunate; people obsessed with health in general and food in particular, whose bodies are, as a consequence of this symbolic logic, bastions of power (McDowell 48). People who construct, and move within, social spaces where the barriers of class and control have been internalized, as they are in the space of the park in the following example:

> [Después de iniciar una conversación con una mujer] Lucy cayó en la cuenta de que no era cuidadora, sino una amiga de la señora, . . . no pudo dejar de sentirse incómoda, como si a partir de ese momento todo lo que hiciera . . . estuviera siendo grabado por la espía . . . , incluso por las cámaras de videovigilancia de los alrededores de la Audiencia Nacional y el Tribunal Superior de Justicia. [[After starting a conversation with a woman] Lucy realized [the other woman] was not a nanny, but a friend of the lady of the house, . . . she could not help feeling uncomfortable, as if from that moment on everything she did . . . would be recorded by the spy . . . even by the security cameras around the Spanish High Courts and the High Court Tribunals.]] (Carrero 34)

From this perspective, the neighborhood and home of her employer become metaphors of an asymmetrical relationship; insistently, street and shop names, advertisements, shop windows and posters and their slogans serve to remind Lucy that this is not her place (the narration articulates this point through focusing on the visual interaction between the nanny and her environment during her comings and goings). And the same is true of the home in which she works, whose layout, without walls to separate the living room and kitchen, for example, is aimed at and succeeds in making the young woman feel insecure and, once again, in alien territory. The story provides an ironic reading of Bachelard's argument that associates home with stability (6) and which McDowell deploys in her essay, enriching it with thought-provoking reflections on "paid domestic labour" (83) and the consequent breakup of the equation home=private=familial.

So close and so distant, in this story, the foundations of community, that elusive abstraction, usually related to a collective project and to solidarity (McDowell 100–101; Jacobs especially 55–73), are broken by prejudices based on status or nationality. Actually, as Simmel (2002) and Wirth pointed out, all that has happened is that community based on caring and goodwill has been replaced by society, built on pecuniary relationships (Wirth 17) and governed by "a spirit of competition, aggrandizement and mutual exploitation" (Wirth 15). To use Bauman's words: community "the kind of world which is not, regrettably, available to us" (3), has been transformed into the *"really existing community:* a collectivity which pretends to be community incarnated" (4, emphasis added). This collective offers security and confidence in exchange for the promotion of attitudes of exclusion and the obliteration of personal freedom.

Carrero's text opts for breaking away: Lucy leaves her job; she seems to reason that only those who wish to be inside allow themselves to be excluded and, in so doing, their options are reduced. With her decision, the young woman resignifies the conflict between security and freedom: by rejecting insider living and its limitations, she opens up to the possibilities of an outside in which life, Life, does not cease to turn and wait round the corner: "Adiós, Olivia García. Hola, próxima esquina" [Goodbye, Olivia García. Hello, next corner] (39).

For García Canclini, cities are always heterogeneous, because they are inhabited by many imaginaries (in Lindón "La ciudad" 91). As has been shown in the previous pages, the subject, through his/her urban practices, may resolve the tensions generated by the clash between his or her own codes and those of the hegemonic representation. In the process, he or she redefines the symbolic tradition which he or she inhabits. If there are no "absolute localizations" (Garcia Canclini in Lindon "La ciudad" 94), it is because the subject exercises his/her capacity for reappropriation and manages to alter a prefixed spatial sense. Lucy, with her attitude, resignifies the neighborhood of Las Salesas in Natalia Carrero's story.

SPATIAL AUTOBIOGRAPHIES

Alicia Lindón ("La construcción socioespacial de la ciudad"10) refers to the "actor territorializado" [territorialized actor] as the "motor de la vida social" [driver of social life] to affirm the interaction between the person who gives a value to a place and the mark that this place leaves on the person. It pertains to a process of identity recomposition which is completely outside the dimension of time. This leads to my second group of texts in the anthology *Madrid, con perdón*: "Gaudeamus porque no nos queda otra" [Gaudeamus because there's no alternative], by Mercedes Cebrián (a skeptical look back on the author's university days); "Puerta Bonita. La forja del barro" [Puerta Bonita. The forging of mud], by *Grace Morales*; "La extraña libertad" [Strange liberty], by Elvira Navarro; and "Una bolsa llena de cómics" [A bag full of comics], by Jimina Sabadú. These works constitute four proposals linked by the trace of autobiography. They share with García Llovet and Carrero the trespassing of limits, both in genre and urban space. They dispense with the framework of genre and, in the case of *Grace Morales* and Elvira Navarro, are set in the periphery, while Jimina Sabadú, in a contrasting approach, explores a gentrified center (Gran Vía/Callao) as a site of generational memory in danger of extinction. [8]

If we are to trust her first lines, *Grace Morales* offers us a fragmentary autobiography: "La costumbre era estar sin un duro e ir andando al centro desde casa" [The custom was to be broke and walk to the city center from home] (*Morales* "Puerta Bonita" 165). But the *auto-* does not take long to become diluted and another biography, that of the district of Carabanchel, occupies the center stage. This in turn soon dissolves into that of the grandmother and the father of the author, before finally returning to the first person. The author explains how her piece makes us understand that, at a deeper level, all these biographies are one:

> La primera [de las razones] es que se trata del barrio de Madrid en que he nacido y crecido, y ahora asisto a su proceso de degradación, antes de que no quede ninguna huella del terreno que yo conocía como escenario de juegos y psicogeografía de mi adolescencia. Pero, sobre todo, es un homenaje a la memoria de mi padre, que murió meses antes de escribirlo y cuya vida va casi en paralelo con ese paisaje del fracaso y de la soledad. Quise que el drama de mi padre, como el de otros muchos madrileños en su situación, el paro producto de la primera reconversión industrial de los años ochenta, el aislamiento personal y familiar quedara reflejado en el texto.

> [The first [of the reasons] is that it is about the neighborhood of Madrid where I was born, and now I am witnessing the process of its degradation, before there is not a single trace left of the territory that I knew as the scene of games and the psychogeography of my adolescence. But, above all, it is a homage to the memory of my father, who died a few months before it was written and whose life runs almost parallel with this landscape of failure and loneliness. I

wanted the drama of my father, like that of many other residents of Madrid in his situation, the unemployment resulting from the first industrial reconversion of the eighties, the personal and family isolation- to be reflected in the text] (*Morales*, Personal email).

On the one hand, and from the perspective of the subject, the strong sense of territoriality that the quote expresses, and which is the origin of "Puerta Bonita. La forja del barro," evokes a spatial logic associated with an extended period of time. Hence the person, the people—the author, her father, and her grandmother—are identified as (they acquire the identity of) having been born, raised and having lived in a place that explains them as individuals and which organizes their social practices:

> Soy de un barrio pequeño, Puerta Bonita. De unas pocas calles en las que se define mi recorrido en el mapa de la rutina y los acontecimientos. . . .
> Sin embargo, los jardines en otoño . . . de Vista Alegre, los muros de ladrillo sin tiempo, las tiendas que resisten, las casas antiguas y el camino desde la plaza del Ayuntamiento por Monseñor Romero . . . hasta el cementerio parroquial, esa ruta que hacía de niña con mi padre y ahora hago sola hasta su tumba, son las únicas cosas tangibles que todavía tienen sentido y significado.
> [I come from a small neighborhood, Puerta Bonita. From a few streets which define my journey in the map of routine and events. . . . However, the autumn gardens . . . of Vista Alegre, the timeless brick, the enduring shops, the old houses and the walk from the Town Hall Square through Monseñor Romero . . . to the parish cemetery, this route that as a child I took with my dad and which now I take alone to his grave, are the only tangible things that still have sense and meaning] (*Morales*, "Puerta Bonita" 180–81).

But, on the other hand, the passing of time introduces into the story the theme of spatial memory and with it, collective imaginings. From this point of view, Puerta Bonita and Carabanchel become a different set, more complex and less placid: they become the landscape of the clash between official History and the counter-memory of the collective, or the landscape of the urban myth that continues to define, persistently, even when circumstances change: "el lugar común de Carabanchel lleva lustros delimitado por la cárcel, la inseguridad ciudadana y el paro" [the commonplace of Carabanchel has been for years delimited by the prison, street danger and unemployment] (*Morales*, "Puerta Bonita" 170).

As García Canclini proposed, the paradigm of urban knowledge has been shifted; to a certain extent, this expert is echoing the approach of de Certeau when he explains that the objective need not specifically be the city, any city, but rather the understanding of "cómo nos situamos respecto de varias ciudades que pueden estar contenidas bajo un mismo nombre" [how we situate ourselves with respect to various cities which might be contained within a single name] (in Lindón "Diálogo con Néstor García Canclini" 92). The text by *Grace Morales* makes clear that urban experiences are not interchange-able in an absolute sense: the subjects, individual and social, provide, through the contribution of historical and biographical time, the successive layers of meaning that turn each place into an imaginary under constant renegotiation.

This layered creation of meanings is central to the next story to be exam-ined, "La extraña libertad," by Elvira Navarro. Set in the Paseo de Extrema-dura, a street which she frequented at a particular point in her life, the writer reflects, from various angles, on the subjective perception of the locality, paying particular attention to the cultural expressions which allow a symbolic (re)interpretation of urban practices.

Hence the text describes, for instance, the journey which begins from the "mera existencia lingüística" [merely linguistic existence] (185) of the places named in the signposts and ends in the real physical sensation she experi-ences when, later, she arrives in them. But it also meditates on the literary, social, and historical echoes—collective imaginaries—that spaces collect over time, and how, in the present, they appropriate the subject and condition his/her life.

Such trajectories are not so strange, but rather to be expected: de Certeau (103–105) explains that toponomy hides a heterodox enterprise: within the subject, the possibilities for movement multiply because, feeling trapped by certain associations and promises, the subject voluntarily changes the direc-tion of his/her steps. In this way a "second, poetic geography" (105), his or her own, enriches his or her dialogue with the environment and redefines it. However, de Certeau also confirms that, "the memorable is that which can be dreamed about a place" (109).

"That which can be dreamed" is, in the end, what can be imagined. And following the theoretical premises of this work, I assume that what can be imagined aspires to be authentic. Hence, as the text seems to suggest, a sense of place is also born of an unresolved tension between past and present, determined by the feeling of loss (Juaristi 279) which, as Navarro expresses with metaliterary implications, not even identity escapes:

> Me interesaba volver a instalarme a través de la escritura en aquella impresión de caos, pérdida y extraña libertad que tenía en aquellos días [en que ya no seguía con su novio y vivía en Carabanchel], o que creo que tenía, pues todo el rato nos estamos inventando las cosas. En definitiva, quería hacer espeleología en la parte de mi subjetividad que se construyó en esos barrios [Paseo de Extremadura y Carabanchel], y que ha generado a través de la escritura algo que no es mi subjetividad ni por supuesto los barrios [I was interested in using writing to take myself back to that impression of chaos, loss and strange sense of freedom I had in those days (when she was no longer with her boyfriend and no longer lived in Carabanchel), or at least I think I had, since we are constant-ly inventing things. I particularly wanted to go potholing in that part of my

subjectivity that was constructed there in those neighborhoods [Paseo de Extremadura and Carabanchel], and that has created through my writing something which is neither my subjectivity nor, of course, the neighborhoods themselves]. (Navarro 202)

CONCLUSION

In the "Prologuillo" [Little Prologue] which opens *Madrid, con perdón*, Mercedes Cebrián cautions that we are about to enter the dark side of the capital of Spain (7). This is clearly the case. But so it must be, if the objective is to draw a cartography of a Madrid beyond the unreal, all-embracing city, through the neighborhoods habitually silenced by hegemonic imaginaries and through the subjects who, with their manners of signifying these spaces, redefine limits and relaunch territories. In this way we are brought to another Madrid, a Madrid inaccessible and unsettling, almost a borderland ("La M–30, gran velada"); one which welcomes newcomers with a deceitful proximity, a concealed weapon of the symbolic power which aspires to perpetuate itself ("Necesidad de doblar esquinas"); one that is the painful result of the combined actions of time and space, aiming to sustain individual memory in the battle against the collective and official ("Puerta Bonita. La forja del barro"); one that knows itself indebted to its cultural constructions, and can doubt its own existence ("La extraña libertad").

Is this the city that, as the slogan of the Regional Government proclaims, is composed of the inclusive "Suma de todos" ["Sum of us all"]? Institutional discourse for this claim is unconvincing. One of the advertisements with which the regional government promotes the idea (https://www.youtube.com/watch?v=02c80KCzJog) merely exploits the commonplace of interculturality through the presence of individuals with different skin color, who together perform the task of painting the flag of the Comunidad Autónoma [autonomous region] of Madrid on the pavement. The colors of the flag, white and red, are used to daub the faces of a young black man or a young Asian woman; perhaps the gesture is meant to be educational, to signify integration, but its image of "happy multicultural land" rings hollow against the current social context and the urban landscape the authors describe in these texts. As the Metropolitan Observatory has claimed, the city and the community are still scenes of difference, inequality and injustice which discriminate equally against nationals and immigrants. However, as I hope I have shown in this article, Madrid is today the sum of us all, including the *her*stories analyzed and the women who appear in them; these writers do integrate traditions, the new, the past and the present, the national and the foreign, the center and the margins of the city. And so they become spokeswomen of a heterogeneity that enriches and questions the overcodified and spectacularized capital that perhaps still believes in its dated postcard image.

NOTES

1. This article is the result of research carried out by the author within the framework of the project of the National Plan of Research (Spain) titled LA CIUDAD FLUIDA: REPRESENTACIONES LITERARIAS DE LA CIUDAD TRANSNACIONAL (reference FF12010-172696). The author wishes to thank Dr. Isabel Carrera Suárez and Dr. María Cristina Valdés Rodríguez, members of the same research group, for their inestimable assistance with the linguistic revision of the English text.

2. The title ironically rewrites the popular saying "De Madrid al cielo, y en el cielo, un agujerito para verlo" [From Madrid to heaven, and in heaven, a little hole to see it through]. It is worth noting that institutional promotion of Madrid as a tourist destination exploits this relationship between Madrid and the ethereal/celestial in a wide variety of ways (see https://www.youtube.com/watch?v=5aW6Fsd4pe0).

3. For a lucid analysis of the effects of mistaken urban planning, see Jacobs (3–25) and Vilagrasa Ibarz.

4. On December 13, 2013, the media released the news that Eurovegas will finally not be built in Alcorcón (Madrid). The central Government of Spain was not prepared to accept the conditions imposed by the magnate Sheldon Adelson.

5. We should remember that one of the great myths of this city is that of the Republican resistance in the face of Franco's troops throughout, more or less, the three years of the civil war. The battle cry of "¡No pasarán!" [They won't get through!] became the symbolic slogan of the community under siege.

6. All these (women) authors give voice to the Spanish literature of the moment. They share interests and concerns (e.g., *Grace Morales* and Jimina Sabadú collaborate in the fanzine *Mondo Brutto*, and Elvira Navarro has reviewed Esther García Llovet's novel *Submáquina* [*Submachine*] and interviewed Natalia Carrero. Generally, they acknowledge the influence of North American realism and frequently cite names such as Clarice Lispector and Georges Perec, while at the same time Spanish literary tradition permeates their works in the form of Galdós, in the case of *Grace Morales*, and Ignacio Aldecoa and Belén Gopegui, in the case of Elvira Navarro.

7. The sacrarium is the receptacle in which are stored the particles which, through the consecration of the Eucharist, are converted into the body of Christ.

8. Jeaveau's "place of memory" deals with the influence of the memory of the experiences as associated with a space, in terms of how they interact in the present with the same place.

WORKS CITED

Augé, Marc. *Non-Places. Introduction to an Anthropology of Supermodernity*. London: Verso, 1995.

Bachelard, Gaston. *The Poetics of Space*. Boston, MA: Beacon Press. 1994.

Bauman, Zygmunt. *Community. Saking Safety in an Insecure World*. Cambridge/Malden, MA: Polity Press/Blackwell, 2001.

Berdoulay, Vincent. "Sujeto y acción en la geografía cultural: el cambio sin concluir." *Boletín de la A. G. E.* 34 (2002): 51–61.

Bourdieu, Pierre. *El sentido práctico*. Buenos Aires: Siglo XXI Editores Argentina, 2007.

Carrero, Natalia. "Necesidad de doblar esquinas." *Madrid, con perdón*. Coord. Mercedes Cebrián. Madrid: Caballo de Troya, 2012, 25–39.

Cebrián, Mercedes, coord. *Madrid, con perdón*. Madrid: Caballo de Troya, 2012.

———. "Prologuillo." *Madrid, con perdón*. Coord. Mercedes Cebrián. Madrid: Caballo de Troya, 2012, 7–9.

———. "Gaudeamus porque no nos queda otra." *Madrid, con perdón*. Coord. Mercedes Cebrián. Madrid: Caballo de Troya, 2012, 41–54.

Certeau, Michel de. "Walking in the City." *The Practice of Everyday Life*. Berkeley: University of California Press, 1984, 91–114.

Cosgrove, Denis. *Apollo's Eye: A Cartographic Genealogy of the Earth in the Western Imagination.* Baltimore: Johns Hopkins University Press, 2003.

García Llovet, Esther. "La M–30, gran velada." *Madrid, con perdón.* Coord. Mercedes Cebrián. Madrid: Caballo de Troya, 2012, 143–54.

———. Personal email communication with the author. August 29, 2013.

Jacobs, Jane. *The Death and Life of Great American Cities.* New York: Random House, 1961.

Javeau, Claude. "Lugares de memoria individuales y estructuración de las interacciones: acerca de los síndromes de Lamartine y de Proust. *La vida cotidiana y su espaciotemporalidad.* Coord. Alicia Lindón. Barcelona: Anthropos–El Colegio Mexiquense–Centro Regional de Investigaciones Multidisciplinarias (UNAM), 2000, 171–86.

Juaristi, Joseba. "El aire de la ciudad postmoderna: identidad, espacio público, cultura y miedo." *La ciudad y el miedo. VII Coloquio de Geografía Urbana.* Coord. Obdúlia Gutiérrez. Girona: Universitat de Girona, 2000, 269–87.

Lindo, Elvira. "Defensa de Madrid." *El País,* October 7, 2013. Supplement "Domingo," 10.

Lindón, Alicia. "La ciudad y la vida urbana a través de los imaginarios urbanos." *Eure* 91 (August 2007): 7–16.

———. "Diálogo con Néstor García Canclini. ¿Qué son los imaginarios y cómo actúan en las ciudades?" *Eure* 91 (August 2007): 89–99.

———. "La construcción socioespacial de la ciudad: el sujeto cuerpo y el sujeto sentimiento." *Cuerpos, emociones y sociedad* 1 (December 2009): 6–20.

McDowell, Linda. *Gender, Identity and Place: Understanding Feminist Geographies.* Cambridge: Polity Press, 1999.

Méndez, Rafael, and Álvaro de Cózar. "De Madrid al suelo." *El País,* October 6, 2013. *Domingo* Supplement, 3–5.

Morales, Grace. "Puerta Bonita. La forja del barro." *Madrid, con perdón.* Coord. Mercedes Cebrián. Madrid: Caballo de Troya, 2012, 165–81.

———. Personal email communication with the author. August 29, 2013.

Navarro, Elvira. "La extraña libertad." *Madrid, con perdón.* Coord. Mercedes Cebrián. Madrid: Caballo de Troya, 2012, 183–204.

Observatorio Metropolitano. *Madrid: ¿la suma de todos? Globalización, territorio, desigualdad.* Madrid: Traficantes de sueños, 2007.

Sabadú, Jimina. "Una bolsa llena de cómics." *Madrid, con perdón.* Coord. Mercedes Cebrián. Madrid: Caballo de Troya, 2012, 247–64.

Simmel, Georg. "The Metropolis and Mental Life." *The Blackwell City Reader.* Eds. Gary Bridge and Sophie Watson. Oxford: Blackwell, 2002, 11–19.

Smith, Neil. "Homeless/global: scaling places." *Mapping the Futures: Local Cultures, Global Change.* Eds. J. Bird. et al. New York: Routledge, 1993, 87–119.

Vilagrasa Ibarz, Joan. "Ciudad y sociedad. ¿Relaciones en transformación?" *La ciudad. Nuevos procesos. Nuevas respuestas.* Coords. Lorenzo López Trigal, Carlos E. Relea Fernández and José Somoza. León: Universidad, 2003, 331–48.

Wirth, Louis. "Urbanism as a Way of Life." *American Journal of Sociology* 44 (1) (July 1938): 1–24.

www.capillatorreespacio.es. Accessed January 20, 2013.

www.esmadrid.com/es/salesas. Accessed January 20, 2013.

https://www.youtube.com/watch?v=02c80KCzJog. Accessed January 18, 2013.

https://www.youtube.com/watch?v=5aW6Fsd4pe0. Accessed July 15, 2013.

Chapter Four

City and Community in María Reimóndez's *O club da calceta*

Pilar Martínez-Quiroga

The opposing concepts of rural and urban have been a crucial diacritical mark in the history of Galician national identity. While the interrelation between the urban and the rural spaces in Galicia has been analyzed from the perspective of geographic, economic, and sociological studies, literary and cultural studies have largely neglected it.[1] Unlike the rest of Spain, where the interest in cultural studies about the city has increased in recent years, in Galicia's case this trend seems to be confined to very specific disciplines because of its particular political situation.[2] Due to Galicia's political status, most cultural studies focus on analyzing Galician national identity, a political circumstance already highlighted by Kirsty Hooper and Helena Miguélez Carballeira. In these authors' words, "Questions of identity, and especially national identity, have always been the driving force in Galician culture and the related discipline of Galician Studies" (202).

However, this "driving force" of Galician studies is not the main reason for the current lack of studies about Galician cities, but rather the fact that the classic nationalist authors considered rural life the "authentic Galician identity," as opposed to the urban space, where traditional Galician habits were lost.[3] This apparently irreconcilable antagonism between the rural and the urban is also supported by the vital debate on the Galician language, which is an essential defining element for nationalism. Linguistic studies show that for many years the rural area was the place with more speakers of the Galician language, while in the city Castilian was the dominant language. In addition, emigration from rural spaces to urban ones was a decisive factor in the decrease of Galician speakers. Clearly, the linguistic situation favored the

43

negative view of the city by the nationalist authors and the lack of studies about the city from a cultural perspective.[4]

This equivalence between Galician national identity and rural space caused two outcomes: on the one hand, it has empowered the mystification of the rural, and extended for many years the trend to set most of Galician literature in a rural environment. On the other hand, it has also contributed to the contempt of the city as an object of study, which is considered an external and imposed space; in other words, the urban was identified as a space "less Galician." At present, Galician nationalism has moved beyond this paradigm and, instead of restricting the definition of national identity to the rural, seeks to create bonds with young, college-educated people, who are mostly urban.[5] This evolution in political nationalism has not permeated the scholarly production on Galician identity. Although Galician cultural studies are now paying more attention to the question of space, an interest derived from a postcolonialist approach that focuses on the opposition between local and global space, known as the "glocal."[6] The concept of the "glocal" provides a view of Galician identity that is not restricted to the isolated, peripheral, and rural space which has been imposed both by the more traditional discourse of nationalism and by the stereotypes about Galician people. In fact, Galician identity breaks up its borders because of the emigration effect, and the permanent contact of the diaspora with Galicia.[7]

The neutralization of the opposition between the rural as synonym of Galician identity versus the urban as an element that is foreign to this identity is one of María Reimóndez's achievements in her novel *O club da calceta* [The Knitting Club], published in 2006. Reimóndez does not resort to the concept of the "glocal," but rather recovers the urban space for Galician nationalism and feminism by providing new ways to look at the city. This article analyzes how Reimóndez assigns an innovative and subversive role to the city of Vigo, the urban space in which the novel is set.[8] First, Reimóndez cancels the division between rural and urban by showing a nonmonolithic and uniform city, which is stratified in neighborhoods inhabited mostly by women who come from rural areas. At a second level of subversion, Reimóndez uses the city to compare the Galician nationalist demands to feminist claims by assimilating the marginalization of Galicia within the Spanish state to the discrimination of the women within society. The last level of subversion is the creation of a feminist community. The displacements through the city provide the characters with the opportunity to meet other women and to create a new form of agency as a community. This chapter focuses on three of the main characters in *O club da calceta* who are representative of the urban and human development of Vigo in the last decades. While Matilde serves to void the division between the urban and the rural, Anxos conveys the tensions and contradictions of the interrelations between the discourses of feminism and nationalism, and finally, Elvira's house, in which the knitting club meets, symbolizes the urban development of Vigo and the creation of new spaces for female agency in the city.

As David Harvey states, "The freedom to make and remake ourselves and our cities is, . . . , one of the most precious yet most neglected of our human rights" (4). This statement is especially true for Galician people—and above all for women—since the combination of national identity and urban space could not be conceived in literary texts until the second half of the twentieth century. It is only in the 1970s when the novel starts to include urban spaces in their plots (Colmeiro, "Smells Like Wild Spirit" 230; Vilavedra 22; Figueroa 47–48). As Dolores Vilavedra points out, it is only in the 1990s that the urban space becomes fully included in the novel: "A miúdo o espazo no que transcorre a acción está a cabalo entre o rural e o urbano, e amosa, ben a invasión do primeiro polo segundo, ben o traslado dos habitantes do campo a cidade e as crises persoais e sociais que dese movemento de poboación se derivan" [Often the space in which the action takes place is divided between the rural and the urban, and shows either the invasion of the first by the second, or the move of the rural people into the city, as well as the personal and social crises which derive from this movement of the population] (Vilavedra 157).[9]

The novels of the 1990s, as analyzed by Vilavedra, reflect an empirical urban situation examined by the architect César Portela and the urban planner Daniel Pino. According to Portela and Pino, the late arrival of the urbanization process to Galicia has blurred divisions between rural and urban, even in the most populated cities like Vigo (30). Thus they classify most of current Galician population as "rurban" (40).[10] The same phenomenon is noticed by the geographer Andrés Precedo Ledo, who takes the concept even further and defines the "rurban" as a "psychological state" of the Galician people (166). The rurban situation is showed through the common practice of Galician urban people of visiting the village (aldea) every weekend, which, as Rei Doval suggests, "Quizais fixese que se perpetuasen ata practicamente a actualidade hábitos e costumes moi propios da vida rural en barrios eminentemente urbanos" [maybe this caused that habits and customs typical of rural life were perpetuated in eminently urban neighborhoods almost until the present]. In order to understand the "rurban phenomenon" (39), we should add that every day there is more frequent contact between the village and the city because of the improvements in the communication systems and transportation. Indeed, in spite of the increase in the urban population in Galicia since the 1960s and 1970s due to the intensity of migration from the rural to the urban (Rei Doval 43), according to the geographer Precedo Ledo, the Galician urbanization still remains low when compared to other developed countries (169).

The human and physical changes that Vigo's city underwent are shown in Reimóndez's novel through the sum total of experiences of the six main characters and the novel's structure, which evokes the organization of one city. The novel is a choral work in which each of the chapters is named for one of the parts that form a sweater. This structure obviously refers to the activity whereby the main characters meet; but it points as well to the social fabric ("tecido social") "interwoven" through the activity of knitting, which is considered traditionally feminine. Thus each chapter focuses on a female character who lives in a certain neighborhood and experiences a particular perspective of the city. These characters manage to break with their previously established spaces and with the behavior assigned to each of them by registering in a knitting course in a modest neighborhood association. The knitting course becomes the origin of a feminist community because it allows characters not only to get out of the roles in which they were trapped, but also to start a new life with the help of the others. Furthermore, they become aware of the need to help other women and they create an association that helps them in different ways, such us achieving economic independence, obtaining legal counsel, or providing a foster home for those who need one. This is reflected in the last chapter entitled "Xersei" ("Sweater"), which sets up the whole piece as a metaphor of the feminist community, as well as a view of the city as a unit shaped by different centers and with different modes of inhabiting it. But at the same time, as the image of the sweater suggests, the perception of the city as a whole is only possible by looking at the sum of the parts. Through a series of synecdoches, the pieces of sweater and the seam lines become the neighborhoods and streets that allow for the creation of alternative spaces, such as the neighborhood association, from which it becomes possible to carry out actions of collective resistance.

Matilde is introduced in the chapter "Elástico" ("Elastic"). Her life represents the migration from the rural to the urban that occurred in the Vigo area in the 1960s and 1970s. Matilde was born and raised in a small village, and then she moved with her family to Vigo. Matilde is described as a very tall and strong woman, in clear reference to a supposed Galician matriarchy linked to rural woman. Matilde's physical aspect prevents her from fitting in the urban space. For instance, she struggles to find clothes of her size and she can never find suitable seats. This interpretation is confirmed by Davinia's ghost whose visits coincide with Matilde's headaches, and with the strange moments in which she does not want to follow her minutely calculated schedule. Davinia visits her niece to remind her of her rural origin and her matriarchal power. [11]

María Xosé Queizán ("A muller en Galicia" 32–33) differentiates between the rural woman who, in spite of living in a patriarchal system, has her own space in the family unit and whose job is appreciated, and the urban woman who is dependent on her husband or works in jobs related to cleaning services, such as Matilde. This division is perfectly applicable to the conflict between Matilde and Davinia. Raimóndez breaks with the idealization of the rural world; even though Davinia is a brave woman from the rural context, she also comes from a violent environment in which she was killed when defending her friend from a rapist. Nobody investigated the assassination; even her own family hid the circumstances of her death. The visits of Davinia's ghost are meant to encourage Matilde, but Davinia's ghost will benefit from the encounters as well. Matilde's new friends, whom she met in the knitting club, will help her to find out who killed Davinia in the village and to demand justice as a posthumous tribute. Finally, after Matilde solves her identity issues, she represents a clear symbiosis of the rural and urban; the supposed Galician matriarchy and the opportunities that the city offers to women.

Matilde represents the "rurban" style of life and the neutralization of the imaginary cultural borders between rural and urban. Her family migrated from the rural to the urban when she was a young adult and her body connects her to the rural Galician matriarchy. But more importantly, it is from the space of the city that she recovers Davinia's memory and legacy. The renovation and normalization of Matilde's bonds with the village are shown in a symbolic trip during which Matilde visits the family house in the village and comes back to the city with Davinia's belongings. This trip to the village to recover Davinia's most beloved belongings—especially her sculptures of women, which will be located in the future store of Matilde—is a metaphorical way to relate the Galician identity shaped in the rural to the new Galician urban reality.

If the cultural opposition between the rural and the urban is superseded by the character of Matilde, the rearticulation of a new Galician identity in relation to labor can be found in the character of Anxos. Scholars have highlighted how Galician feminism has been committed to the political agenda of Galician nationalism but the commitment has not been reciprocal, since Galician nationalism has always given preference to other political issues and has even rejected the equal representation quotas.[12] As Hooper argues, in spite of the limited participation of women in public life, Galician nationalism has appropriated the woman's body and the language of reproduction. Hooper states that the usurpation of the female body by Galician nationalism is shown in the use of the metaphor of the woman as mother of the nation and also in the theoretical construction of the nation in terms of family ("Alternative Genealogies" 46–47). Certainly, the appropriation of the female body by the nationalist discourses is not exclusive to Galician nationalism, but a common feature to all nationalisms based on a colonial situation (Blanco 75–76). The Galician case is remarkable because both discourses, nationalist and feminist, reclaim the same figure: Rosalía de Castro. Blanco points out that, even though both the feminist and nationalist commitment are present throughout Castro's work, in her first poetry book *Cantares gallegos* (1863) the focus is on national identity, while in her second book *Follas novas*

(1880) it is the feminist agenda that predominates (73). For this chapter the focus on *Cantares gallegos* is relevant because Castro exalts the Galician community through a woman's voice that sings for a feminine audience. Reimóndez seems to take this foundational work of nationalism to emphasize the choral feminist voice, and then she moves this collective voice to the city, thus proposing both a new Galician nationalism and feminism, whose common struggles now take place in the urban setting. Reimóndez not only tries to break the exclusive link that Galician nationalism has established with the rural, but also aims at freeing women from the impositions of a nationalist discourse that links the rural woman with the symbol of the Galician nation.

In Reimóndez's novel, the character who reveals this dysfunctional relation between feminism and nationalism is Anxos. She is forty years old, and is an economics professor at the university. She should be happy, since she has a good job and is married to Damián—her inseparable comrade in the nationalist party since her time as a university student. However, an old picture of her college days suddenly makes her realize that her commitment to feminism during the Transition has adapted to peaceful university feminism and has been reduced to a limited intellectual circle. Anxos's double political affiliation as feminist and Galician nationalist is reflected in her progressive disengagement from both her marriage to Damián and the nationalist party. Anxos perceives the standstill of the relationship between Galician nationalism and feminism through a dull conversation with Damián: He has just returned from a meeting of the nationalist party; he tells Anxos that, as usual, women have demanded equal representation in the party; and finally he concludes by stating that the most urgent political issue is the party itself. At this point, Anxos realizes that the party has been giving women the same response for twenty-five years. When she realizes that, after all this time, the party has not changed its position on this issue, she attends a meeting in which she defends women's right to equal representation and then resigns immediately afterward. Anxos does not want a sedentary life, but wants to be in contact with real life, which she finds on the street. Influenced by the knitting club women, she realizes that her life in the party has been sedentary; and, as she says, "para a cal [*vida sedentaria*] hoxe ela non ten espazo, quere andar, correr, percorrer as rúas da cidade. As coñecidas e as descoñecidas. Vellas e novas. As que están en obras. As intransitables. As sen saída. Todas elas. Camiñar, camiñar, camiñar e camiñar. Soa na celebración" [for which [*for the sedentary life*] she has no room today; she wants to walk, run, and explore the streets of the city. The known and the unknown. Old and new. Those that are under construction. The impassable. Those that have no way out. All of them. Walking, walking, walking, and walking. Alone in the celebration] (84).

By the action of "walking, walking, walking, and walking" the city provides these characters with what Michael Hardt and Antonio Negri have called "encounters." According to these authors, the "encounters" are passive and spontaneous acts which are typical of the metropolis and allow the multitude to find a place in which to organize and participate in the political life, as occurred in the Greek *Polis* (254). Hardt and Negri do not argue that all "encounters" in the city are desirable—quite the contrary, they consider that most of them are troublesome. However, some "encounters," like the knitting club in *O club da calceta*, are "felicitous"—in Hardt and Negri's words—and "result[s] in a new production of the common—when, for instance, people communicate their different knowledges, different capacities to form cooperatively something new. The felicitous encounter, in effect, produces a new social body that is more capable than either of the single bodies was alone" (254–55). In *O club da calceta*, the spontaneous and felicitous "encounter" of the main characters occurs in a neighborhood association in which Elvira teaches a knitting course.

These kinds of communities formed by spontaneous "encounters" coincide with what the feminist Marilyn Friedman calls "communities of choice." Friedman differentiates these kinds of communities from what she calls "communities of place," which are constituted by more primitive communities such as family, church, neighborhood, or school, and are based on oppressive gender politics. According to Friedman, the city benefits the "communities of choice": "Like friendship, many urban relationships are also based more on choice than on socially ascribed roles, biological connections, or other nonvoluntary ties. Urban communities include numerous voluntary associations, such as political action groups, support groups, associations of cohobbyists, and so on" (200). Furthermore, Friedman indicates that an essential feature of the "communities of choice" is their influence on identity construction (199). This characteristic can be observed in *O club da calceta*: every woman arrives at this community with her own fears and concerns, and by talking to each other they seek the solutions to their respective problems together. For instance, Matilde solves the murder of her aunt, overcomes the traumas related to her physical appearance, obtains her financial independence by opening a yarn store, and finds her artistic side in her sculptures. Anxos divorces her husband and leaves the nationalist party. Elvira—the knitting teacher—is an old woman who lives alone in a rundown house; her new friends repair the house, and some members of the knitting club such as Anxos and Luz even move there. According again to Friedman, the city "can provide women with jobs, education, and cultural tools with which to escape imposed gender roles, familial demands, and domestic servitude. The city can also bring women together, in work or in leisure, and lay the basis for bonds of sisterhood" (201). Ultimately, the city enables the "encounters" of the main characters and makes possible the creation of a feminist community. Initially, this community meets in the neighborhood association, and later in the renovated house of Elvira.[13]

To conclude I would like to focus on Elvira's house as a metaphor for the achievements of this feminist, nationalist, and urban community. At first, the house was renovated in order to help Elvira, who in turn welcomes Anxos and Luz. Ultimately, the house ends up being the new headquarters of the knitting club, where all these women meet every week. The location of the club changes because they want to provide other women like them the opportunity to meet and organize themselves in their space of the neighborhood association. Thus they conceive the association as a transitional, dynamic, and open place. Elvira's house is the place where the relationship between these women continues, becoming a *chora* space. This space is defined as active, and is related to the maternal body and the feminine ethic of care. [14] The *chora* space carries a subversive function not only because of these associations, but also, as Grosz states, because the *chora* "is the space in which place is made possible" (116). [15] In Reimóndez's novel, Elvira's house represents a *chora* space, and works as a subversive space in several levels; the first one is related to the overcoming of the rural/urban divide through the introduction of a rurban space. The house is located downtown, and it remains a one-floor structure, while all the neighbors have to sell their houses to construct large buildings, many of which are empty. However, the cohabitants of Elvira's house stay and decide to recover a small orchard, which is an obvious symbol of the rural assimilation of the members and a new style of living the city. In this sense, the community recovers the right to influence the city development, as previously proposed by Harvey. A second level of intervention is the creation of a feminist and nationalist community. Traditionally, women have been confined to the private space of the house, while men have ruled the public space. In this new *chora* space, the main characters have taken the streets of the city, and have returned to the space of the house in order to transform it. At present, the house is inhabited by three women without family bonds between them, forming what Friedman has named a "community of choice," which is voluntary, opened to other members, and regulated by a feminine ethic of care. Elvira's house is not inhabited by a traditional family and is therefore not based on blood bonds. Elvira's house in *O club da calceta* thus symbolizes the Galician rurban reality at the same time that it reimagines this spatial process as the possibility to create a space that can be both feminist and nationalist, as well as an alternative family and home.

NOTES

1. Many of the geographic and economic studies that deal with the Galician urban situation have a European Union approach because Galicia—along with Portugal—is considered a peripheral Euroregion; and therefore it qualifies for subventions to its development. Along these lines, in 2002 the well-known Galician Journal *Grial* (number 155) published a special issue about the city entitled *Galicia, cidade atlántica*. An exception to this economic and social trend

is identified in an article by Anxo Tarrío, which approaches the issue from a literary and cultural perspective.

2. Galicia is one of the communities recognized as a "historic community" ("Comunidad histórica")—along with Catalonia and Basque Country. According to the Constitution of 1978, this special status concedes Galicia the right to have its own language—Galician—which is an official language along with Castilian. The 1981 Statute of Galicia transferred many powers from the state to the regional government.

3. For more information on this issue, see Jacobo García Álvarez.

4. For more information on the use of the Galician language in the city, see Gabriel Rei Doval.

5. Even though current Galician nationalism is focused above all on the college educated and urban electorate, Reimóndez reminds us that the conservative party ("Partido Popular") has governed in Galicia from 1990 to 2005. In recent years, the socialist and nationalist parties only governed during the 2005–2009 term. The "Partido Popular" returned to power in 2009 through the present. According to Reimóndez, the "Partido Popular," led by Manuel Fraga, contributed to the creation of the rural image of Galicia through the promotion of the St. James Way (El camino de Santiago) ("Whose Heritage Is It, Anyway?" 194).

6. The term "glocal" was coined by Néstor García Canclini, and afterward was used by many scholars. For the purpose of this chapter, I follow José Colmeiro's proposal to apply the concept of "glocal" as "the deterritorialization of the Galician cultural map to overcome long-established exclusions based on gender, national origin, language, or territorial demarcation, and the disjointing of the center/periphery dichotomy that has relegated Galician culture to the margins. In essence, it is an attempt to address the perceived necessity of opening Galicia and Galician Studies to the world" ("Peripherical Visions" 214).

7. On Galician Emigration and diaspora, see Hooper ("The Many Faces" and "Galicia desde Londres") and Eugenia R. Romero.

8. The name of the city is never said in the novel, but there are clear references to Vigo. The most obvious clues are the journal fragments included by Reimóndez at the beginning of the novel. These events happen in well-known places in Vigo, such as "Praza de América" or the port. Also, Fernanda, one of the main characters, lives in "Zamáns," which is an actual parish of Vigo.

9. All translations from Galician are mine.

10. According to Xelís de Toro, regarding urban Galician culture, we cannot forget the role played in the 1980s by the "movida galega" (347–48), whose center was Vigo, the same city chosen by Reimóndez. The rurban feature of the Galician cities was also pointed out by José Colmeiro to analyze the cultural movement of the 1990s called "movimiento Bravú" ("Smells Like Wild Spirit" 229).

11. As Avery F. Gordon states, "the ghost is primarily a symptom of what is missing. It gives notice not only to itself but also to what it represents. What it represents is usually a loss, sometime of life, sometimes of a path not taken" (63–64). This assertion can be applied to Davinia, since she represents not only the injustice related to her assassination—she was killed when defending her friend from a rapist and the crime was never prosecuted—but also she symbolizes the injustice of women's situation in general and the lack of courageous women who follow her example. Yet, according to Gordon, there is also a positive interpretation of the ghost, since it can also signify the possibility of a future and therefore of hope (64). Both justice and hope for the future are the reasons for which the ghost of Davinia appears to Matilde. In this sense, Davinia's feminist behavior was a threat in the past, and still is, because, as Jacques Derrida wondered, "Is it the difference between the past world—for which the specter repre-sented a coming threat—and a present world, today, where the specter would represent a threat that some would like to believe is past and whose return it would be necessary again, once again in the future, to conjure away?" ("Specters of Marx" 48). This quotation from Derrida seems to justify the need of the feminist movement in the past, present, and future, a need represented in Reimóndez's novel by the ghost of Davinia. For an analysis of how the literary figure of the ghost serves to articulate Galician collective identity, see María do Cebreiro Rábade Villar.

12. See Mónica Bar Cendón, Carmen Blanco, Lupe Cês, Helena González Fernández, and María Xosé Queizán ("Racionalismo político").

13. Vigo holds a tradition of fostering the creation of associations in which women demand their rights both as workers and feminists. A good example is the "Asociación de Mulleres Dorna," which was created thirty years ago in the working-class neighborhood of Coia (Bar Cendón 99).

14. The concept of *chora* space was studied by Julia Kristeva, Elizabeth Grosz, and Adriana Cavarero. These authors relate this platonic concept to the mother's womb, and to a language based in rhythms and not in words. Also, these authors grant it a subversive function above all because of its connections with the feminine solidarity, and because it is a space out of the reach of the father. According to Grosz, the *chora* space cannot be defined by its shape because it is amorphous; if it were defined, it would lose its properties. We can only know its functions, "as the receptacle, the storage point, the locus of nurturance in the transition necessary for the emergence of matter, a kind of womb of material existence, the nurse of becoming, an incubator to ensure the transmission" (114). The concept was also applied to the field of architecture by Jacques Derrida, see *Khôra*.

15. In *Space, Place, and Gender*, Doreen Massey states that the dichotomy between Space/Place reflects a gender division, in which place is defined as "local, specific, concrete, descriptive" (9) and is related to the feminine gender, in opposition to the masculine space that is characterized as "general, universal, theoretical/abstract/conceptual" (9).

WORKS CITED

Bar Cendón, Mónica. *Feministas galegas. Claves dunha revolución en marcha.* Vigo: Xerais, 2010.

Blanco, Carmen. *Sexo y lugar.* Vigo: Xerais, 2006.

Cavarero, Adriana. *For More Than One Voice: Toward a Philosophy of Vocal Expression.* Trans. Paul A. Kottman. Stanford, CA: Stanford University Press, 2005.

Cês, Lupe. Feminismo e independentismo." *Para umha Galiza independente: Ensaios, testemunhos, cronologia e documentaçom histórica do independentismo galego.* Coord. Domingos Antom García. Santiago: Abrente Editora, 2000, 153–64.

Colmeiro, José. "Smells Like Wild Spirit: Galician *Rock Bravú,* Between the 'Rurban' and the 'Glocal'." *Journal of Spanish Cultural Studies* 10(2) (2009): 225–40.

———. "Peripheral Visions, Global Positions: Remapping Galician Culture." *Bulletin of Hispanic Studies* 86(2) (2009): 213–30.

Derrida, Jacques. *Khôra.* Trans. Horacio Pons. Buenos Aires, Argentina: Amorrortu Editores, 2011.

———. *Specters of Marx.* Trans. Peggy Kamuf. New York: Routledge, 1994.

Figueroa, Antón. "Between Politics and Art: The Recovery of a Galician National Literature." *Contemporary Galician Cultural Studies: Between the Local and the Global.* Eds. Hooper and Puga Moruxa. New York: Modern Language Association of America, 2011, 46–53.

Friedman, Marilyn. "Feminist and Modern Friendship: Dislocating the Community." *Feminism and Community.* Eds. Weiss and Friedman. Philadelphia: Temple University Press, 1995, 187–207.

García Álvarez, Jacobo. "Territorio, paisaje y nacionalismo: la construcción geográfica de la identidad gallega." *Paisaje, memoria histórica e identidad nacional.* Ed. Ortega Cantero Madrid: Ediciones UAM, 2005, 171–212.

González Fernández, Helena. *Elas e o paraugas totalizador: Escritoras, xénero e nación.* Vigo: Xerais, 2005.

Gordon, Avery F. *Ghostly Matters: Haunting and the Sociological Imagination.* Minneapolis: University of Minnesota Press, 1997.

Grosz, Elizabeth. *Space, Time, and Perversion.* New York: Routledge, 1995.

Hardt, Michael, and Antonio Negri. *Commonwealth.* Cambridge, MA: Harvard University Press, 2009.

Harvey, David. *Rebel Cities: From the Right to the City to the Urban Revolution.* London: Verso, 2012.

Hooper, Kirsty. "Galicia desde Londres desde Galicia: New Voices in the 21st-Century Diaspora." *Journal of Spanish Cultural Studies* 7(2) (2006): 171–88.

———. "The Many Faces of Julio Iglesias: 'Un canto a Galicia', Emigration and the Network Society." *Journal of Spanish Cultural Studies* 10(2) (2009): 149–66.

Hooper, Kirsty, and Helena Miguélez Carballeira. "Introduction: Critical Approaches to the Nation in Galician Studies." *Bulletin of Hispanic Studies* 86(2) (2009): 201–11.

Kristeva, Julia. *Revolution in Poetic Language.* Trans. Margaret Waller. New York: Columbia University Press, 1984.

Massey, Doreen. *Space, Place, and Gender.* Minneapolis: University of Minnesota Press, 1994.

Portela, César, and Pino, Daniel. "A Galiza entendida como síntese do rural e o urbano: apontamentos para um debate necessário." *Para umha Galiza independente: Ensaios, testemunhos, cronologia e documentaçom histórica do independentismo galego.* Coord. Domingos Antom García. Santiago: Abrente Editora, 2000, 39–43.

Precedo Ledo, Andrés. *Geografía humana de Galicia.* Barcelona: Oikos-tau, 1998.

Queizán, María Xosé. *A muller en Galicia.* Sada, A Coruña: Ediciós Do Castro, 1977.

———. *Racionalismo político e literario.* Vigo: Xerais, 2004.

Rábade Villar, María do Cebreiro. "Spectres of the Nation: Forms of Resistance to Literary Nationalism." *Bulletin of Hispanic Studies* 86(2) (2009): 231–47.

Rei Doval, Gabriel. *A lingua galega na cidade no século XX: unha aproximación sociolingüística.* Vigo: Xerais, 2007.

Reimóndez, María. *O club da calceta.* Vigo: Xerais, 2009.

———. "Whose Heritage Is It, Anyway? Cultural Planning and Practice in Contemporary Galicia." *Contemporary Galician Cultural Studies: Between the Local and the Global.* Eds. Hooper and Puga Moruxa. New York: Modern Language Association, 2011, 190–201.

Romero, Eugenia R. "Amusement Parks, Bagpipes, and Cemeteries: Fantastic Spaces of Galician Identity through Emigration." *Journal of Spanish Cultural Studies* 7(2) (2006): 155–69.

Tarrío Varela, Anxo. "Espazos culturais e literatura na Galicia contemporanea." *Boletín Galego de Literatura* 36–37 (2006): 169–98.

Toro Santo, Xelís de. "Negotiating Galician Cultural Identity." *Spanish Cultural Studies: An Introduction.* Eds. Helen Graham and Jo Labanyi. New York: Oxford University Press, 1995, 346–51. Print.

Vilavedra, Dolores. *A narrativa galega na fin de século: Unha ollada crítica dende 2010.* Vigo: Xerais, 2010.

Chapter Five

Street, City, and Region as Global Contact Zones: Glocalized Self-Identities and Stereotypes in the Graphic Novel *El Nord*

Raquel Vega-Durán

> One evening not long ago I was sitting in an outdoor restaurant by the water. My chair was almost identical to the chairs they have in restaurants by the Vltava River in Prague. They were playing the same rock music they play in most Czech restaurants. I saw advertisements I'm familiar with back home. Above all, I was surrounded by young people who were similarly dressed, who drank familiar-looking drinks, and who behaved as casually as their contemporaries in Prague. Only their complexion and their facial features were different for I was in Singapore.

These words, chosen by Czech president Václav Havel to open his commencement address at Harvard University on June 8, 1995, exemplify how the idea of globalization leads us to think of a single world society characterized by cultural homogenization. Twenty years ago, Havel had already perceived some of the most characteristic effects of globalization. Nevertheless, globalization is a complex phenomenon and not only forges a sense of being at home in the world, but is also a "process that generates contradictory spaces, characterized by contestation, and internal differences" (Sassen xxxiv). This is clearly visible when we consider the unprecedented level of migratory movements in the world today. We do not need to look at a map of global migrations to understand the current mobility of people, nor is there a need to examine one of the so-called global cities, such as Tokyo, New York, London, or Singapore, to evaluate the consequences of migratory movements. We don't even have to turn to smaller global cities, such as Barcelona or Boston, to fully understand the paradoxes of immigration. Globalization is so omnipresent nowadays that it can be sensed at a variety of levels. As Held, McGrew, Goldblatt, and Perraton argue in the introduction to *Global Trans-formations*, "Although in its simplest sense globalization refers to the widening, deepening and speeding up of global interconnection, such a definition begs further elaboration. . . . Globalization can be located on a continuum with the local, national and regional" (Held et al. 14–15). The Catalan graphic novel *El Nord* (2007) (North Street), written by Miquel A. Bergés and illustrated by Josep M. Cazares, can help us think through how a work of literature understands identity construction at several levels of this continuum.[1] Set in Lleida, a medium-size city in the west of Catalonia, Spain, *El Nord* focuses on the interactions of the Spaniard Ludovico and the Moroccan Muslim immigrant Nawal on North Street, where they both live. Through their exchanges in a common space, *El Nord* illustrates what Saskia Sassen has called "a new geography of centrality and marginality," a space of contradictions where cultural encounters are generating new complex national and foreign identities. In a world where both nationals and immigrants are tied to a global process, what happens to their sense of belonging? In *El Nord*, Catalonia, Lleida, and North Street become contact zones, territories where cultural negotiations take place within asymmetrical power relations, and thereby spaces that represent the art of encounters between Spaniards and North African immigrants.[2] Through different spatial levels (the region, the city, and the street), *El Nord* presents a complex global locality where the receiving society imposes a stereotyped global identity on the Muslim immigrant in order to explain itself at a local level.

El Nord detects and unravels the global in the local by focusing on the experiences of two neighbors, Ludovico and Nawal. Ludovico is an aspiring Catalan historian who is writing a book about Andrés Laguna, a Spanish physician who practiced in sixteenth-century Europe. Nawal is a Moroccan woman who arrived in Spain hoping to find her place in the world and to become rooted, which is, as Simone Weil put it, "perhaps the most important and least recognized need of the human soul" (Weil 41). Both of them live on North Street, located in the historic center of Lleida, a street that has become home to a large number of North African immigrants who have gradually settled in Spain over the last two decades. Divided into eleven chapters, *El Nord* takes the reader into the intricacies of the migrant experience by dedicating each chapter to a particular aspect of the migration experience, and combining past and present events to understand the future of immigration in Spain. For example, *El Nord* dedicates individual chapters to people from the past, such as the emigrants "Sindbad" the Sailor (chapter 1) and "Andrés Laguna" (chapter 4), and the author puts them in dialogue with the contemporary characters of "Ludovico" (chapter 2) and "Nawal" (chapter 3). By placing the stories titled "Nawal" and "Ludovico" in between the lives of

Sindbad and Laguna, *El Nord* suggests both that immigration in Spain, which tends to be perceived as a new phenomenon, is part of a continuum of history, and that, to interpret what is happening at a local level, we must simultaneously consider a more global scale.

El Nord also dedicates several chapters to "Europe" (chapter 6), "The City" (chapter 9) and "The Street" (chapter 11), pointing out the importance of spaces for the understanding of migratory experiences. This article will analyze how, parallel to the structure of the novel, the gradual decrease in size of the areas Ludovico and Nawal share coincides with their crescendo in importance. That is, while Catalonia is obviously a larger area than North Street in Lleida, this street becomes the space where the most vivid encounters between Spaniards and immigrants take place. Homi Bhabha has conceptualized the idea of a hybrid third space in which cultures can encounter each other without being in opposition. But the antagonistic encounters between Spanish and immigrant cultures in Catalonia, Lleida, and North Street are highly relevant in *El Nord*. Thus, the space where they meet is rather a "contact zone," a space defined by Mary Louise Pratt as:

> the space in which peoples geographically and historically separated come into contact with each other and establish ongoing relations, usually involving conditions of coercion, radical inequality, and intractable conflict . . . "contact zone" is an attempt to invoke the spatial and temporal co-presence of subjects previously separated by geographic and historical disjunctures, and whose trajectories now intersect. (6–7)

Hence, the contact zones in *El Nord* are not hybrid spaces, but areas where the lives of Spaniards and immigrants intersect, and where encounters among different cultures are characterized by power inequality. Moreover, these spaces are characterized by what Gilles Deleuze and Félix Guattari have labeled "deterritorialization" and "reterritorialization," two processes distinguished by constant transformation, as globalization itself is. In the novel, immigrants are deterritorialized by losing spatial references after their departure from their homelands, but their settlement on North Street, a street where they can find some familiar faces and culture, is a form of territorialization. Immigration implies first a dislocation, and then a relocation. When the "North" receives new immigrants, it does not concern itself with their deterritorialization; meanwhile, questions of territorialization and reterritorialization seem to evoke different responses. The contact zone Ludovico and Nawal share is home to episodes of both territorialization and reterritorialization; on the one hand, the emigration of Nawal brings a sense of displacement to her life, and she tries to alleviate this feeling by territorializing her new place in order to call it home; on the other hand, this territorialization is in turn perceived by Ludovico as a threat, as an invasion of *his* land. He then tries to reterritorialize, not the contact zone they inhabit, but the identity of the immigrants in it, by setting up his own definition of the immigrant as a threatening presence.[3]

At first sight, one might say that the novel revolves around the relationship of Ludovico and Nawal, and their insistence on transforming the territory they inhabit, since most of the chapters of the novel deal with their interactions. The city, and particularly the street where they live, however, also become characters in this novel, because it is mainly here where we come to understand the complexity of the encounter between the national and the foreigner. Ludovico, who shares his name with the Visigoth king who conquered Lleida from the Muslims in 801, CE, is obsessed by the sixteenth century, a period characterized by the continuous fight against the Turks in Europe and by the fear of crypto-Muslims (Moors who converted to Christianity). He thus perceives the presence of North African Muslims on North Street as a repetition of this turbulent history, referring to this street as an "Islamic ghetto," and drawing a clear divide between "that world" and his. Moreover, Ludovico exploits the globalized view of Islam as an aggressive religion in order to justify his conception of Muslim immigrants in Spain as a threatening transnational identity. On the other hand, Nawal perceives Ludovico as a closed-minded *other* whose hostility prevents her and her compatriots from finding their place in Spain. The novel's own literary representations of the urban landscape, however—particularly through Ludovico and Nawal's walk through Lleida, when he lectures her on the city's Muslim past, and later a reunion at Nawal's apartment to mourn her father's death—undermine Ludovico's and Nawal's homogeneous view of the *other*. Thus, in this graphic novel, the negative perceptions that Ludovico and Nawal have of each other do not lead to a fruitless struggle. The street functions as a contact zone where these homogeneous beliefs enter into a complex dialogue that unfolds the complexities of the encounter and coexistence of apparently different identities. North Street is an intricate contact zone; on the one hand it does not merely celebrate hybridity; on the other hand, the street does reveal the impossibility of perceiving the contemporary world in either-or terms. North Street is thus presented as a puzzling space where cultures meet but cannot assimilate.

El Nord refers to the common contemporary perceptions among Spaniards that Moroccan Muslim immigrants are threatening outsiders because of their religion. The graphic novel links this feeling to two main sources: the belief that Spain was invaded by North African Muslims in 711 (and the omnipresent idea of the Reconquest as a victorious struggle against them for almost eight centuries), and the September 11 attacks that took place in the United States in 2001 (reinforced later by the March 11, 2004, bombings in Madrid, and the London bombings in 2005). This Islamophobia, a perception of Muslims as a threat to "Western" society, has shaped a negative social imaginary imposed on the Moroccan immigrant in Spain. This grand narrative connecting Islam to religious fundamentalism has constructed an idea of a Jihadist globalism that can also be felt at a local level. As Nawal says in *El Nord,* "Todo cambió con el 11-S, con el atentado de las torres gemelas. . . . A partir de entonces, el mundo occidental nos ha visto, además de como pobres, como potenciales agresores" [Everything changed on September 11, with the attack on the Twin Towers. . . . From then on the West has seen us, not only as poor people, but also as potential attackers] (128).[4] This kind of West that imposes on Muslims a global stereotyped identity as terrorists is embodied in the character of Ludovico.

This fear of the foreigner recurs throughout *El Nord.* One example takes place during the first long conversation between Ludovico and Nawal, soon after her arrival in Lleida. While lecturing her on the city's history, he points to the area where North Street is:

> Mira, por allí, al final de la calle de al lado, asaltaron la ciudad los franceses el año 1707, una noche cerrada de octubre. Ahora vivís vosotros allí: temo que no hemos sabido defender la ciudad tan bien como nuestros antepasados . . . y tampoco sé si vosotros la defenderíais, si nos atacasen . . . claro que los únicos que nos pueden atacar vienen de donde vosotros. [Look, over there, at the end of the street next to us, the French troops attacked the city in 1707, during a dark October night. Now you live there: I am afraid we have not been able to defend the city as well as our ancestors did . . . and I don't know if you would defend it, if we happened to be attacked . . . of course the only ones who could attack us come from the same place as you]. (150)

Nawal remains silent, but in her thought bubble we can read: "Un motivo recurrente: todos los musulmanes somos terroristas. ¡Y se quedan tan anchos! Si todos los millones de musulmanes fuéramos terroristas, el mundo sería nuestro" [A recurrent motif: all Muslims are terrorists. And they do not show any sign of remorse! If all us millions of Muslims really were terrorists, the world would be ours] (150). These two comments—one by a non-Muslim Spaniard and one by a Muslim Moroccan who lives in Spain—fit into much larger and complex discourses about the construction of group identities. Ludovico tends to perceive Spain as a country that has been fighting against enemies for a long time.[5] Now the "Spanish identity"—which he never defines—is *again* in danger, since "the enemies" have returned. By stating that "the only ones who could attack *us* come from where *you* are from" (emphasis added), he establishes an analogy between the medieval Muslims and the Muslim immigrants who are currently settled in the city. But would Ludovico's potential attackers come solely from Moroco, where most immigrants on North Street are from? According to Sander Gilman, "The deep structure of our own sense of self and the world is built upon the illusionary image of the world divided into two camps, 'us' and 'them.' 'They' are either 'good' or 'bad'" (17). Ludovico's division of the world allows him to make a clear distinction between "us" and the "other," thus establishing a polarized conception of the world divided into the "West" and "the Rest" (where he places *all* contemporary Muslims). His comment reflects the rhetoric surrounding the September 11 attacks—a rhetoric that soon became global, establishing itself as a truth which since then has been profusely used to justify rejection of the Muslim. This logic appears, for example, in Anthony Gidden's statement that "prior to . . . [September 11, 2001] no heartlands area in a Western state had been attacked by a non-Western force for over three centuries" (*Runaway* xv). As noted before, the attack of 2001 sparked an artificial analogy between Islam and fundamentalism, leading to the idea of Muslims as a threatening presence in Western countries, and Ludovico adopts it to justify his rejection.

If Ludovico shares this global stereotype of the Muslim, he concocts his own version of it by seasoning the global idea of Muslim threat with some local ingredients, primarily the arrival of North African immigrants in 711 to the Iberian Peninsula (presented by Ludovico as an invasion, thus framing the Muslim as a historical enemy). Gilman's work on stereotype is again useful here: "Patterns of association are most commonly based . . . on a combination of real-life experience (as filtered through the models of perception) and the world of myth, and the two intertwine to form fabulous images, neither entirely of this world nor of the realm of myth" (21). As a historian, Ludovico bases his arguments on history. But it is a history full of never-questioned negative stereotypes where Muslim identity is fabricated anachronistically as a combination of past and present perceptions. Ludovico combines negative views of the Muslim across countries and centuries, circumventing his anachronistic (and unfounded) perception of the Muslim by connecting events across space and time—a practice that Anthony Giddens sees as the core of globalization, arguing that globalization is "the intensification of worldwide social relations which link distant localities in such a way that local happenings are shaped by events occurring many miles away and vice versa" (*Consequences* 64). Such connections allow Ludovico to blend the local and the global to control the swirl of data for his own convenience, creating a negative identity of the Muslim as a way of generating a positive space, where he then positions himself. In *El Nord* this process of stereotyping takes place in a multidimensional account—region, city, and street, and it is in these spaces that the reader can see "the way in which this stretching of social relations affects the character of the localities that they typically inhabit" (Tomlison 107). The street is part of the city, and in turn the city belongs to the region. An analysis of these spaces will show how, even though they could be perceived as part of a single space (Catalonia or Spain), they function as individual contact zones used by Ludovico to construct his identity in opposition to the Muslim immigrant.

THE GLOBAL AT THE REGIONAL LEVEL

El Nord asks us to think about the dangers of stereotyped thinking by displaying the illogical rationale followed by Ludovico. For example, the global view of the Muslim as a threat to the "West" can be perceived on a regional scale, where Ludovico is presented as a character obsessed with the ninth and the sixteenth centuries. He defines himself as an expert on Andrés Laguna, a sixteenth-century doctor who lived in an age marked by hostility against the Turks in Europe and the *moriscos* in Spain. The clichéd picture of the Muslims that Ludovico has in his head originates for him in the ninth century when Louis the Pious (known in Spanish as Ludovico Pío), son of Charlemagne, tried to conquer what is today Catalonia.[6] Ludovico's distrust of Muslims is underlined by his very name, whose rarity in Spain leads us to think that this name was not randomly chosen by the author.[7] Ludovico is captivated by this historical period—marked by the confrontation with the Muslim presence in Catalonia—and he tends to explain everything in terms of this encounter.

His obsession with fights against Muslims throughout history and the symbolism of his name shape his perception of the current Muslim immigration in Spain. Drawing a connection between the *Reconquista* narrative and the contemporary Muslim presence, however, is not uncommon in Spain. For example, textbooks still tend to show the *Reconquista* (presented mainly as the fight against enemy Moors) as one of the pillars of the national identity, and it is common to hear taglines such as: "the Muslims were in Spain for almost eight centuries, but then they were expelled in 1492" or "The Reconquest started in Covadonga." Even though these statements are rooted in "some shadow of . . . reality" (Gilman 28), what Joshua Fishman has called "a kernel of truth" (cited in Ramírez Berg 16), their oversimplification of Spanish history aids in the construction of a solid Christian Spanish identity. On the one hand, they suggest, for example, that Covadonga was a stronghold where all the Christians gathered and decided to fight against their enemies (leaving us to believe the rest of the Peninsula was inhabited by Muslims, which was not the case); on the other hand, they present 1492 as the year when Spain "returned" to being Spanish (even though Spain did not have a sense of national identity in 711, when North Africans arrived at a peninsula that was inhabited by many different peoples). Ludovico adopts this distorted vision of the history of the country and applies it to Catalonia, reducing the long historical period called *Reconquista* to a single protracted fight between two apparently coherent, unmixed, and firm identities. By presenting this as truth, Ludovico uses "history as a legitimator of action and cement of group cohesion" (Hobsbawm and Ranger 12). This cohesion is based on the "fixity" of identity, which is key "in the ideological construction of otherness" (Bhabha 94), and Ludovico uses it in order to define the Mus-

lim immigrants as invaders. He bases this definition, in other words, on a
Hobsbawmian invented tradition, whose repetition implies continuity with
the past (Hobsbawm and Ranger 1). Ludovico takes the reduced traditional
portrayal of Muslims as enemies of Spain as a legitimator of his perception
of the present-day Muslim immigrants in Spain, whom he perceives both as
phantasmagoric presences of a menacing past and as contemporary threats to
the whole "West," where he positions himself. The homogenization of the
Muslim as a solid and fixed negative identity helps the West in turn to define
itself as part of the in-group "us," who are threatened by the out-group
presence. It is interesting, however, that Ludovico never defines what he *is*
(or what the "West" is), but exclusively what he and the "West" *are not.*
Even though it is undeniable that the four-century Muslim presence in Catalonia left a strong legacy, by adopting the stereotype of the Muslim as enemy
and different, Ludovico makes "fast, firm and separate what in reality is
fluid" (Dyer 16). His own definition of himself could never be complete
without drawing links to the Muslim past of the city.

THE GLOBAL AT THE CITY LEVEL

El Nord does not merely show how Ludovico's stereotypes draw in national
histories, however; Ludovico projects them on to the city as well, imagining
Lleida as a microcosm of the grand historical narrative of the Reconquest.
During the long walk in which Ludovico tells Nawal the story of Lleida, he
offers a conflicting account of the history of the city. The following extract
from their conversation gives the reader a sense of his inconsistency:

> *Ludovico*: Otro día te enseñaré La Suda. ¿Sabes que los moros goberna-
> ron Lleida durante más de 400 años? Del 716 al 1149. Vuestro palacio era
> La Suda.

> *Nawal*: ¿Y vosotros erais también buenos creyentes musulmanes en esos
> años?

> *Ludovico*: Pues claro que sí, toda la ciudad estaba repleta de mezquitas,
> empezando por la mezquita mayor que se levantaba donde ahora tenemos
> la catedral. Y todos los leridanos íbamos en aquellos años con turbantes y
> babuchas.

> *Nawal*: Ja, ja, ja . . . No te imagino vestido como un musulmán, Ludovico.
> Ja, ja . . . yo pensaba que los árabes solo habían conquistado Andalucía.

> *Ludovico*: ¡Ignorante! Todos los huertos que rodean la ciudad son un
> recuerdo de la labor civilizadora de los musulmanes medievales.

[*Ludovico*: I will show you La Suda another day. Do you know that the Moors ruled over Lleida for more than 400 years? From 716 to 1149. Your palace was La Suda.

Nawal: And you were also good Muslim believers during those years?

Ludovico: Of course, the whole city was filled with mosques, starting with the Main Mosque, which stood where we now have the cathedral. And all the people of Lleida wore turbans and slippers.

Nawal: Ha, ha, ha . . . I cannot imagine you dressed like a Muslim, Ludovico. Ha, ha . . . I thought the Arabs had only conquered Andalusia.

Ludovico: Ignorant! All the vegetable gardens that surround the city are a reminder of the civilizing work of the Medieval Muslims.] (151).

Ludovico appears to be troubled by a Muslim history he praises and rejects at the same time. On the one hand, it is evident that he admires the engineering works and the architectural achievements of the medieval Muslims in Lleida. In this respect, he identifies himself as part of that powerful and successful society by including himself as part of "all the people of Lleida" (151). The present vegetable gardens, remnants of a flourishing Muslim identity he selectively appropriates (and deliberately frees of any negative connotation), allow Ludovico to enjoy his own Baudelarian modernity, "a place in which the link between the present and the past, the old and the new, is still visible" (Augé, paraphrased by Tomlison 110). This selected past ("good" Muslims) and present clashes nonetheless with the *other* one, the past of the *other*. This latter history that he connects to the Muslim immigrant is presented as negative, inhabited by the "infidel ancestors" of the present Muslim immigrants in Spain (who of course are not the descendants of the Medieval Muslims). That is, Ludovico presents both himself and the present-day Muslim immigrants as coming from the same origin: the medieval Muslim.

This medieval "self," however, is then divided by Ludovico into two branches, a "good" branch and a "bad" branch. Undoubtedly, Ludovico determines he is a descendant of the "good" side, leaving "them," by process of elimination, as heirs of the dark side. This is another example of how Ludovico lightly regulates the identity of the present-day Muslim immigrant in Spain. At a regional level, Ludovico presents the immigrant as a villain, combining perceptions that are both local (as Ludovico's own archenemy during the "Reconquest") and global (adopting the idea of the Muslim as a terrorist). At the city level, Ludovico conceives the identity of the Muslim immigrant as a product of infidelity. That is, their lineage derives from the "infidels" who inhabited Lleida and were finally eventually defeated by one of Lleida's Christian heroes, the fourteenth-century Count Ramón Berenguer

IV. This unfettered reconstruction of history allows Ludovico to fashion his own particular identity that legitimates the devaluation of the out-group whenever necessary.

THE GLOBAL AT THE STREET LEVEL

The last chapter of the novel helps the reader understand the transformation of identities by offering a brief history of the street. North Street came into existence in 1860 and acquired that name because it led to North Station, used by trains coming from and going to the North. (Interestingly, nowadays its residents come also from the "South.") During the 1990s, this dynamic area saw two substantial transformations; on the one hand, the boom of the real estate market convinced many Spaniards to move away to the newly built suburbs; on the other hand, immigration started to boom in Lleida. Male immigrants, mainly of Moroccan origin, started to rent out the empty apartments on North Street, and by the mid-1990s their families joined them. As fewer and fewer Spaniards were willing to stay on North Street, more and more immigrants moved there. By the end of the 1990s, Moroccans were joined by Palestinians, Iraqis, and Algerians. Western clothes mingled with djellabas and chadors (Bergés and Cazares 176), many of the stores were run by immigrants and catered to immigrant customers, and the first mosque opened in a small warehouse. Of course not all the Muslim immigrants in Lleida live on this street. But as Nawal points out during a meeting that takes place at her apartment with other immigrants and Ludovico, "Lo bueno de esta calle es que la llegada a destino es menos traumática, porque pueden venir como si estuvieran todavía en su país" [The good thing about this street is that the arrival is less traumatic, since they can feel as if they were still in their own country] (127). Whereas immigrants, perceived as *others*, are envisioned by Ludovico as "the other within," Nawal sees North Street as their (first) home outside their homeland.

The positive connotations of Nawal's words find a negative counterpart in Ludovico's opinion: "Esta misma calle: parece que funciona como si fuera un gueto islámico, una especie de microciudad que funciona al margen de la ciudad a la que, queráis o no, pertenece esta calle" [This very street: it seems to work as if it were an Islamic ghetto, a kind of micro-city that works at the margins of the city to which, whether you want it or not, this street belongs] (117). Thus, Ludovico does not understand Nawal's constructive framing of the street, in which it is a welcoming gateway into Lleida; on the contrary, by using the word *ghetto* he portrays it as a segregated place, detached from the rest of the city. Ludovico blames the Muslim immigrants for their own marginalization, adding that "parece que no os esforcéis demasiado para integraros" [you do not seem to be working very hard to be integrated] (117). This is another example of the contradictory perceptions that inhabit North Street, where the presence of Muslims is thus understood from opposing viewpoints; what some see as a springboard for inclusion and integration, others see as a cause of separation.

Finally, *El Nord* draws our attention toward an even more local level. The title of the graphic novel refers to the "Carrer del Nord," that is, North Street. It is here that both Spanish and immigrant characters meet and live side-by-side. First, the very name of the street shows the complexity of the space. It is a place (Europe) perceived as North by the so-called South; but it is also a place seen as South (as a street invaded by Africa and the Middle East) by the so-called North. Moreover, during the era of colonization, the North invaded the South, territorializing it; now, in what Anthony Giddens calls reverse colonization, "non-Western countries influence developments in the West" (*Runaway World* 16). That is, now the South has arrived in the Carrer del Nord—in the North.

FINAL REMARKS

As Saskia Sassen has argued, globalization has led us to imagine new geographies, including a geography of centrality and marginality. For centuries, migrating meant saying goodbye to your motherland to arrive and settle in another place. Nowadays, most immigrants no longer have to cut off all ties with their home country; on the contrary, they tend to stay in touch with their hometown and family, and thereby develop a new kind of transnational identity. By being both here and there, they are part of an *in-between* category of actors who now have become a new presence in Spain as in other countries. These in-between identities, "geographically and historically separated" (Pratt 6), influence in turn the countries they live in, bringing about new identities that result from encounters in the contact zone. In *El Nord*, region, city, and street all function as contact zones. The characters in the novel perceive these spaces as strange (inhabited by "them"), hybrid (where connections are established between "us" and "them"), and familiar (as a home for "us"). This complexity, however, turns into simplicity with Ludovico's polarized conception of the world. By positioning himself as the holder of knowledge, he uses that power as a legitimator to define the *other*, whose identity he constructs by selecting aspects from local and global perceptions. This selection is not arbitrary—by choosing specific aspects, he appropriates what is convenient for the identity he is trying to construct, molding it, and ultimately using it to define himself in opposition to it. He articulates the difference by producing an image of otherness, where apparently that *other* is the antithesis of the self. This *other* is no other than the Muslim, whom he perceives as the "black one," the epitome of difference. Thus, he creates a binary world in either-or terms, a world formed by poles, by black and white, not allowing space for different tonalities.

At first sight, *El Nord*—itself inked in black and white—is a graphic novel with a somewhat didactic tone as it clearly shows how illogical Ludovico's claims and actions are. Nevertheless, a closer look at the novel reveals that it has an intricate structure. For example, even though the textual worlds in the bubbles reveal a polarized world, and the vignettes are drawn using two colors—black and white—the life on North Street is not visually presented in just two colors. In fact, black and white are constantly combined, creating different tones of gray which result from the "encounter" of black and white, the main colors of the novel. Both metaphorically and visually, the predominant use of different hues of gray throughout the novel indirectly reminds the reader of the commonalities, fusions, and connections that take place in a contact zone.

This novel also has a polemical value. It is a text directed at a reader from a country that has a long relationship with migrations; as Ludovico explains, in the 1950s (as well as the 1960s and 1970s), Spaniards emigrated to Northern Europe, ending up as *others*; now this same society coexists with other *others*, the present-day immigrants who have become around 15 percent of the country's total population. This relationship of *others* with *others* shows how "places are no longer the clear support of our identities" (Morley and Robins 87) since these two identities are constructed in terms of at least two spaces, a homeland and an intended new home. In an era in which people are remarkably mobile, where do we belong? The complexity of the identities of the characters in *El Nord* makes us wonder if it is still possible to have a local identity after we have entered into contact with transnational subjects (or after having been them ourselves); do we indubitably belong to a global world, or do we have to start thinking in terms of hybridity, or an identity where global and local meet? If Ludovico needs to construct an *other* in order to exist, it seems necessary to ask if the will to find ourselves actually leads us to the need for an other. If this is the case, can that other, in this globalized world, be completely different from ourselves? Can *selves* and *others* exist in this world shaped by encounters?

NOTES

1. *El Nord* has received media attention as a novel that deals with immigration and the controversial use of the burka in Catalonia. Moreover, it was awarded the *Premi Lleida de Narrativa* (Lleida Prize in Narrative) in 2007. The novel, however, has attracted little scholarly attention.

2. Immigration has become a common theme in contemporary novels, films, and plays. In recent years graphic novels have echoed this trend, paying particular attention to the mobility of people with works such as Shaun Tan's *The Arrival*, Gene Luen Yang's *American Born Chinese*, and Henry Kiyama's *The Four Immigrants Manga: A Japanese Experience in San*

Francisco, 1904– 1924, among others. This tendency has also been reflected in Spanish cultural production with novels such as Elia Barceló, Jordi Farga, and Luis Míguez's *Futuros peligrosos*, Hernán Mogoya and Joan Martín's *Olimpita*, and Miquel A. Bergés and Josep M. Cazares's *El Nord*. The terrain of the graphic novel offers an alternative way of presenting a story, combining both literary and visual elements to represent complex migrant experiences. Among these examples, *El Nord* does a particularly good job of connecting the local aspect of immigration in Spain to the globalized conception of migratory movements, presenting immigration as a multifarious experience that affects both immigrants and Spaniards.

3. An analysis of Ludovico's own perception of the immigrants is provided in the next pages.

4. All citations of the graphic novel come from the Spanish edition of *El Nord* (Calle del Norte) published in 2010.

5. It is significant that the term "invasion" is predominantly used in reference to immigrants from North Africa, mainly Maghrebian immigrants. Maghrebian immigrants are numerous in Spain, but they are outnumbered by immigrants from Eastern Europe and Latin America. The Spanish press, however, seems to have bestowed the invasion discourse on Maghrebian immigrants, the only ones with which Spain has a history of "invasion."

6. In 1922 Walter Lippman denominated this kind of cliché picture as "stereotype." He dedicated the entire third chapter of his work *Public Opinion* to expanding on this idea (79–157).

7. The Frankish King Ludovico Pío (778–840), King of Aquitaine and Holy Roman Emperor, besieged Lleida in 801, trying to seize it from Muslim control, but he was soon defeated by Amrus Al-Leridi.

WORKS CITED

Augé, Marc. *Non-Places: Introduction to the Anthropology of Supermodernity*. London: Verso, 1995.

Barceló, Elia, Jordi Farga, and Luis Míguez. *Futuros peligrosos*. Madrid: Edelvives, 2008.

Bergés, Miquel Àngel, and Josep Maria Cazares. *Calle del Norte*. Lleida: Milenio, 2010.

———. *El Nord*. Lleida: Pagès editors, 2009.

Bhabha, Homi. *The Location of Culture*. New York: Routledge, 1994.

Deleuze, Gilles, and Félix Guattari. *A Thousand Plateaus: Capitalism and Schizophrenia*. Trans. Brian Massumi. Minneapolis: University of Minnesota Press, 1987.

Dyer, Richard. *The Matter of Images: Essays on Representation*. New York: Routledge, 1993.

Giddens, Anthony. *Runaway World*. New York: Routledge, 2003.

———. *The Consequences of Modernity*. Cambridge: Cambridge University Press, 1990.

Gilman, Sander. *Difference and Pathology: Stereotypes of Sexuality, Race, and Madness*. Ithaca, NY: Cornell University Press, 1985.

Havel, Václav. "Vaclav's Havel Commencement Address at Harvard University." June 8, 1995. Accessed December 12, 2013, http://www.vaclavhavel.cz/showtrans.php?cat=projevy&val=190_aj_projevy.html&typ=HTML.

Held, David, et al. *Global Transformations*. Cambridge: Polity Press, 1999.

Hobsbawm, Eric, and Terence Ranger. *The Invention of Tradition*. New York: Cambridge University Press, 1992.

Kiyama, Henry. *The Four Immigrants Manga: A Japanese Experience in San Francisco, 1904–1924*. Berkeley, CA: Stone Bridge Press, 1999.

Lippmann, Walter. *Public Opinion*. New York: Free Press Paperbacks, 1922.

Mogoya, Hernán, and Joan Martín. *Olimpita*. Barcelona: Norma Editorial, 2008.

Morley, David, and Kevin Robins. *Spaces of Identity; Global Media, Electronic Landscapes and Cultural Boundaries*. London: Routledge, 1995.

Pratt, Mary Louise. *Imperial Eyes: Travel Writing and Transculturation*. New York: Routledge, 1992.

Ramírez-Berg, Charles. *Latino Images in Film: Stereotypes, Subversion, Resistance*. Austin: University of Texas Press, 2002.

Sassen, Saskia. *Globalization and its Discontents*. New York: New Press, 1998.

Tan, Shaun. *The Arrival*. New York: Arthur A. Levine Books, 2007. Print.

Tomlison, John. *Globalization and Culture*. Chicago: University of Chicago Press, 1999.

Weil, Simone. *The Need for Roots: Prelude to a Declaration of Duties towards Mankind*. New York: Ark, 1987.

Yang, Gene Luen. *American Born Chinese*. New York: First Second, 2006.

II

Migration, Space, and Tourism in Documentary Films

Chapter Six

Immigration and Rhizomatic Itineraries of Resistance in the Global City: Reflections on two films: *Si nos dejan* and *Raval, Raval*

Megan Saltzman and Javier Entrambasaguas

> A rhizome can be broken, shattered at a given place, but it will start up again on one of its old lines, or on new lines . . . and these lines always tie back to one another.—Gilles Deleuze and Felix Guattari[1]

Immigration produces constellations of inclusion and exclusion, which, for many cultural theorists, is increasingly polarized by our neoliberal economic conditions.[2] Interdependent boundaries crisscross nations, cities, and neighborhoods. Etienne Balibar in *We the People of Europe* upholds that:

> The borders of new sociopolitical entities, in which an attempt is being made to preserve all the functions of the sovereignty of the state, are no longer entirely situated at the outer limit of territories; they are dispersed a little everywhere, wherever the movement of information, people, and things is happening and is controlled for example, in cosmopolitan cities. (1)

Global (or "glocal") space is characterized by a mobility that is rapid, fluid, virtual, and flexible. Dominated and organized by a dynamic network of capital and information, glocal mobility traverses traditional national boundaries, reconfigures relations, and grounds them physically in cities.[3] It is in these global cities where we find growing economic inequality, the highest demand for cheap labor, and the highest concentration of immigrants (Borja 287; Sassen, "Whose City" 206–10). The international circulation of goods, capital, and information is facilitated, while the international movement of women and men in search of improving their lives is made difficult to the point of criminalization, incarceration, or violence. According to Sassen and most cultural geographers, this division results from a globalizing "politics of exclusion" that only "represent[s]and valorize[s] corporate actors as participants" (206). Within the European context, for instance, governments and private industries are investing in a plethora of mechanisms of control: walls, coiled wire fences, airport and sea surveillance, rubber bullets, watchtowers, infrared rays, fiber-optic thermal sensors, police, guards, and the media simply to try to regulate immigrant bodies and what we know about them (Pabón 578). [4] Barriers on paper, in other words, legal documents, can bar an individual from entering the country, receiving medical assistance, or securing a job or a place to live. [5] But *papeles* alone are hardly the only factor that dictates one's citizenship. (By citizenship, we are referring to personal and collective memberships and identities that are always in the making; they can be constructed and manifested legislatively, i.e., *papeles*, and also through our everyday surroundings, i.e., communities, barriers. [6]) In public spaces the sensorial barriers that influence citizenship become more evident (skin color, speech, clothing, smell, economic class). These can determine the level of racism, xenophobia, distrust, and adversity that an individual faces. [7] Spain does have official legislation that is supposed to protect subjects from systematic forms of marginalization (such as Articles 8 and 9 of the Constitution and the Organic Law), but they have lost legal value. [8]

As of 2011, roughly 17 percent of both greater Barcelona and Madrid consisted of immigrant populations (Ajuntament, Ayuntamiento). With the exception of José María Rodríguez Zapatero's 2005 amnesty *regularización* (an amnesty that came as a response to entrepreneurs' complaints that there were not enough legal workers to hire), immigrant needs have been largely absent from Spanish government agendas (Pabón 582). [9] The last time immigration emerged in a national political discourse was in 2013 when the Partido Popular decided to overtly convert citizenship into a commodity for the upper classes. As of May 2013, a foreigner can now purchase Spanish residency for 500,000 euros (EFE).

In spite of an unprecedented crackdown on immigration—resistance, counter-narratives, and pro-immigrant action groups maintain a presence in Spanish cities and on global screens. This article will discuss two examples of cultural resistances, two recent low-budget independent films from Barcelona: *Si nos dejan* (*SND*) by Ana Torres (2003) and *Raval, Raval* (*RR*) by Antoni Verdeguer (2006). Both directors employ public spaces as contemporary and dynamic locations where human differences incessantly culminate, contend, arrive, depart, share, and negotiate at a rapid pace. Unlike the stereotypical stories we tend to hear from the mainstream media and politicians, both of which tend to demarcate "*un ellos-negativo y un nosotros-positivo*" [a negative-them and a positive-us], *SND* and *RR* reject this dichotomy, and present immigrants within a contentious space of flows that is intimately shared with locals (Dikj and Zapata 10, Castells).[10] *SND* and *RR* provide an abundance of catalysts for discussing social heterogeneity. Torres and Verdeguer exploit both content and "genre bending" forms (montage, fragmentation, meta-stories, etc.) to cram their feature-length films with a polyphony of voices, languages, ethnicities, religions, spaces, conflicts, and life processes (Martí 137). The films personalize and humanize immigration experiences, giving immigrants visibility, history, discursive time and space to tell their own stories. Against the surveillance, gentrification, and a narrow limitation of what is permissible and who can be visible in the city, public spaces in these films still function as what Michel de Certeau called in 1980 "spaces of enunciation"—they are the everyday milieux where lesser-known discourses can unfold and be discerned (98). Outside in the plazas, on the benches, sidewalks, and streets, these films focus on immigrants whose mundane conversations, itineraries, and practices interpellate social exclusion. Their presence resists politically as it "makes visible what had no business being seen, and makes heard a discourse where once there was only place for noise" (Ranciere, *Disagreement* 30). However, given the conditions, many of the filmed subjects live in fear and many of the spaces they appropriate are rapidly transformed. Hence, enunciation and visibility, as we will see, entail an ongoing human struggle, one that constitutes resistance to neoliberal domination, and in doing so inevitably keeps politics and questioning in motion.[11] By exposing how spatial practices of immigrants in the neoliberal city are responses to exclusion, we hope to also demonstrate how the rights for citizenship and equality converge with what Henri Lefebvre coined and David Harvey has revived as "the right to the city." The right to the city could offer a more integrated and democratic political platform from which to advocate better living conditions for urban dwellers—locals and immigrants alike.

Chema Castiello's book *Los parias de la tierra: Inmigrantes en el cine español* [The Damned of the Earth: Immigrants in Spanish Film] tells us that films about immigration in Spain have been too oriented on Spain and Spaniards; that is, they have only been filmed by Spanish directors and these directors have not allowed immigrants to speak for themselves (38–39). Coincidentally, around the same time that Castiello was publishing his book, Argentine director Ana Torres was illegally in Barcelona filming *SND*, a documentary that would allow immigrants to tell their own story with less mediation. *SND* is composed of dozens of overlapping interviews with illegal immigrants as well as a several autochthonous urbanites. While the locals provide their general opinion on immigration in Spain, the immigrants speak casually about their personal journey to Spain and their experiences living without legal documents. In *SND*, Torres achieves a rare and challenging accomplishment as an artist. By compiling a wide range of authentic voices, spatial practices, raw emotions, and opinions, she manages to dismantle stereotypes and present us with an inclusive and very humane reflection of the conflicting experiences and spaces related to Barcelona's contemporary immigration situation.

While *SND* reveals a variety of rhizomatic journeys across countries and disjunctured parts of Barcelona, *RR*, a bit like José Luis Guerín's *En construcción*, zooms in and speaks to us of the top-down effects of global pressures in a single neighborhood, which is none other than the mythical Raval—Barcelona's most compact, sociohistorically diverse, and emblematic neighborhood where immigrants and their small businesses have been present since the late 1980s. A striking characteristic of *RR* is that the Catalan director manages to take heterogeneity and inclusivity to even more hyperbolic levels than does Torres, both thematically and technically. Furthermore, its genre is hybrid—*RR* includes a mix of documentary genre (in which many of the characters play themselves), fictional genres, montage, short skits, and meta-representation (Martí 137). This *"memoria coral"* [choral memory], as Martí-Olivella describes it, encompasses 110 characters of different age groups and eight different languages (137). Verdeguer ambitiously interweaves a dozen fictional narratives that map realistic conflicts of today's immigrant population in European cities—unemployment, poverty, racism, segregation, family separation, and housing discrimination. These general problems intermix with others that align themselves more singularly with Barcelona: speculation, *mobbing*,[12] mass tourism, pick-pocketing, and small-scale violence. The film cuts quickly from one dramatic narrative to the next in a nonlinear fashion. What holds together such diverse stories is that, on an everyday basis, all the characters dwell and share the same dynamic public spaces of the Raval, particularly the Rambla del Raval, where the seemingly disparate modes of storytelling merge into the aforementioned constellations of inclusion/exclusion.

Both films bring us to the historic quarter of the city, and *SND* includes the periphery as well. The center of most global cities translates to heightened visibility, land value, and material history. While heterogeneity in Barcelona is being pushed to the outskirts by gentrification, mass tourism, exclusive housing prices, and increased surveillance, the historic quarter continues to be the privileged location where the majority of locals and foreigners traverse and learn about citizenship and positions of power from their sensorial surroundings.[13] In these central public spaces, immigrants may encounter a stronger sense of rejection, as it is here where their visible difference is a more salient political intervention in the "normal order of things" (Rancière, *Disagreement* 12). In other words, it is here where precarious immigrant difference can disturb the pristine urban image that corporate leaders and politicians strive to maintain and sell. The center is where Ali and his Moroccan friends in *RR* cannot find housing; and it is where the police pursue Ali and his friends. Downtown, on and off screen, is where *manteros* must circulate to find customers, but the same location drives them to attach strings to their merchandise display sheets to disappear quickly when police approach. Beyond the tourists' view, we can find the ethically controversial immigration detention centers and where viewers meet Nana of *SND*, an undocumented immigrant from Ghana, who seeks refuge in the Torres i Bages *okupa* house (before it was demolished). [14] In front of the house, Nana tells us poignantly, articulating each word in English, "I'm not a prisoner, but I don't have any place to go, and I don't have nothing to do, all I have to do, is to keep myself there, inside, in order to avoid any problem." The films suggest an invisible barrier is growing between the center and periphery, and although the police may pass a blind eye in the latter, certain immigrants are made to feel uncomfortable on either side.

SND and *RR* introduce us to dozens of fast-paced individual journeys that are typical of neoliberal spatial practices. Many of the immigrants in *SND* describe veritable rally races around the global map, jumping from country to country, city to city—leaving a country is easy, entering is complex. The city of Barcelona in these films is not presented in its Gaudí glamour, but rather just as another checkpoint and possibility on an international search for decent living conditions. *SND* maps the rhizomatic movement of deterritorialization, the controls that attempt to maintain it, and the subjects who, intentionally or not, resist these controls. [15] Andrej, for instance, a Ukrainian native, recounts how, after paying the required 400 euros to cross the German border into England, he was intercepted and held for one year at an immigrant detention center. After one year of detention, he gave up on his application for asylum and was returned to the Ukraine. Shortly afterward, he crossed into Western Europe again, passed through the Pyrenees, and entered Spain illegally. Another case is Maricarmen, a Venezuelan national who entered Spain without getting her passport stamped (a common tactic). Maricarmen's parents are Spanish emigrants living in Venezuela, hence technically she should be able to obtain Spanish citizenship. However, she works full time at a bar in Barcelona and cannot afford the price or time that would be required to return to Venezuela and wait a minimum of four years for the visa. Maricarmen's case is symbolic of the real-life situation we have heard countless times—the situation of the hundreds of thousands of immigrants in Spain who initially try the legal route to obtain residency, waiting in the long outdoor lines for extended periods of time, but later find that the most viable solution is to sidestep the slow bureaucracy of the Spanish immigration system and settle illegally.

A local woman at the beginning of *SND* explains how she allowed undocumented immigrant friends (including the director herself), as well as their undocumented friends, to temporarily stay at her house (an illegal practice). She explains that so many foreigners ended up coming and going through her home that she is unable to recall most of their names or where they were from. At the end of *SND*, viewers learn that the director can no longer locate the whereabouts of Nana. Overall, the majority of the undocumented immigrants in these films appear and disappear to highlight exclusion in the same weakly indicative way that Benjamin's "true picture of the past flits by . . . flashing up at a moment of danger" (255). Against their wishes, these "floating subjects," as Rancière calls them, lack the spatial stability or temporal duration needed to create a meaningful identity and membership (*Disagreement* 100). Cata, an American-Catalan interviewee who lived in many countries and married Andrej so that he could gain legal residency, tells us that "*mi nacionalidad es inmigrante*" [my nationality is immigrant]. While Cata and these rally races around the globe allude to a single, global, egalitarian identity of the future, they also suggest that deterritorialization is producing ephemeral relationships and root-less identities that put those with little economic capital in increasingly vulnerable legal and spatial situations. [16]

SND and *RR* offer a critical response to how neoliberal politics have appropriated space over the last three decades in Barcelona and beyond (*Disagreement* 100). As many cultural geographers assert, there is a general assumption that, in the face of a virtual economy and globalizing marketplace, space has become neutralized and has lost its sociohistorical relevance. [17] Many incoming actors of the global economy—entrepreneurs, tourists, immigrants, and politicians—engage in less long-term commitment in the urban center (increasingly true in times of economic crisis). This leads to what Harvey has termed "time-space compression": the process by which the duration of any physical material is shorter and shorter every day. The more profitable a space, the more quickly it will be transformed into something new and/or privatized. Much research has been conducted on the disappearance of historic spaces and local signifiers in globalizing cities, as well as on their replacement with sterile "non-places" (Augé, Jameson). Too often we witness governments, multinational corporations, and architects joining together without the public's consent to implement large-scale urban renewal and "starchitecture" plans. [18] They publicize their projects as initiatives that will improve the city for the public good, yet entire lower-income neighborhoods are razed, historic downtowns are converted into predictable consumer opportunities for tourists and investors, and immigrant and middle and lower-income communities—along with their small businesses and places of memory—are eliminated or dispersed. [19] It is ironic, the epitome of neoliberalism, that as heterogeneity is washed away, it is replaced by a commodified form of heterogeneity that is replicated internationally. For instance, in Barcelona's historic quarter and international downtowns around the world, many "ethnic" food chains and "exotic" clothing stores are opening (Balibrea 8). Furthermore, while *RR* exposes the daily malaise of gentrification, *mobbing*, speculation, police surveillance, and eviction in the Raval, *SND* briefly satirizes the destructive hypocrisy of the 2004 "Forum of Cultures" which urbanized the historic Poble Nou district and arrested 160 homeless immigrants.[20] Contemporary forms of spatial control that appear as the backdrop of these two films abate the emancipatory components in the city, namely spontaneity, creativity, possibility, community, and difference. The rights to housing and protest are also pushed aside.

Many different theoretical neologisms exist for this type of space that is designed and monitored by an abstraction of media, corporations, and governments. Marc Augé coins it "non-place"; Don Mitchell calls it a "landscape"; both share some characteristics with Guy Debord's classic "spectacle." These terms coincide in pointing out that contemporary spatial design drowns out any noise or contention. As Mitchell says, "the very purpose of "landscape . . . is often precisely to mask the relationships of control that govern the production of landscape. . . . The *illusion* of landscape is a seamless zone of pleasure" (105). Created for private profit and semipublic use, usually neoliberal space appears fixed, seamless, optimistic, clean, orderly (and superficially multicultural). Most contemporary urban design—of which the Barcelona Model and tourist image are examples *par excellence*—attempts to cover up precisely what *SND* and *RR* uncovers: conflict, contradictions, workers' conditions, surveillance, disorder, and precariousness. In both films the presence of immigrants, more specifically the precarious spaces many of them occupy, demystify the mass-produced spectacle of Barcelona. The most striking example from these films is when Torres interviews Nana while juxtaposing scenes of poverty and decay with Barcelona's tourist image. We observe large piles of garbage, clothes hanging from pipes, and old shopping carts around the Torres i Bages *okupa* home, and then, in the foreground, Nana admits that after risking his life to come to Europe, he has discovered that the image and the reality have nothing in common: "now we are in Europe, where is the dream now?" Immediately after his question viewers are faced with a postcard of Barcelona and, subsequently, a series of panning shots over the Sagrada Familia and the yachts and cruise ships at the port.

SND and *RR* exploit film techniques in an attempt not only to vocalize as many immigrant stories as possible within a limited filmic time, but also to highlight the positive potential of contentious, heterogeneous space. Torres frequently uses montage to jump from response to response, person to person, cutting their sentences in half and returning to them later. Certain scenes are rewound, others are played in fast motion; many scenes are recorded with a jittery handheld camera. The sound is often interrupted by background noise and wind blowing into the camera microphone, further fragmenting the interviews that are recorded outdoors. Both films play Manu Chao's upbeat multicultural music while showing a hodgepodge of everyday human movement in the city—immigrants playing soccer, skateboarding, running from the police, getting arrested; large crowds walking briskly, riding bikes; police frisking.

As a cornucopia of stories, characters, languages, emotions, conflicts, and everyday public spaces, both films come across as very explosive thematically, often overwhelming the viewer. In our reading of *RR*, Verdeguer and Torres are presenting chaotic montages as a collective dynamism—a way of countering the oppressive constraints of Barcelona's particular relationship with the international economic pressures. Many scholars who have written about the importance of heterogeneity in space prescribe that we not interpret this chaos in the way that many real estate speculators, politicians, urban planners or architects do, that is, as something negative, unappealing, and worth zoning or gentrifying. Rather, they suggest the opposite: that we conceptualize messy or heterogeneous spaces as something positive—inclusive and conducive for democratic potential. Messiness disrupts the externally imposed or prescribed paradigms, binaries, and barriers, and it can reveal power relationships and contradictions.[21] It may sound obvious, but it is worth repeating—when disorder and disagreement are manifested, contention creates possibilities for debate and democratic change. The moment disorder and disagreement stop, the moment space becomes deterritorialized, political possibility stagnates or freezes all together, and oppression and inequality become more easily consolidated by those in power.[22]

If not made invisible by politicians, police, and urban speculators, many undocumented immigrants, including those in our films, are driven to keep a low profile to circumvent the law and avoid deportation, including in cases in which immigrants have urgent medical or security needs. The director Torres is injured while making the film, and Nana suffers from diabetes, but neither seeks assistance for fear of their status being discovered; both are aware that they are excluded from the institutions that offer civic protection.

The same nebulous threat that keeps undocumented immigrants from approaching a police officer or hospital for help, also triggers immigrants to engage in quasi-legal spatial practices to earn money. As Sassen and Appadurai and Holston attest—a contradiction of the global economy is that it creates and relies on a "disempowered" and usually illegal lower-income market, thereby putting the most economically vulnerable into a state of legislative limbo ("Whose City," 210–12; 198–99). Nana, in *SND*, is not far off when he tells the director that economic pressure in Africa forces Africans to immigrate to Europe, creating a contemporary "form of slavery." Nonetheless, on and off screen, we view how undocumented immigrants can navigate a space that, for them, is in limbo.

Once they have entered the country, many immigrants find themselves highly mobile with the most economic and natural form of mobility—their own two feet. We can see subjects crisscrossing the public spaces in evasive and sporadic fashion. Often these *on-the-go* spatial itineraries through the veins of the city are motivated by fear of authority and/or economic need (such as Ali running from the police or running from tourists from whom he swiped a camera). The urban niches, heterogeneity, and the crowd facilitate the anonymity and semi-invisibility needed to carry out small quasi-legal economic activities. "To walk is to lack a space," as de Certeau describes in relation to tactical practices in the city (37). Those who lack a space "vigilantly make use of the cracks" (103). In *SND*, Juanita, an illegal immigrant from Latin America, sells ice cream back and forth along the Barceloneta beach, a *chatarrero* pushes a shopping cart full of discarded metal to resell, and *manteros* sell black-market products on retractable sheets on the sidewalk. (*Manteros*, off screen, have developed a creative linguistic and spatial network to advise one another when one sees a police approach so that they can rapidly sweep up their goods and disappear).[23]

If certain immigrants cause "one world to be lodged onto another," as Rancière states of how "politics" emerge, then *RR* shows us that one world is not so different from the other ("Ten" 10). As we progressively observe in Spanish cities, locals join the ranks of economic vulnerability and they too participate in elusive spatial-economic itineraries such as *chatarrero* work or prostitution (which have gained public visibility with the current economic crisis). Verdeguer utilizes the intermixing in the microcosm of the Raval's public spaces as an opportunity to expose how the lives of low-income individuals—*both immigrants and locals*—are subjected to violence and social exclusion, thus integrating the "us versus them" dichotomy mentioned earlier. Without downplaying the struggle of the immigrant status, *RR* portrays a widespread urban malaise that transcends legal paperwork, citizenship, or nationality. For instance, in separate narratives, Ali and an older Catalan man struggle to maintain housing and eventually are evicted as they cannot afford rent. Around the corner a Spanish *mafioso* pays Ali to help him destroy a studio that belongs to someone who owes money. In other scenes we view both Sub-Saharan African and Catalan prostitutes.

The immigrants who appear in these two films function as a synecdoche for the more than two million undocumented immigrants that are currently living in Spain.[24] Their *civitas*, citizenship, as well as ours, is still politically constituted in cities (even despite our involvement with computer technology). Appadurai and Holston tell us that:

> Crowds catalyze processes which decisively expand and erode the rules, meanings, and practices of citizenship. Their streets conflate identities of territory and contract with those of race, religion, class, culture, and gender to produce the reactive ingredients of both progressive and reactionary political movements. (188)

Discussions on immigrant citizenship are usually left out of academic and political discussions on urban spatial politics (such as public space, gentrification, and the right to the city). However, recent discourses and actions related to the right to the city and Spain's *15M* can offer a discursive bridge and urban commonality between the two. Lefebvre coined this phrase in his book of the same title in 1969, and it was recently revived in David Harvey's analyses of historical and global urban revolutions in *Rebel Cities* (2011). Lefevbre and Harvey did not elaborate on "citizenship" and "immigration" per se,[25] but the concept of the right to the city seems to us to be an inclusive and feasible plan from which to advocate and embrace both immigrant and local needs. In the face of an increasing alienation between desire and possibility, the growing domination of a nebulous threat forces immigrants and locals to carry out quasi-legal economic strategies and live a precarious existence without decent housing, medical assistance, or freedom in the space they inhabit and invest in economically (through taxes) and affectively (through experiences). As opposed to focusing on singularity or a specific protagonist, *RR* and *SND* address human heterogeneity in all its contentious differences. The pluralistic content and form of the films resonates very closely with many of the demands that were vocalized globally in 2011 by the Occupy and Spain's *15M* movement: widespread social inclusion, equality, horizontalism, and dissidence in the public space. The right to the city is a collective demand to allow everyone the opportunity to participate in an ongoing decision-making process in the places where our lives become, whether it be in an actual city, or a neighborhood or workplace. The right to the city would recognize our basic rights, it would recognize every person as a dignified human being and it would entail the freedom to manifest harmless difference without being chased by police or incarcerated in an immigrant detention center. What the right to the city potentializes for public space and human citizenship is so *transformative* and *possible* that much of the immigration control apparatuses that we mentioned in the introduction was applied and heightened in 2011 when the Occupy movements temporarily reclaimed public space.

While the connection between people and space is rapidly diminishing, the right to the city calls for wider political agency in space so that we can bring people and space back together and work towards the messy task of "mak[ing] a city more after their own heart's desire" (Harvey xvi). This is precisely what the *chatarreros* do when they push their grocery carts from garbage container to garbage container, what Nana does when he takes refuge in the *okupa* house, or, in *RR*, when Javed, a Pakistani child, and dozens of international neighbors do when they join together in a community center in the Raval to sing their "*canto a la integración*" [song for integration] "*El Raval es plural, un Raval original, un Raval cultural, el Raval es un cidral*" [the Raval is plural, an original Raval, a cultural Raval, the Raval is a forest]

(Martí 137). They appropriate and regain control of a small portion of shared space, but only briefly, and with apprehension.[26]

This writing effort is dedicated to Jinhwa Chang, Diane Aretz, and all the humans who made possible the production and distribution of these films.

NOTES

1. Our translation. Original: "Un rhizome peut être rompu, brisé en un endroit quelconque, il reprend suivant telle ou telle de ses lignes et suivant d'autres lignes. . . . Ces lignes ne cessent de se renvoyer les unes aux autres." From *Capitalisme et schizophrénie: Mille Plateaux*, 27–28.
2. For instance, please see the works referenced in the bibliography by Etienne Balibar, David Harvey, Saskia Sassen, and Joan Subirats.
3. This definition was compiled from the writings of cultural theorists Appadurai, Castells, Sassen, and Manuel Delgado.
4. Ceuta and Melilla, for instance, are circumscribed by fences (Pabón 257).
5. On April 24, 2012, the Spanish government passed the law 16/2012 which requires legal documents (an official health card, *la tarjeta sanitaria*) for someone to be attended at a medical facility (Amnestía "*Violaciones*").
6. We formed this definition of citizenship from the writings of Sassen, Balibar, and Appadurai and Holston. Besides membership and identity, citizenship is also intimately related to participation and representation. Balibar adds that the components of citizenship are usually polarized.
7. Rodríguez i Villaescusa in *Inmigración y política urbana en la región metropolitana de Barcelona* claims that immigrants that come to Spain from wealthy countries are treated much better by locals than those that come from poorer countries (91).
8. More specifically, we are referring to the following legal documents: the United Nations Charter (1945), the Universal Declaration of Human Rights (1948), the Spanish Constitution (1978, Articles 8, 9, and the Organic Law), and the Treaty of Amsterdam (1999).
9. Much has been discussed about Spain's largest amnesty *regularización* in 2005, which granted legal status to 700,000 illegal immigrants that met labor and residence requirements. However, this was only a small part of the larger "labor" policy to redefine and toughen up a national immigration policy. On June 26, 2009, a new Immigration Law was passed, the fourth in eight years, which facilitated the persecution of irregular immigration over humanitarian aid. In addition, it specified a maximum period of sixty days in a *Cies* (immigration detention center), and it complicated the procedure for family reunion (Amneistía 4; Cáritas 6). For an exhaustive explanation of the 2005 *regularización* see Pabón López.
10. For more on public media coverage of recent immigration in Spain, see the first three chapters of Van Dijk and Zapata, and Martínez Lirola. Also, Olivella's article touches on the critical incorporation of television and radio references in *RR*.
11. In the end credits of *SND* we learn that fear impeded many immigrants from participating in the documentary.
12. *Mobbing*, in Spanish, is a term used to describe speculation harassment, specifically the unethical ways real estate agents and landlords try to evict tenants, usually in order to gentrify the building or to increase rent.
13. In 2005 the City Council of Barcelona instated civic laws ("*Ordenances de Civisme*") to limit behavior in public spaces. See http://www.bcn.cat/conselldeciutat/pdf/plenari_22novembre_projecte_ordenanca.pdf.
14. At its height, over one thousand immigrants lived at the Torres i Bages *okupa* house before it was demolished in February 2004 (Blanchar). Nana's comment coincides with Andrej's experience of having been "imprisoned" in an immigrant detention center.

15. By "deterritorialization" we mean a general contemporary disconnect between space and history—a disappearance of social meaning in space. See endnote 17.

16. We do not have space here to expand on this, but undocumented immigration opens the doors to important connections with Giorgio Agamben's and Michel Foucault's concepts of bare life and biopolitics.

17. For more on this general claim, see the bibliography for Augé, Castells, Harvey, Jacobs, Jameson, Mitchell, and Soja.

18. Starchitecture is a term used to describe the very expensive name-brand buildings designed by famous international architects ("starchitects").

19. Barcelona, the "Barcelona Model," has been at the forefront of this urban strategy. A plethora of critical texts on the Barcelona Model exists; some that we recommend are: Balibrea, Capel, Delgado, and Marshall.

20. The Forum, funded by multinational corporations and public funds, was publicized as an international opportunity to create a month-long event of exhibits and conferences on multiculturalism. To construct the buildings for this poorly attended and expensive event, much of the historic Poblenou neighborhood was demolished. In relation to our argument, we should add that during the preparations for the Forum, the police shut down a metro station where homeless immigrants were living, surrounded the station, and arrested 160 immigrants (Delgado, "El gran").

21. For more on the social benefits of disorder in urban planning, see Jacobs, Mitchell, Steven Pile, Richard Sennett, and Karen Franck, and Soja's concept of "third space."

22. Many progressive cultural theorists have expressed this need for perpetual dissent and heterogeneity to constitute democratic emancipation; many of them locate this potential in public urban space. For instance, see Harvey, Chantal Mouffe, Rancière, and Sennet.

23. As of October 2011, it is illegal to rummage through the trash in Spain, in spite of an increasing number of locals doing so (Fernández).

24. This estimated number is from 2010. For more information see *"Inmigrantes en España."*

25. Harvey does briefly conjoin immigrant rights with the right to the city in *Rebel Cities* when he discusses the 2006 immigration reform protests in the United States.

26. Although it is clear that wide, systematic, grassroots action is needed to address the situation we have described, we would like to mention a couple of Spanish texts that offer specific, practical solutions that need to be developed in order to make public space more socially inclusive: *"Ciudadanía e inclusión social frente a las inseguridades contemporáneas."* by Joan Subirats; *La ciudad conquistada* by Jordi Borja; and many of the reports produced yearly by Cáritas and Fundación Foessa. The following three foundations online also offer recent publications and current activities related to specific actions for social inclusion: *Observatorio Metropolitano* (http://www.observatoriometropolitano.org), *Traficantes de Sueños* (http://www.traficantes.net/), and *Fundación de los Comunes* (http://fcomunes.communia.org/).

WORKS CITED

Ajuntament de Barcelona. "Informes Estadístics. La población estrangera a Barcelona. Gener 2011." December 30, 2013. http://www.bcn.cat/estadistica/catala/dades/ inf/pobest/pobest11/pobest11.pdf.

Amnestía International. *Hay alternativas: No a la detención de personas inmigrantes: Comentarios al borrador del Gobierno sobre el reglamento de los centros de internamiento de extranjeros.* Madrid: Sección española de Amnistía Internacional, February 2013. December 30, 2013. https://doc.es.amnesty.org/cgi-bin/ai/BRSCGI/ Informe%20CIEs?CMD=VEROBJ&MLKOB=32229590404.

———. "Violaciones de derechos humanos, caos y estigmatización de inmigrantes, resultados de la reforma sanitaria." July 4, 2013. Accessed November 18, 2013.
http://www.es.amnesty.org/noticias/noticias/articulo/violaciones-de-derechos-humanos-caos-y-estigmatizacion-de-inmigrantes-resultados-de-la-reforma-s/.

Appadurai, Arjun. "Disjuncture and Difference in the Global Cultural Economy." *Public Culture* 2 (2) (Spring 1990): 1–24.

Appadurai, Arjun and James Holston. "Cities and Citizenship." *Public Culture*. Chicago: University of Chicago Press, 1996, 187–204.

Augé, Marc. *Non-Places: Introduction to an Anthropology of Supermodernity*. Trans. John Howe. London: Verso, 1995.

Ayuntamiento de Madrid. "La población extranjera en la ciudad de Madrid: Dossier de magnitudes básicas." February 25, 2011. Accessed December 30, 2013. http://www.madrid.es/UnidadesDescentralizadas/Inmigracion/EspInformativos/MadridConvive/Observatorio/Publicaciones/Datos%20poblaci%C3%B3n%20extranjera/Ficheros/Magnbasicas2011.pdf

Balibar, Etienne. *We, the People of Europe? Reflections of Transnational Citizenship*. Princeton, NJ: Princeton University Press, 2004.

Balibrea, Mari Paz. "Urbanism, Culture and the Post-Industrial City: Challenging the 'Barcelona Model.'" *Journal of Spanish Cultural Studies* 2(2) (2001): 187–210.

Benach Rovira, Núria. "Diferencias e identidades en los espacios urbanos." *Inmigración, género y espacios urbanos: Los retos de la diversidad*. Eds. Mary Nash, Rosa Tello, Núria Benach. Barcelona: Edicions Bellaterra, 2005, 71–83.

Benjamin, Walter. "Theses on the Philosophy of History." *Illuminations*. Ed. Hannah Arendt. New York: Schocken Books, 1968, 253–64.

Blanchar, Clara. "Punto final a los cuarteles de Sant Andreu, refugio de los 'okupas'." *El País*. February 10, 2004. Accessed November 8, 2013. http://elpais.com/diario/2004/02/10/espana/1076367625_850215.html.

Borja, Jordi, Belil Mireia, et al. *Ciudades: una ecuación imposible*. Barcelona: Icaria Editorial, 2012.

Capel, Horacio. *El modelo Barcelona: un examen crítico*. Barcelona: Ediciones del Serbal, 2005.

Cáritas. *Informe de acciones en el proceso de la reforma sobre la Ley de Extranjería*. November 6, 2009. December 30, 2013. http://www.san-pedro.org/corcho/caritas/DEFInformeAccionesProcesoReformaLOEX06Nov09.pdf.

Castells, Manuel. "The Space of Flows." *The Castells Reader on Cities and Social Theory*. Edited by Ida Susser. Oxford: Blackwell Publishers, 2000, 314–66.

Castiello, Chema. *Los parias de la tierra: Inmigrantes en el cine español*. Madrid: Talasa Ediciones, 2005.

Certeau, Michel de. *The Practice of Everyday Life*. Berkeley: University of California Press, 2002.

Delgado, Manuel. "El gran circo de las culturas." *El País*. September 11, 2002. Accessed November 16, 2013. http://elpais.com/diario/2002/09/11/catalunya/1031706444_850215.html.

———. *Sociedades movedizas: Pasos hacia una antropología de las calles*. Barcelona: Anagrama, 2007.

———. *Elogi del vianant*. Barcelona: Edicions de 1984, 2005.

Deleuze, Gilles, and Felix Guattari. *Capitalisme et schizophrénie: Mille Plateaux*. Paris: Les Editions de Minuit, 1980.

EFE. "El gobierno establece el permiso de residencia para los extranjeros ricos." *Público.es*. May 24, 2013. Accessed November 8, 2013. http://www.publico.es/455969/el-gobierno-establece-el-permiso-de-residencia-para-los-extranjeros-ricos.

Fernández-Pacheco, Alba. "La crisis de Zapatero la paga el chatarrero" *El Mundo*. October 11, 2011. December 20, 2013. http://www.elmundo.es/elmundo/2011/08/11/madrid/1313039922.html.

Gilbert, Liette, and Mustafa Dikeç. "Right to the City." *Space, Difference, Everyday Life: Reading Henri Lefebvre*. Eds. Kanishka Goonewardena, et al. New York: Taylor and Francis, 2008. 250–63.

"Inmigrantes en España: Un millón de ilegales y un 30% de paro entre los legales." Diario Crítico, October 7, 2010. Accessed December 30, 2013. http://www.diariocritico.com/general/231302.

Jacobs, Jane. *The Death and Life of Great American Cities*. New York: Vintage Books Edition, 1992.

Jameson, Fredric. "Postmodernism and Consumer Society." *The Anti-aesthetic: Essays on Postmodern Culture*. Ed. Hal Foster. New York: New Press, 1998, 111–25.

Martí Olivella, Jaume. "El Raval Como Mito Urbano Y/en El Cine Catalán Reciente." *Fotogramas para la multiculturalidad: Migraciones y alteridad en el cine español contemporáneo*. Eds. Cantero-Exojo, Maria Van Liew, and José Carlos Suárez. Valencia: Cine Derecho, 2012, 129–52.

Martínez Lirola, María. "Aproximación a las noticias sobre inmigración." *Revista Nuevas Tendencias en Antropología* 3 (2012): 75–89.

Marshall, Tim, ed. *Transforming Barcelona: The Renewal of a European Metropolis*. New York: Routledge, 2004.

Mitchell, Don. "Metaphors to Live By: Landscapes as Systems of Social Reproduction." *Cultural Studies: An Anthology*. Eds. Michael Ryan and Hanna Musiol. Oxford: Blackwell Publishers, 2008, 101–23.

Mouffe, Chantal. "Artistic Activism and Agonistic Spaces." *Art amd Research: A Journal of Ideas, Contexts, and Methods*. Accessed December 30, 2013. http://www.artandresearch.org.uk/ v1n2/mouffe.html.

Pabón López, María. "Immigration Law Spanish-Style: A Study of Spain's Normalizacion of Undocumented Workers." *Georgetown Immigration Law Review* 21(4) (2007). December 31, 2013. http://ssrn.com/abstract=1172057.

Pile, Steve, et al., eds. *Unruly Cities: Order/Disorder*. London: Open University, 1999.

Rancière, Jacques. *Disagreement: Politics and Philosophy*. Minneapolis: University of Minnesota Press, 1999.

———. "Ten Theses on Politics." *Theory & Event* 5:3. December 30, 2013. http://www.scribd.com/doc/21247046/Ten-Theses-on-Politics-by-Ranciere.

Rodríguez i Villaescusa, Eduardo. *Inmigración y política urbana en la región metropolitana de Barcelona*. Barcelona: Fundació Carles Pi i Sunyer, 2002.

Sassen, Saskia. "The City in a Global Digital Age." *Cluster*. Accessed November 16, 2013. http://www.cluster.eu/the-city-in-a-global-digital-agela-citta-nellera-digitale-globale/.

———. "Whose City Is It? Globalization and the Formation of New Claims." *Global Culture* 8 (1996): 205–23.

Sennett, Richard. *The Uses of Disorder: Personal Identity and City Life*. London: Allen Lane, 1970.

Soja, Edward. *Postmodern Geographies*. New York: Verso, 1989.

———. *Thirdspace* . New York: Blackwell Publishers, 1996.

Stevens, Quentin, and Karen A. Franck. *Loose Space: Possibility and Diversity in Urban Life*. London: Routledge, 2007.

Subirats, Joan, Eva Alfama, and Anna Obradors. "Ciudadanía e inclusión social frente a las inseguridades contemporáneas: La significación del empleo." *Documentos de trabajo* 32 (2009): 133–42.

Van Dikj, Teun, and Ricard Zapata Barrero, eds. *Discursos sobre la inmigración en España: Los medios de comunicación, los parlamentos y las administraciones*. Barcelona: Edicions Bellaterra, 2007.

Chapter Seven

Madrid as a *Glocal* Enclave in *El otro lado: un acercamiento a Lavapiés* by Basel Ramsis

Alicia Castillo Villanueva

Noticeable presence of immigration in Spain began in the late twentieth century, but had a greater impact on Spanish society in the early years of this century, with the arrival of about four million immigrants from different countries (Valero Escandell 45). This steady volume of immigration in most areas of Spanish cities has affected aspects of education, health, and work and also the transformation of urban neighborhoods. It also appears to have a significant effect on the demographic profile, as the Spanish population grew considerably in a decade (Verdugo and Swanson 23). Between 1998 and 2008, the total population of Spain changed from 39.8 to approximately 46.1 million, taking into account the year 2000 as an important point of departure when the Spanish population began to grow dramatically. In the same decade, the immigrant population of Spain had increased from an estimated 637,085 to 5,268,762, accounting for 11.5 percent of the total population of the country by 2008. These numbers explain an extraordinary growth of immigrant population by 727 percent between the mentioned years and consequently a substantial impact on population change in Spain (Verdugo and Swanson 26–27).

In 2002 the Egyptian-born director Basel Ramsis produced the documentary *El otro lado: un acercamiento a Lavapiés*, a district of *Embajadores* characterized by the rapid impact of transnational immigration evidenced by an extraordinary increase from 4.90 percent to 35.16 percent of foreign population between 1991 and 2006 (Barañano et al 61). The rapid increase in transnational immigration raised key issues related to spatial and symbolic reconfiguration of this popular neighborhood in the center of Madrid. [1] In this context, the documentary, produced by both national and transnational directors, has emerged as a genre that tackles critical issues related to spaces as a focal point for the meeting of both the established local community and the recently arrived global immigrants. The city of Madrid has been the preferred location for many directors for the setting of films, documentaries and docudramas that represent various aspects of transnational immigration.[2]

The overarching objective of this article is to foreground documentary media production as a valuable evidence-based discipline. This work comprises both the capacity to mirror the urban transformation and open a space for reflection within a multicultural context in the city of Madrid. To this end I will analyze Basel Ramsis's documentary *El otro lado: un acercamiento a Lavapiés* (2002), in which the director reflects on the complex process of the reconfiguration of physical, symbolic and imaginary spaces stimulated by the encounter of new and traditional identities in the specific area of Lavapiés.[3]

The growth of the capital responds to an increasing dynamism that has recorded a strong process of economic and social modernization throughout the years. This process has elevated the metropolis to the status of "global city" (28) in the terms proposed by Saskia Sassen, in which the globalization of economic activity entails a new type of organizational structure. The accelerated development of communication, international firms, and information networks through globalization has facilitated the mobility of both types of transnational immigration: highly qualified professionals and laborers. Sustained economic growth between the mid-1990s and 2007, at rates generally above the European Union average, was the main driver behind the dramatic rise in the number of immigrants in the country (Arango 3). Thereby, the consequences of economic activity have been reflected in the urban renewal and the change of functional space, such as the transformation of residential areas into space occupied by offices. The immediate effects have been, on the one hand, a strong progressive loss of the collective use of the city as an area of public gathering. On the other hand, driven by its selective nature, it has caused a drastic impact on other contiguous neighborhoods occupied by social groups considered to be marginal, such as the elderly or foreign minorities (Estébanez, Molina, and Pérez 184). Madrid's strategic location for transnational immigration has experienced an intense transformation of local spaces within the current course of globalization. The ongoing restructuring process has had an impact on uprooting social phenomena and re-articulating previous spatial-temporal groundings (Barañano 425). According to Barañano, "space and time, far from constituting a sort of immutable undercurrent of social evolution, shift as profoundly as society does and present its same plurality and complexity" (52).[4] The underlying question is if we are seeing a process of inexorable territorial disembedding in which global connections are seen as a development that involve the triumph of culturally homogenizing forces over all others (Robertson 25).

This view may often involve a lack of concern with local issues as it looks primarily at the presence of the universal within the particular. To that effect, the need to introduce the concept of *glocalization* arises from the considera- tion of globalization as a process that overrides locality with the irreparable loss of identity, specificities, and localisms (Robertson 26). Furthermore, transnational immigration establishes significant links connecting the territo- ries of departure and arrival, the later evolving *translocal* characteristics (Smith and Guarnizo 11–12). Therefore, the *global* and the *local* tendencies are mutually implicated. The analysis of the documentary argues that the reconfiguration of the physical, symbolic, and imaginary spaces in Lavapiés is best understood not as a process of globalization, but as a process of *glocalization*, with a specific set of relations established between the global and the local communities that coexist in this area.

Basel Ramsis's documentary is a milestone for various reasons. First, it is the foremost of its kind in which an enormous diversity of nationalities who work and live in Lavapiés is represented. Second, his nonfiction film breaks a major barrier creating complicity between immigrants who are recorded and a filmmaker who, in turn, is an immigrant. As Ramsis states in an interview: "in the end it is an immigrant who speaks with another immigrant" (Romero "Meto la mano"). Although he acknowledges an extended rejection of the testimony in the documentary format, Ramsis recognizes the relevant role of these in his production. The importance of being an immigrant direc- tor leads to an egalitarian relationship with the characters while adding an interesting perspective that prevents a paternalistic gaze of the *other*.[5] The documentary allows Basel Ramsis to show the reality of Lavapiés and also, as he declares, to talk about a subject of his concern through the discourses of both transnational immigrants and autochthonous residents in this area (Ro- mero "Meto la mano"). According to Dapena, D´Lugo and Elena, *El otro lado* is a "full-length documentary that gives a lucid account of the country's new multicultural reality" (45). Furthermore, the nonfiction production shows how the process of globalization and transnational immigration has driven a restructuring of the physical and symbolic spaces in this metropoli- tan quarter, which makes Lavapiés an ideal case study of transfers that occur between the global and the local communities. With this work Ramsis collab- orates in the construction of a new collective imaginary in the neighborhood and offers a valuable portrait of immigrant settlements in the historic center of the Spanish capital.

The release of the documentary in 2002 coincides with the remarkable increase of immigrants arriving in this district previously characterized by an aging local population. As a result of these flows, there has been a revitaliza- tion of the historic center of Madrid. Lavapiés had experienced a sharp de- cline and loss of the autochthonous population in the past decades due to the migration to peripheral residential areas in response to other needs such as bigger houses and green spaces. The quarter is presented as attractive to transnational immigrants for both the proximity to the center of Madrid and the low cost of rents due to the substandard housing conditions. The high number of immigrants arriving in Lavapiés has made the place with the highest foreign-born population in Madrid. Moreover, it remains in the social imaginary as a genuine area that, in conjunction with multiculturalism, appeals to artists and intellectuals who have also settled there.

The division of the documentary into eight tales adds a poetic element to the production that contrasts with the testimonies of the people who live and work in the neighborhood. This organization responds to the need to raise questions related to issues such as the confluence of old and new identities, social and spatial segregation, ghettoized spaces and the devastating consequences for the future of the inhabitants under the Plan for Urban Development for Madrid (1997) promoted by the Mayor's Office.

Among key informants are the group of transnational immigrants represented by Africans, Arabs, Ecuadorians, Colombians, Argentines, Cubans, Bengali, Brazilian, and only one representative of the Chinese community.[6] The discourses offer each particular view on how the different collectives perform and interplay in public spaces. To reinforce the idea of equal treatment of individuals Ramsis avoids giving the name and origin of the informants in the documentary to prevent a stereotypical categorization of members of the communities represented in the film. From those representing the group of Spaniards are people with deep roots in the neighborhood, squatters established recently and representatives of the local Emilia Pardo Bazán Elementary School. The dialogues present a range of views that vary considerably on the impact caused by the arrival of new residents in Lavapiés. The collective formed by new youth also named as "alternatives" live as unlawful inhabitants in the so-called laboratories. These occupied and self-managed spaces provide a venue for art, theater, education, and political activism. This community is compounded by the presence of "activists whose ideologies and socio-political practices occur at the margin of the system" (Gómez 3). The majority is educated at university level, and their objective is the integration of all the collectives living in Lavapiés. Similarly, the theater company "Sala Triángulo" focuses on a specific cultural policy of integration. Another group with representation in the documentary is the association of neighbors "La Corrala" that focuses on a struggle in favor of the improvement of the district while avoiding the expulsion of its residents. This association, dating back to the last years of the dictatorship, was integrated by students against the regime and transformed Lavapiés into space of activism (Barañano et al. 80–82).

The testimony of informants offers a direct reflection on the sociospatial configuration of the quarter in physical, symbolic, and imaginary terms that contrasts with the narrative voice used to tell the story of a Jewish neighborhood with a long historical tradition and strong identity.[7] By means of the stories of the indigenous and the narrative voice, the director reconstructs the etymology of the word Lavapiés and the Jewish origin of the area formerly called *Avapies*. Several interviewees speculate that the name derived from a fountain, close to the synagogue where today stands the Church of San Lorenzo, in which people washed their feet as a gesture of purification. Through these stories the director invites the spectator to reflect on the place as a dynamic space in a constant re-inscription of its spaces throughout history. As Ringrose states, "Lavapiés has maintained during different centuries its function as a home for immigrants and other marginal populations that arrived in Madrid throughout different periods and in the late twentieth and twenty first centuries" (298).[8]

The images of the quarter captured by establishing shots reveal the transformative power of globalizing processes of transnational immigration that coexist with unique strong local traditions. The *glocal* character can be perceived in several ways through a camera that witnesses the socio-demographic and urban changes taking place in Lavapiés. The streets of the densely populated district exhibit a collage of colorful nationalities that demonstrate the increasing heterogeneity compared to a relatively stable situation in the past. Straight-on angles of mothers of different cultures with their children in the parks, elderly people sunning themselves on the street benches, and street musicians, among others, show the daily pacific contact of the collectives in shared places. While interaction between the groups appears to be superficial, Torres observes that this situation does not constitute a lack of sociability, but peaceful relationships regulated by social conventions established in the collective imaginary (377). However, it seems immigrants are often required to maintain an active search for personal interaction which would not be required among the local population (García Armand 129). The absence of social segregation is proven through the long shot of the heart of the neighborhood, *La Plaza de Lavapiés*, a crossroads for residents, workers, and passersby, but also a meeting point for leisure. The locked shot draws the attention of the audience to the fact that they are eyewitnesses of the multicultural reality of this area in which the square functions as a space of intersection and confluence. This area has always been known as a place with plenty of interaction, lively streets, and social circles, elements that the immigrants have integrated into their social routine. Perhaps this is due to the substandard housing as one interviewee notes, "the small space of the apartments invites the people out on the street."

Specific activities such as leisure, worship, and business bring into the Lavapiés new music, colors, names, and decoration that have dramatically changed the significance of these places, thus leaving behind the notion of static, unified, and homogeneous spaces. As a result, the incorporation of new pluralistic and multiethnic transnational identities has favored the process in which traditional spaces become *glocal* by means of interpenetration between the local and the global peculiarities. The documentary shows the physical and also symbolic reconfiguration through the transformation of businesses with a strong repercussion in the local economy. A clear example is the hairdresser at *Los Amigos*, owned by a Moroccan, whose shop front signage is written in both Arabic and Spanish. The name of the business retains the *castizo* essence that characterized Lavapiés in order to attract both local and global clients. The emergence of new businesses, mostly owned by people of Chinese and Arabic origin, is comprised of traditional shops and wholesalers as *La Muralla Long* that provides a range of products, such as bags and shoes, for many customers in the area. In the past decade there has been a proliferation of ethnic shops, cultural and retailer associations that contribute to the development of new patterns of mixed business with both national and international products. A substantial number of Moroccans and Senegalese were the first groups to settle in the quarter and began a number of small enterprises. Due to the proliferation of butcher shops, restaurants, and bazaars in Lavapiés the Moroccan community was conferred with a key role in the area. As a result, an image of a Maghreb neighborhood was created that still remains, although other collectives, such as Ecuadorians, outnumber them. The exchange of music, food, sports, cultural, and artistic activities has benefited not only the immigrants, but also the autochthonous people who until a few years ago did not know what a *Kebab* or *falafel* was, as one of the interviewee states. Nowadays these businesses not only signal an identity of the historical center of Madrid, but also find new customers from outside the area attracted by the multicultural and unique features of the district.

In the documentary the different discourses affect not only the metamorphosis of the space, but also the identity reconfiguration of the neighborhood. Imaginary representations differ among the testimonies of the interviewees captured by a sequence of medium shots that can vary from single, group, and two shots. Ramsis also introduces over-the-shoulder and close-up shots for a more intimate communication with the audience when personal experiences of xenophobia, racism, or marginalization are expressed by the informants. In collecting opinions from different members of the African, Arab, Chinese, Hispanic, and autochthonous groups, among others, Ramsis creates an image that initially may lead the viewer to perceive a fragmentation among the inhabitants of Lavapiés. The informants reflect on the questions "How do the ghettos function in the district" and "What is Lavapiés?" in order to find a common definition derived from the multiple conceptions offered. Individuals and collective views fall into an expressive axis in which respondents highlight their own experiences as immigrants, natives, passersby, and neighbors. Initially Ramsis gives the testimonies of interviewees who perceive Lavapiés as a set of *ghettos* and colonies within the area in which

customs and different languages prevail, and therefore impede the establishment of a full common coexistence among ethnic groups. A Spanish-born
woman declares that "although there is a visual mix of collectives in different
spaces, separate groups prevail in the quarter." Additionally a Romanian
woman explains the formation of ghettos due to racism and xenophobia
experienced by the communities of the same culture. Locals offer different
perceptions that range from those who see immigrants as "separate ethnicities living in their own ghetto" to those signaling the need to reinvent the
language and the term "ghetto" to endow it with a positive connotation. A
member of the African community also has a positive view that highlights
how "in the so-called ghettos many leading pan-African projects have
emerged." Manuel, head of studies of the Emilia Pardo Bazán Elementary
School, draws attention to the same tendency to grouping of the Spanish
national and transnational migration in the recent past. As he notes, "this
tendency is reproduced in migratory flows and not only in Lavapiés, but
eventually these groups will disperse." The quarter is an important point of
arrival of transnational immigration as many of them are chain immigrants
who wish to live with or near family and other members from their own
country of origin. Consequently there is a trend for particular collectives to
concentrate in specific locations without a uniform distribution throughout
the population.

The major challenge faced by this historic district is to re-actualize its
identity, which is also an important step on the way to recognition and
integration of its members (Barañano et al. 17). Benwell and Stokoe define
identity as an "essential, cognitive, socialized, phenomenological or psychic
phenomenon that governs human action" (3). Based on this, other questions
arise such as "what" identity people possess and "how" they may be distinguished from one another (3). To answer the question "what is Lavapiés" is a
difficult task due to the complexity of different collectives coexisting there.
Ramsis collects a wide range of discourses of oneness organized around three
main arguments which are the identification of the inhabitants with the
neighborhood, the identification of the groups, and the imaginary identity
fostered outside Lavapiés, mostly spread by the media.

The construction of identity of the quarter is created by the testimonies of
the informants while the spectators draw their own conclusions. In general,
transnational immigrants perceive it as the ideal place to live for reasons,
mentioned before, such as location or cheap rental market. Although opinions may vary, interviewees commonly recognize the "popular character" of
Lavapiés with which they identify while they feel supported by other members of the same communities, as a Spanish-born declares. A Senegalese man
identifies with the neighborhood as it reminds him of his own in Africa. The
new youth are attracted to Lavapiés as the multicultural nature of the area
offers new forms of expression and knowledge of other cultures. For this

group the district represents a way of living. The more nostalgic autochthonous group feels that Lavapiés was a much nicer place to live before the arrival of transnational immigration as there has been a loss of "authentic Madrilenian" uniqueness, and to a lesser degree, Spanish distinctiveness. Lavapiés has a rich history of representation in Spanish theater that has played a key role in constructing popular notions of a Madrilenian character articulated by *castizo* types (Feinberg 40). Parson also points out that *lo castizo* refers to an urban identity similar to that of the London cockney that is principally associated with the working class inhabitants of areas as Lavapiés or La Latina (184). These informants perceive an inevitable death of the quarter and its identity; however, it can be argued that the arrival of transnational immigration has resulted in a significant revitalization of the area.

Identification of the groups also varies one from another depending on the common elements they may share, such as religion in the case of Arabs, or language within the Hispanic community. Other collectives, such as the Moroccans and Chinese, perceive themselves as being the group that best integrates with other communities and with the autochthonous respectively. A minority of local residents with deep roots in the neighborhood are more cautious because they sense Lavapiés as more dangerous with the arrival of transnational immigration. This stigmatized vision of immigration related to criminal activities, is also shared by the member of the Chinese community, Leti Long. On one hand, these discourses show the indispensable reflection by the Spaniards on a multicultural reality and, on the other, they expose the tension between homogeneity and heterogeneity derived by the transition from an autarkic Francoist Spain to a global society (Martínez Carazo 265).

Basel Ramsis reveals a reality distorted on many occasions by both the stigmatized vision shared by a minority of the residents and the representation of Lavapiés in the media. The documentary puts emphasis on a nondisruptive image of the district, although some very marginal areas, such as the Plaza de Cabestreros, have been reported as conflictive due to clashes between socially excluded groups that constitute a minority in the neighborhood. This view is shared by most of the informants, who suggest that the cause of several problems is due to the conditions of exclusion and poverty of a number of immigrants. Manuel, head of studies of the elementary school, notes that these groups were already marginalized in their countries of origin. Many of the interviewees, linked to social movements of immigrants, appeal to the Mayor's Office to promote appropriate integration policies in order to end these marginal spaces in the quarter. Throughout these testimonies, the director breaks the demonized image of immigrants, particularly of Moroccans, constructed in the imaginary that links immigration with crime and extensively broadcast not just by the media, but also manipulated by some politicians seeking electoral victories and the removal of immigrants and squatters from Lavapiés. The Plan for Urban Development for Madrid

(1997), promoted by the Mayor's Office, has subjected Lavapiés to a process of gentrification that will result in higher housing and rental prices. This will have serious consequences not only for the displacement of the current transnational residents, who are anxious about their future in the quarter, but also for a new process of physical, symbolic, and identity reconfiguration of the area.

After analyzing these testimonies, we can deduce that discourses of identity are constructed on a multicultural conception of Lavapiés. Although some of the views manifest certain skepticism about this multicultural reality, the inhabitants allege it is too early to appreciate a shift in perception of transnational immigration in the collective imaginary. What qualifies Lavapiés as a multicultural neighborhood is not merely the presence of different national and ethnic groups in a common space, but also the existence of the current cultural exchanges and peaceful coexistence among their residents (Barañano et al. 115).

The end of the documentary raises concerns related to education, social integration, and the future of transnational immigrants in Lavapiés. Ten years later, a study done in 2011 shows that the district still boasts a high number of transnational individuals, 31.1 percent, with eighty-eight different nationalities (Schmidt 3). At present, Lavapiés is still an attractive place for the settlement of transnational people in established communities that can provide networks and key contacts for new residents in the area (Barañano et al. 222).

El otro lado is a significant contribution of Basel Ramsis to visualize the social, demographic, and urban changes taking place in the downtown of Lavapiés under the influence of globalization. The arrival of new neighbors has driven a process of physical and symbolic transformation of the space reconfiguring both old and new identities. Transnational immigration, squatters, artist, and autochthonous population with deep roots in the area have consolidated a kaleidoscopic reality of a unique popular and multicultural neighborhood in the heart of Madrid. As a result, contemporary Lavapiés should be understood as a *glocal* space comprised by the local, the national, and the global communities.

NOTES

1. Like Madrid, the three other major cities of Spain—Barcelona, Valencia, and Seville—have experienced the same concentration of transnational people in their neighborhoods.

2. Barcelona has attracted the attention of filmmakers such as José Luis Guerín in his documentary *En construcción* (2001). The nonfiction film, set in the old area of the city and known as *El Raval*, shows the transformation of the neighborhood in the past decades due to the arrival of transnational immigration and the urban renewal promoted by the major office.

3. Other documentaries and docudramas in which Madrid urban spaces become a remarkable part of the production are *Extranjeras* (2003) by Helena Taberna, *Pobladores* (2006) by Manuel García Serrano and *Cantando bajo la tierra* (2004) by Rolando Pardo.

4. All translations are by the author of this chapter unless otherwise indicated.

5. In the last decade the number of filmmakers with immigrant origin and links has proliferated significantly. Among others are Ana Torres, Rolando Pardo, Omer Oke, and Santiago A. Zannou.

6. The Chinese community rejected the possibility of being interviewed as a collective. Only one member volunteered, as Basel Ramsis explains in the documentary.

7. Historic tradition and strong identity of the neighborhood are determined by the fact that its buildings were built prior to 1920, as Schmidt states (11).

8. Ringrose explains that Madrid has been a city of immigrants since it became the capital of Spain through the present day (233).

WORKS CITED

Arango, Joaquín. "Exceptional in Europe? Spain's Experience with Immigration and Integration." *Migration Policy Institute*. March 2013. Web October 2013.

Barañano Cid, Margarita. "Escalas, des/re-anclajes y transnacionalismo. Complejidades de la relación global-local." *Las encrucijadas de la diversidad cultural*. Ed. Antonio Ariño, Madrid: Centro de Investigaciones Sociológicas, 2005, 425–51.

Barañano Cid, Margarita, et al. *Globalización, Inmigración transnacional y reestructuración de la región metropolitana de Madrid. Estudio del barrio de Embajadores*. Madrid: Fundación Sindical de Estudios, Ediciones GPS, 2006.

Benwell, Bethan, and Stokoe Elizabeth. *Discourse and Identity*. Edinburgh: Edinburgh University Press, 2006.

Dapena Gerard, D'Lugo Marvin, and Elena Alberto. "Transnational Frameworks." *A Companion to Spanish Cinema*. Eds. Jo Labanyi and Tatjana Pavlović. Oxford: Wiley-Blackwell, 2013, 15–49.

Estébanez Álvarez, José, Molina Ibáñez, Mercedes, and Pérez Sierra, Carmen. "Madrid, configuración de una ciudad global." *Geographicalia* 30 (1993): 177–90.

Feinberg, Matthew Isaiah. "Lavapiés, Madrid as Twenty-First Century Urban Spectacle." Diss. University of Kentucky, 2011.

García Armand, Asunción. "El rol de las mujeres en el devenir de un barrio intercultural: el Raval de Barcelona." *Inmigración, género y espacios urbanos*. Eds. Mary Nash, Raquel Tello and Nuria Benach. Barcelona: Edicions Bellaterra, 2005, 123–40.

Gómez, Mayte. "El barrio de Lavapiés, laboratorio de interculturalidad." *Dissidences: Hispanic Journal of Theory and Criticism*. September 2006. Web. January 2014.

Martínez Carazo, Cristina. "Cine e inmigración: Madrid como espacio de encuentro/desencuentro y su representación en *Extranjeras* de Helena Taberna." *Hispanic Research Journal* 6(3) (2005): 265–75.

Parson, Deborah. "Fiesta Culture in Madrid Posters, 1934–1955." *Constructing Identity in Contemporary Spain*. Ed. Lo Labanyi. Oxford: Oxford University Press, 2002, 178–205.

Pereda, Carlos, Walter Actis, and Miguel Ángel Prada. *Inmigrantes nuevos ciudadanos ¿Hacia una España plural e intercultural?* Madrid: Fundación de las Cajas de Ahorros (FUNCAS), 2008.

Ramsis, Basel, dir. *El otro lado: un acercamiento a Lavapiés*. Dayra Arts, 2002. DVD. Courtesy of Basel Ramsis.

Ringrose, David. "Madrid, capital imperial (1561–1833)." *Madrid: historia de una capital*. Eds. Santos Juliá, David Ringrose, and Cristina Segura. Madrid: Alianza, 2000, 155–314.

Robertson, Roland. "Glocalization: Time-Space and Homogeneity-Heterogeneity." *Global Modernities*. Eds. Michael Featherstone, Scott Lash, and Roland Robertson. London: Sage, 1995, 25–44.

Romero, Jessica. "Meto la mano en zonas que son tabúes en el mundo árabe." Interview with Basel Ramsis. *Periodismo Humano*, March 31, 2010. Accessed March 23, 2013.

Sassen, Saskia. "The Global City: Introducing a Concept." *Journal of World Affairs* 2 (2005): 27–43.

Schmidt, Hebe. "Lavapiés. Fenómeno migratorio y claves de la convivencia." *Cuadernos de la Epic, Comunidad de Madrid,* March 7, 2012. Accessed June 2013.

Smith, Michael Peter, and Luis Eduardo Guarnizo. *Transnationalism from Below.* New Brunswick: Transaction Publishers, 1998.

Torres Pérez, Francisco. "Los nuevos vecinos en la Plaza. Inmigrantes, espacios y sociabilidad pública." *Revista de Antropología Iberoamericana* 3 (2008): 366–97.

Valero Escandell, José Ramón. "Los espacios de mayor inmigración en los centros históricos:algunos ejemplos en las grandes ciudades españolas." *Cuadernos de geografía* 83 (2008): 27–38.

Verdugo, Richard R., and David Swanson. "Immigration and its Effects on Demographic Change in Spain." *The Open Demography Journal* 4 (2011): 22–33. Web.

Chapter Eight

Ecuadorian Immigration and the Transformation of Religious and Civic Space in Madrid in *La Churona: Historia de una Virgen Migrante* by María Cristina Carrillo Espinosa

Maryanne L. Leone

The immigration of Ecuadorians to Spain has brought a contiguous migration of spiritual practices that have redefined public and religious space in the city of Madrid. María Cristina Carrillo Espinosa's documentary *La Churona: Historia de una Virgen Migrante* (2010, 82 mins.)[1] tells of the veneration of a Marian figure in Ecuador and the transfer of that worship to Madrid, where approximately 120,000 of the 400,000 Ecuadorian immigrants in Spain reside (Gobierno de España 18, 26, 33, 52).[2] Her film highlights Ecuadorians in the heart of Madrid, at the center of iconic spaces.[3] Through an analysis of the film *La Churona*, this chapter discusses Ecuadorians' active role in creating and asserting a place for themselves in twenty-first century multicultural Spain, resistance and acceptance of Ecuadorian immigrants in Madrid, and the impact of global migration on urban spaces, religious practices, and local and national identities.

Distribution of *La Churona: Historia de una Virgen Migrante* has been successful in alternative circuits to commercial theater. The film has been selected for inclusion at film festivals in seven different countries (Bolivia, Ecuador, Cuba, México, Colombia, Uruguay, Finland) and at events on Ecuadorian film in New York City, New Jersey, Connecticut, Georgia (Russia), Barcelona, and Paris. *La Churona* also has been shown at six universities, in the United States, Murcia, Spain, and in Quito, Ecuador, as well as at commercial cinemas in Quito and in Loja, Ecuador, and at Casa de América in Madrid, Spain. Reception has been positive. [4] At Cine 8 y Medio [Eight and One-Half Cinema] in Quito, the film's run was extended by a week, and at Casa de América the one night showing at the one hundred-seat theater sold out with dozens of spectators still in line. [5] The migration from Ecuador of over one million people in the 1990s and 2000s has reshaped communities in Ecuador, in Spanish cities, and in other immigration destinations (Jokisch). Carrillo's representation of the impact of the figure of La Churona and the use urban space to create inclusion in an environment of exclusion for Ecuadorians in the diaspora has claimed the interest of audiences with direct and indirect connections to this transnational exchange.

Contemporary, postcolonial, and colonial migration and travel intersect in the figure of the Virgin of El Cisne, who appeared to the indigenous people of El Cisne, Ecuador, in 1594. [6] Today 150,000–200,000 people walk the three-day, seventy-two kilometer pilgrimage route from El Cisne to Loja that originated with a decree Simón Bolívar issued in 1829. [7] Worshippers call the Virgin of El Cisne "La Churona," which means "The Curly-Haired One," and she holds a military rank and the nickname "the General," suggesting she symbolizes not only religious faith but also Ecuadorian independence and national pride. Fast-forward to Madrid, Spain, more than four hundred years after the miraculous appearance of the Virgin. An Ecuadorian family asks their parish priest if they may place a framed image of the Virgin in the church, and then Carmen Ballagán, an Ecuadorian woman residing in Madrid, asks if she may place a statue in the sanctuary. The priest agrees and Carmen returns to Ecuador to bring a statue of La Churona to Spain so that she and her compatriots may publically express their devotion to this Virgin in their new place of residence. This replica and La Churona's immigration to Spain transform the rituals and cultural practices at the Church of San Lorenzo in Lavapiés, a neighborhood generally associated with Spain's working classes and more recently with Madrid's immigrant population. As portrayed in the film, this Marian figure symbolizes the precarious position of Ecuadorian immigrants without legal status and the formation of community in the diaspora. She also provokes anxiety on the part of Spanish nationals from the more visible presence in Madrid of residents of foreign origin and changing cultural practices.

A symbol of the ambiguous situation of many immigrants, La Churona legally enters Spain, papers in hand, but then finds herself homeless and at the center of a local, parochial controversy about dominion over her. Carrillo's documentation of the statue's trajectory from factory to flight leads to reflection on national identity and the patrol of borders. Antonino Jaramillo, who works at a factory in San José, Ecuador, dedicated to the fabrication of religious iconography, describes what he calls "el procedimiento más adecuado" [the most suitable method] (24:06–24:08) to transport statues of the

Virgin. He carefully wraps her outstretched arm to protect it from breakage, covers her head in clear plastic, places the statue in a black plastic bag, and uses a second one to cover her head "para que no se vea" [so that she cannot be seen] (23:09–23:12). Antonino advises that travelers acquire permission from the airline in advance and that they inform check-in agents of their possession of the Virgin before passing through security, where she will be subject to X-ray examination. Highlighting control and suspicion at the borders, the artisan's suggestions insinuate that even if one has obtained permission, it is best not to call attention to oneself when emigrating.

Antonino's knowledge of the process to prepare a replica of the Señora del Cisne for air travel points to the commonality of the voyage and her transnational status. Indeed, a writer from Loja explains that the Virgin of El Cisne also is known as "la Viajera . . . porque es como si ella fuera a acompañar los que han emigrado" [the Traveler . . . because it's as if she traveled with those who emigrated] (21:43–21:54).[8] Alluding to her migratory identity, Antonino notes that the accessories—the baby Jesus and a crown, for example—easily fit in one's suitcase and, with the Virgin wrapped as he suggests, "llevas un bulto que es manejable" [you travel with a package that's easy to handle] (23:29–23:35). Nonetheless, reverence for La Churona is such that some travelers buy a seat for her rather than store her in the overhead compartment. The election to film the back of the person transporting the statue in the airport, later presented as Carmen, with the Virgin facing backward rather than forward toward her destination as she passes under the bright yellow "Migration" sign, suggests that this migrant's story is not hers alone; she represents the many Ecuadorians leaving their country despite their desire to stay and carrying with them their cultural identity and practices. The documentary also stresses impediments to immigration and the surveillance of migrating people and practices when Carmen later speaks about her journey with the Virgin and the steps she took to have her documents notarized to avert possible problems with migration. For Carmen, notarization also signifies authentication of the spiritual value of the replica and the cultural practice that she transports to Madrid. As we will see however, migration alters the rituals and significance of the Virgin to produce a transnational figure with spiritual and civic potency.

La Churona's migration to Madrid along with hundreds of thousands of Ecuadorians has contributed to changes in the space of the city. Henri Lefebvre argues that people produce space and that urban spaces in particular highlight this social production.[9] Although seemingly removed from twenty-first century Spain, parallels may be seen between Lefebvre's thirteenth-century example of a "newly engendered spatial relationship" (78) in the transformation of land use and production in Tuscany and the globalization of Madrid. As greater numbers of immigrants came to Spain in the 1990s and the first decade of the twentieth century than ever before in response to economic demand and unfavorable situations in their home countries, foreign migrants occupied positions formerly filled with Spanish laborers and brought change to the use and character of social spaces. [10] At the same time that space is a tool to dominate and control, "the social and political (state) forces which engendered this space seek, but fail, to master it completely" (26). The documentary emphasizes La Churona and her followers' alteration of public and spiritual social spaces— streets, squares, a park, and Catholic churches.

The filming of Ecuadorian migrants in the streets and squares of Madrid as well as in the internal spaces of churches stresses movement. Michel de Certeau contrasts the panoramic view of the city with the perspective from the streets, where people enact diverse uses of the urban spaces that escape the totalizing city seen from above: "one can follow the swarming activity of these procedures that, far from being regulated or eliminated by panoptic administration, have reinforced themselves in a proliferating illegitimacy, developed and insinuated themselves into the networks of surveillance" (96). In Carrillo's *La Churona*, if the bird's-eye view is of a fictitious hegemonic Spanish identity, the street view reveals a global city in which colonialist histories interact with the present, culture undergoes transformation, and power is multidirectional, collective, and individual, rather than emanating only from Spanish authorities and autochthonous citizens or only from Ecuadorians. [11]

The Virgin of El Cisne's migration from Ecuador to Madrid revitalizes the Church of San Lorenzo and facilitates the creation of a spiritual and transnational space for Ecuadorians and other Latin Americans, yet the micro-view reveals that her transnational move also invokes interactions colored with colonialist undertones. According to Lefebvre, products mask the labor that produces them and "also the social relationships of exploitation and domination on which they are founded" (80–81). Carrillo's film exposes the material production of La Churona statues, as previously described, and examines points of contact between Ecuadorians and Spaniards in contemporary Madrid to better understand the former's experiences of migration and highlight the importance of familial and cultural ties to community formation. [12] Father Emilio Regúlez, a priest at San Lorenzo's Church for eighteen years, expresses his desire to serve the needs of this new group of parishioners and he exhibits adaptability in the sermons and liturgies he delivers and rituals he develops. With broad smile and amiability, Father Juan José Arbalí, a younger priest at the parish, reaches out to Ecuadorians in numerous ways throughout the film, such as visiting homes to bless them and offer a portrait of La Churona to grace their walls and showing new immigrants the dresses and accessories for the Virgin, kept in a former broom closet the priests have transformed to house the collection. Without question, the priests welcome the Ecuadorian community to their church; yet, Carrillo's presentation also suggests their paternalism and simplification of a multicultural church and city. While Father Emilio adapts the use of space in the church, his words and gestures when he describes the introduction of the Virgin to the sanctuary at San Lorenzo—hands up as if holding a frame and bouncing up and down slightly—suggest that he infantilizes the Ecuadorians and their devotion rather than view their faith reverently: "Vamos a entrar, en lugar de ponerlo, un poco procesionalmente. Pues entramos allí, cantando un poquito, hasta ponerlo y colocarlo en un retablo" [Instead of just putting her there, we decided to do it with a little procession. We sang a little bit and then placed the image in an altarpiece] (32:38–32:47). Seated in a circle with a small group of parishioners, Father Juan José comments on the similarities of design among the small plastic flags linked in a chain under the image of La Churona and explains: "Esto es para mostrar que la iglesia es la misma en Nicaragua, Bolivia, Colombia, España. Todos sitios. . . . [T]e acogen en Nicaragua, te acogen en España" [This is to show that the church is the same in Nicaragua, Bolivia, Colombia, Spain. Everywhere. . . . They welcome you in Nicaragua the same way they do in Spain] (31:38–31:48). Despite good intentions, this scene immediately preceding Father Emilio's description of his introduction of La Churona to the sanctuary suggests that the priests simplify or avoid a more difficult discussion of the frustrations that Latin American immigrants face in Madrid and express in later scenes when the priests are not present. Furthermore, Ecuadorians are agents of change in Madrid, reshaping practices and constituting religious space, not just filling pews; yet the priests seem to see themselves as the innovators and as shepherds of a naïve flock in need of guidance, a view that may not be limited to the Ecuadorian worshippers, but nonetheless brings to the surface a colonialist epistemology. [13]

Processions with La Churona place Ecuadorians and their spiritual practices in the city's historic center and create a parallel with processions of Marian figures associated with Madrid, such as her female patron saint, the Almudena, whom some in the film assert has exclusive rights to proceed into the Plaza Mayor, and the more populist Virgin of la Paloma, whose accompaniment in her annual journey through the Latina district of Madrid by a squadron of the Corps of Firefighters recalls the military's association with La Churona in Ecuador. New compositions of social space do not erase previous networks of relationships, market structures, and historical experiences, but rather build upon past layers: "Social spaces interpenetrate one another and/or superimpose themselves on one another" (Lefebvre 86–87). The procession of La Churona retains traces of the pilgrimage in Loja yet realizes a new ritual for Ecuadorians in the diaspora, and expands the virginal association with Madrid's Plaza Mayor to include the Ecuadorian Virgin. [14] De Certeau argues that people assess what is possible, necessary, and prohibited as they walk known paths and create new ones: "Walking affirms, sus-

pects, tries out, transgresses, respects" (99). Walking alters spatial organization and meaning in the city. In the case of La Churona, her network of
worshippers assigns new meaning and makes patent the visibility and vitality
of Madrid's Ecuadorian population as they gather en masse to walk the city
streets to the Plaza Mayor. The practice of a pilgrimage route in Madrid
opens the city's historic central square to a symbolic association with Ecuadorian identity, faith, and culture that moreover reshapes cultural practices.
Whereas de Certeau emphasizes that walking facilitates the manifestation of
old and development of new expressions of identity, Lefebvre argues more
generally that social space, "itself the outcome of past actions, . . . is what
permits fresh actions to occur, while suggesting others and prohibiting yet
others" (73). A journalist from the newspaper *Latino* notes her surprise at the
high turnout and the diversity of attendees, who hail not only from Loja, but
also from many regions of Ecuador and may not have worshipped La Churona in their home country. The presence of a city councilor from Madrid's
central district (Luis Asúa Brunt), Father Emilio, and Carmen Ballagán on a
platform at the veneration in the Plaza Mayor suggests that Ecuadorian migrants comprise a constituency worth courting to advance political or institutional agendas. The councilor recognizes the priest for his work on integration and elicits cheers from the crowd when he calls out: "¡Viva Ecuador!,
¡Viva!, ¡Viva Madrid!, ¡Viva!, ¡Viva España!, ¡Viva!, ¡Viva la Virgen del
Cisne!" [Long live Ecuador!, Hurrah!, Long live Madrid!, Hurrah!, Long live
Spain!, Hurrah! Long live the Virgin of El Cisne!, Hurrah!] (34:22–34:28)
The call alludes to harmony and equality; nonetheless, the film exposes
cracks in the veneer of integration, despite cheers from the crowd of Ecuado-
rian migrants celebrating in the Plaza Mayor.

Paralleling the reception that many immigrants experience in the diaspora, two years after her arrival the Virgin finds that she is not welcome in her
new place of residence. As recounted by Spanish parishioners and the report-
er for *Latino*, Father Emilio no longer allowed her in the church once Carmen, the woman who brought her from Ecuador, placed her in a glass case
with a box whose donations she intended to collect for her private association
in honor of the Virgin.[15] Carmen moves the statue to a bar that she owns in
Lavapiés, a location whose incongruity with the Virgin's status highlights
her dislocation.[16] Javier de Lucas argues that a guarantee of the rights of
citizenship, education on mutual responsibility, and the recognition of cultural symmetry form the basis for a just intercultural society; yet that Spain's
immigration and integration policies fall short.[17] The uprooting of the spiritual figure of La Churona implies that the Spanish national body, as individuals, institutions, and community groups, fails to offer a rightful place to
immigrants. The Virgin's localization in Lavapiés, a social space in which a
diversity of ethnicities have displaced the formerly Spanish working class
identity of the neighborhood, relates to an identity in flux. Through the figure

of the seventeen-year-old Jonathan, whose mother left her three children with her parents seven years prior to seek work in Spain, the documentary connects the Virgin of El Cisne's lack of place to the impact of migration on families left in the country of origin. At the end of the film, the children leave Quito and reunite with their mother in Murcia, Spain; a subtitle at the end of the film, however, explains that Jonathan plans to return to Ecuador, suggesting his physical, emotional, and cultural dislocation. The subtitle that follows, which also provides the final words in film, communicates that the European Parliament has passed the "Shame Directive" (1:19:10), a policy that would return immigrants without residency permits to their home country. The closing words of the film underscore multilayered manifestations of global displacement, from the local context of a Madrid neighborhood to all countries of the European Union to the communities of those left behind in the country of origin.

The debate that ensues in the church and neighborhood about the Virgin of El Cisne's rightful place reveals tensions that result from anxiety among some Spanish parishioners over not only the place and space that the Virgin of El Cisne occupies, but also the Ecuadorians' place and influence at the Lavapiés church and in broader Spanish society. One parishioner comments that "we" moved our virgin, the virgin of los Colores, to make a place for the Ecuadorians' Virgin. Another woman alludes to the debt she believes immigrants owe the priests: "Si les han abierto los brazos, les dan de todo, les dan de comer, les buscan trabajo. . . . Quiero decirte que les han acogido con cariño" [They welcome them with open arms. They give them everything. Food, work, shelter . . . I'm saying that they have been given a warm welcome] (38:03–38:15). Not all the neighbors hold this view however. One woman interjects that the disagreement over the Virgin is separate from assistance received and an older man at the bar is skeptical that such a large church has no space for the Virgin. Javier de Lucas has argued that associating multiculturalism with current migration to Spain negates an already existing diversity in society and breeds the erroneous perception of a preexisting superior, homogeneous culture in the receiving society (36). Contrary to de Lucas's affirmation that "todos tenemos la palabra para proponer, negociar, decidir" [we all have a say, to propose ideas, negotiate, decide] (41), at least some of the neighbors view themselves as the de facto gatekeepers of the physical and spiritual space of San Lorenzo's parish.

While arguments for whether Carmen or Father Emilio had the right to donations given in honor of the Virgin within the bounds of the church can be made for each side, more importantly, the disagreement highlights the extra-spiritual benefits that the Virgin of El Cisne confers to persons associated with delivering her to worshippers. In addition to monetary rewards, the priests at San Lorenzo gain parishioners at a time of lower church attendance among Spaniards. The film highlights that the redistribution of power to an Ecuadorian woman produces unease not only within the establishment at San Lorenzo, but also within the Catholic Diocese of Madrid. After a second church, María la Reparadora, located near the Gran Vía and the Plaza de España, accepted the Virgin and welcomed her with ceremony and applause, the Diocese ordered her removal. When describing major shifts in the social organization of space, Lefebvre notes the rise of conflict due to some who see "a new representation of space" and others who "continue to experience space in the traditional emotional and religious manner" (79). We see this division in *La Churona* among the parishioners at San Lorenzo's and in the bishop's reaction to worship of the Virgin of El Cisne and perhaps Carmen's competing power. The camera looks toward and foregrounds a spokeswoman for Carmen's association, who explains to a crowd of Ecuadorians with the same vantage point as the camera—that the bishopric threatened to put the Virgin of El Cisne on the street. In the background, the shot shows an official announcement on the church door from the Diocese that the bishop of Ecuador had to cancel his visit to Madrid for that same day. The contrast of the bureaucratic, impersonal tone of the notice, which speaks for an Ecuadorian bishop, with the spokesperson's plaintive voice, and the view from the Ecuadorians gathered on the street, suggests that *La Churona*'s director empathizes with the Virgin's devotees. In the previous scene, a journalist for RTVE's social chronicle *España Directo* observes that La Churona has been called "la virgen de los sin papeles" [the virgin without documentation] (39:36–39:38) and, in this scene outside the Church of María la Reparadora, Ecuadorians compare the Virgin's situation to the treatment they themselves have received: "Vale si nos humillan a nosotros, pero no a la Virgen" [We don't mind if they humiliate us, but not the Virgin] (40:46–40:48). At this point, the camera points at the Ecuadorians, capturing the distress on their faces and their verbal protests. The film's silence on the Diocese's rationale further leads the viewer to side with the Ecuadorians while a camera shot of a parked police car and another one driving by alludes to the distrust with which Spanish authorities view immigrants and the prejudices immigrants face. When juxtaposed with the reason for their gathering, to worship a Marian figure, the officers' patrol and the Diocese's response appear unjust. The Virgin's rejection signals condescension, incomprehension, and anxiety on the part of Spaniards in response to a more ethnically diverse society.

While Carrillo exposes anxieties in the Catholic institution and among some Spanish parishioners over the political and spiritual power of the Ecuadorian community, she also confounds a duality that would elevate Carmen, the Ecuadorian woman responsible for the statue's migration to Madrid. Although Carmen claims: "Siempre he estado peleando por que se respete la fe de la junta ecuatoriana" [I have always fought so that people respect Ecuadorian community's religious beliefs] (41:30–41:35), the film casts doubt on the singularity of her motives. While she indeed facilitates a trans-national devotion to La Churona through bringing a carved image of her to Madrid, the film suggests that Ms. Ballagán also seeks renown within the Ecuadorian community. [18] Kept at her house after the disagreement, Carmen organizes a procession for La Churona at Our Lady of Lluc Parish in Ciudad Lineal, a working class neighborhood that also has seen a notable influx of residents from Latin America. The camera position transmits the sensation to the viewer that he or she is one of the pilgrims who walks from the church to festivities at a nearby park, recalling de Certeau's assertion that "practition-ers of the city . . . compose a manifold story that has neither author nor spectator" (93). At the park's entrance, several women who sell tickets to the festival on behalf of Carmen's association complain that people are entering through another side of the park without paying. Although Carmen organizes the event, neither she nor the priests at San Lorenzo's nor the Diocese can direct all of the practices related to La Churona that unfold. Later, the film shows footage of Carmen stating that she seeks to show Spain and Europe the rich art and culture of Ecuador and then, highlighting her desire for popularity, cuts to a beauty contest that Carmen organizes as part of the festivities for the Virgin. The fact that the contest includes a question on how Spanish authorities should treat immigrants makes patent a common experi-ence of discrimination. Carrillo's documentary attests to heartfelt devotion to La Churona and the merging of the popular with the spiritual, yet also to the use of the Virgin to bolster individuals' political ambitions. A still frame at the end of the film explains that Carmen ran the second beauty contest in 2009, with no homage to the Virgin of El Cisne, and that she ran for a seat on the National Assembly of Ecuador in Europe.

Carrillo's production presents the Virgin of El Cisne as a paradoxical force and symbol in relation to the contemporary migration of Ecuadorians to Spain. She enables her supporters to attain social power, from Carmen who seeks political office to the masses of Ecuadorians who, revering the Virgin, influence parish priests in Madrid to reform cultural practices in the spiritual spaces they oversee. The Virgin of El Cisne creates a home for Ecuadorians in the diaspora despite desire to return: "Mucha gente aquí nos miran como si fuéramos extraños, pero viendo a mi país, a la Virgen, qué bonito, es una casa donde uno se vuelve a vivir" [Many people here look at us as if we were strange, but when I see my country, the Virgin, how wonderful, it's familiar, like I've come home again] (1:08:59–1:09:14). [19] The documentary suggests, too, that La Churona enables reconciliation and a space of coexistence among Spanish and Ecuadorians. In an interview in the film, Father Emilio notes his conversion into a devotee of the Virgin of El Cisne and observes the powerful effect of union that the Virgin has had on the parish. Carrillo's filming supports this view, showing one of the women who criticized the Ecuadorians receiving communion at mass and following with a shot of a letter from the sanctuary of the Virgin of El Cisne in Loja, Ecuador, offering blessings of the image to be venerated in Madrid. Father Juan José traveled to Loja to learn about the Virgin of El Cisne and the faith of her followers, take part in the pilgrimage, and bring back to his church "una copia lo más posiblemente exacta" [the most accurate copy possible] of the Virgin (44:12–44:17). We see this priest as well walking with Ecuadorians, enveloped in a procession through Lavapiés. The filming suggests, however, that venerating the Virgin of El Cisne in Madrid does not replicate the experience in Loja. A panoptic view of Lavapiés that leads into a scene of the dedication of this replica insinuates misinterpretations and recalls the colonizing project. Inside the church most—though not all—of the shots replicate Father Emilio's view looking from the altar out to the people, who fill this religious space. Father Juan José, standing off-center on the altar, announces Ecuadorians of different regions—such as Cayambe, located 700 kilometers from Loja—in traditional costume who present food and dresses for the Virgin to a visiting monsignor from Loja. De Certeau speaks of a "misunderstanding of practices" and simplification of complexities from the voyeur's view, which the folkloric offering suggests (93). La Churona's audience widens, she brings exuberant parishioners and revitalizes the parish of San Lorenzo, and she broadens ritualistic ceremonies to include her cult and the cults of other Virgin Marys; yet Carrillo's documentary implies that her welcome into this religious space is conditioned, at least in part, on her delivery of benefits to the parish.[20]

Outside religious spaces, the film connects La Churona to Ecuadorians' assertion of their right to a political voice in civic Madrid and recognition as equal citizens. A sequence of scenes moves from La Churona's transatlantic voyage to Carmen's description of the notarized paperwork she carried for the Virgin to the director of an Ecuadorian community association's observations on the emigration of memory and popular practices, and finally to a newscast announcing ETA's bombing of the T-4 parking lot at Madrid's Barajas airport and the search for two Ecuadorian citizens. Carrillo's documentary juxtaposes the media's implication of the Ecuadorians' involvement in the December 30, 2006, bombing with a scene of protest and peace. The camera follows a man with an Ecuadorian flag draped over his shoulders as he walks along the Paseo de Recoletos, past the El Espejo restaurant, to Madrid's Cibeles, with shots of the Telecommunications Palace (now called Centro Centro) and the Puerta de Alcalá in the background. The camera's position gives the viewer the sense that she or he is with the Ecuadorian people on the street, sharing their perspectives, participating with them in asserting Ecuadorians' rights. Staging the protest next to iconic architectural symbols of Madrid reinforces the verbal and printed messages of integration and solidarity with Spain. Signs read: "POR LA PAZ, CONTRA EL TERRORISMO" [FOR PEACE, AGAINST TERRORISM] while protestors shout in unison: "Ecuador, España, unidos por la paz" [Ecuador, Spain, together for peace] and "¡Esos muertos no eran de segunda!" [Those who died were not second-class citizens!] (29:18–29:39). The calls of solidarity with *madrileños* and pronouncements of Ecuadorians' civil rights and contributions to a diverse Spanish nation demand the kind of inclusive, plural, egalitarian, and collaborative society that de Lucas advocates (47). By holding the protest in Madrid's Cibeles, a highly trafficked location that is a site for both public outcry and celebrations of local and national reach, from marches against budget cuts related to gatherings to revel in Real Madrid's win of the Spanish title or Spain's win of the Copa de Europa, Ecuadorians assert their voices to the discourse on citizenship to reshape the public narrative on Ecuadorian migrants.

Carrillo's film documents the impact of Ecuadorian migration on sociopolitical relations in religious and civic spaces of urban Spain. This exploration of some layers of Madrid's "flaky *mille-feuille* pastry" reveals the protagonism of a migrant Virgin in the realization of spiritual and public spaces in which Ecuadorian migrants inscribe their right of place, cultural and religious identities, and political voice in a shifting multicultural Spain.[21] As Ecuadorian migrants seek a place for their variation of *marianismo* in the capital city and articulate national pride and community through the figure of La Churona, some Spanish citizens manifest apprehension over the growing presence and power of the Ecuadorian community in Madrid and others negotiate a role for themselves in this cultural and spiritual expression. The film emphasizes tensions in a multicultural society under construction rather than the harmonious resolution asserted by the priests at the Church of San Lorenzo, *La Churona: Historia de una virgen migrante* also reveals new "constellations of social space" that cross national borders as a result of the global migration of people and their cultural practices (Prakash 2). While a panoptic view produces an asymmetric society, greater contact in everyday practices on Madrid's streets may lead to an intercultural Spain in which the novel—La Churona and Ecuadorian citizenry—becomes convention, beats in the rhythm of global Madrid's urban landscape.

NOTES

1. I gratefully acknowledge María Cristina Carrillo Espinosa, director of *La Churona: Historia de una virgen migrante*, and Ecuador para Largo for allowing me to use direct quotes from the film.

2. Political crisis in Ecuador, a crash in oil prices, and the effects of El Niño hurricanes led to increasing poverty in Ecuador in the 1990s while demand for manual labor and favorable residency laws animated men and women from all regions of Ecuador to immigrate to Spain, a shift from mostly rural men migrating to Canada, the United States, and Venezuela in the 1970s and 1980s. For a description of stages of Ecuadorian migration to Spain, see Gómez Ciriano.

3. Carrillo was studying in Madrid and was struck by the ongoing process of Ecuadorians arriving to Spain and the surprise of Spaniards. She filmed *La Churona* between 2007 and 2009

(Carrillo, "Migrant"). Carrillo is completing a doctorate in anthropology at the Universidad Autónoma de Madrid and has published on the impact of migration on Ecuadorian families and on the role of photography in maintaining community bonds. She has a bachelor's degree in anthropology from the Pontificia Universidad Católica del Ecuador and in film from the Escuela de San Antonio de los Baños, La Habana, Cuba. She completed her master's degree in gender and migration from the Facultad Latinoamericana de Ciencias Sociales (FLACSO), Ecuador, to where she returns regularly to teach (Carrillo, Curriculum).

4. Carrillo facilitated a list of distribution venues and prizes. The official blog and website note some of this information and comment on public reception of the documentary (Carrillo, "La Churona," "Re: artículo"; "La Churona," Ecuador). See also Pérez, Puga, and Villarruel, and news articles "Esta noche," and "'La Churona' regresa." In his brief review, Pérez commends the film for a multidimensional treatment of migration that exposes contradictions stemming from the colonial legacy with Spain and from desire to return to Ecuador.

5. Primary contributors to the film's $150,000 budget include the National Counsel of Cinematography of Ecuador, Ecuador's Ministry of Culture, and Flacso (Latin American School of Social Sciences) (Villarruel). Carrillo's film has garnered two prizes, one from the National Counsel of Cinematography of Ecuador in 2007 for full-length documentary and the other at the International Festival of New Latin American Film in La Habana, Cuba, in 2009, for postproduction. Carrillo's script was granted a Development of Latin American Scripts Project scholarship from the Carolina Foundation and the Casa de América in Madrid to support production.

6. Lizardo Herrera provides a fascinating analysis of the significance of baroque and neobaroque Latin American aesthetic elements to the film's representations of national identity, colonialism, popular customs, and social inclusion, and he concludes that *La Churona* exposes the failure of the Ecuadorian nation to provide a national home for its citizens.

7. According to the legend, when the Royal Court ordered the people of El Cisne to emigrate on account of famine, the Virgin came to them from Portugal and asked them to stay and build a church in her honor ("Romería a Loja"). As the film documents, contemporary faithful vividly display their devotion with street decorations, confetti, and the release of doves in the towns along the route.

8. In the diaspora, the spiritual function of the Virgin of El Cisne has expanded to a social one. The Ecuadorian Community Virgin del Cisne of Connecticut, for example, has a Facebook page that informs "friends" of religious ceremonies and of its soccer league.

9. "(S)ocial space is a (social) product," Lefebvre states (26). In dialogue with Marxist ideology, Lefebvre's theory of space accentuates the human labor and "repetitive gestures" (75) of production implicit in cities and the buildings, squares, roads, monuments, and other structures that compose them. He describes the shift from serfdom and slavery to a *métayage* system in which those who farmed the land kept a share of production and supplied agricultural products to growing areas. This change spurred a new spatial distribution, with the *métayer* houses circling the landowner's mansion, and symbolic imagery. The use of cypress trees as property markers not only changed the physical appearance of the land but also became symbols of wealth and contributed to artistic developments in perspective.

10. Although restaurants are of course used for the same purpose, the foods offered in neighborhoods such as Lavapiés have changed as a result of the ethnicity of residents. As another example, in parks such as Madrid's Retiro, one finds many families of Latin American origin picnicking on a Sunday and not many of Spanish origin eating lunch in that manner.

11. I thank Gema Pilar Pérez-Sánchez for her suggestion that de Certeau's theory on walking in the city would enhance my analysis and that Madrid's Virgin of la Paloma, discussed later, also might be compared with Loja's Virgin of El Cisne.

12. See Villarruel's interview of Carrillo.

13. Walter Mignolo proposed not only that globalization began in the colonial period rather than in the modern era and moreover constitutes a space in which local histories and peoples of "the colonial difference" (3) confront and revise Western paradigms of knowledge. I am grateful to Jill Robbins for suggesting this connection with Mignolo and recognize that this line of analysis merits more development than the extension of this article permits.

14. The first celebration in Madrid in honor of the Virgin of El Cisne, in 2005, included a ceremony at the Plaza Mayor, a procession from the Plaza to the Church of San Lorenzo, and a mass during which the statue was welcomed to the sanctuary. The events were repeated in 2006. In 2007 and again in 2008, because of a disagreement between Carmen and Father Emilio, discussed later in this chapter, processions and masses were held both at San Lorenzo, in Lavapiés, and Our Lady of Lluc, in Ciudad Lineal, a neighborhood with approximately 15,000 Ecuadorian residents at the time. A frame at the end of the film notes that, in 2009, the route from the Church of San Lorenzo grew in length (Paz y Miño; Rodriguez Hidalgo; Sánchez).

15. In her presentation of the film at Assumption College, Massachusetts, in October 2012, Carrillo explained that the priest refused to discuss the controversy with her, preferring instead to talk about unification. In the film, he alludes to the disagreement as "algunas cosas de estas, sin ninguna importancia" [one of those things, unimportant problems] (44:46–44:48).

16. I learned from e-mail correspondence with Carrillo that Carmen's bar is located on the same street as the Church of San Lorenzo, a spatial fact that heightens La Churona's dislocation. She was situated close to her destination, yet excluded. Carrillo also informed me that Carmen no longer owns the bar and has moved from Spain.

17. De Lucas, professor of law philosophy at the Universitat de València, where he founded and directed the Institute of Human Rights, has written extensively on immigration politics and immigrants' rights ("Francisco Javier de Lucas Martín").

18. Some of the people gathered outside the Church of María de la Reparadora also question Carmen's motives, wondering if she has taken La Churona to her bar to improve its profits.

19. The Church of San Lorenzo has become a spiritual home for people from other Latin American countries as well. During a visit in July 2013, in addition to the Virgin of El Cisne, I observed statues of Virgin Marys and accompanying letters on the altarpiece from parishes in Paraguay (the Virgin of the Miracles of Caaupé) and Bolivia (the Blessed Virgin of Cotoca and the Virgin of Urcapiña), and a baby Jesus from Bogotá, Colombia.

20. Carrillo's training as an anthropologist appears to have conditioned the documentary's focus on popular practices and the implicit critique in this scene of the Westerner's simplification of folkloric customs and regional identity.

21. "Flaky *mille-feuille* pastry" is Henri Lefebvre's metaphor for the multiple, diverse layers of urban social spaces (86).

WORKS CITED

Barroso, F. Javier, and Jorge A. Rodríguez. "ETA revienta la tregua con un atentado en Barajas que deja dos desparecidos." *El País.com*. Ediciones El País, S.L., December 31, 2006. Accessed October 4, 2013.

Carrillo Espinosa, María Cristina, dir., prod., screenwriter. *La Churona: Historia de una virgen migrante*. Ecuador para largo, 2010. Film.

———. Blog. "La Churona: Historia de una virgen migrante." *WordPress.com*, n.d. accessed December 29, 2013.

———. Curriculum vitae to the author. October 20, 2013. E-mail.

———. "Migrant Virgin: La Churona. Historia de una virgin migrante." Assumption College, Worcester, MA. October 10, 2012. Presentation.

———. "Re: artículo sobre La Churona." Messages to the author. December 28–30, 2013. E-mail.

Communidad Ecuadoriana Virgen del Cisne, Connecticut, USA. *Facebook.com*. Facebook, Accessed October 30, 2013.

De Certeau, Michel. *The Practice of Everyday Life*. Trans. Steven Rendall. Berkeley: University of California Press, 1984.

De Lucas, Javier. "Sobre la gestión de la multiculturalidad que resulta de la inmigración: condiciones del proyecto intercultural." *Migración y interculturalidad: De lo global a lo local.* Eds. Joan Serafí Bernat and Celestí Gimerno. Castelló de la Plana (Spain): Publicacions de la Universitat Jaume I, 2006. 31–51.

"Esta noche se estrena el filme 'La Churona'." *El comercio.com.* Grupo El Comercio, June 24, 2011. Accessed December 29, 2013.

"Francisco Javier de Lucas Martín." *Institut Universitari de Drets Humans. Universitat de València.* Institut Universitari de Drets Humans. Universitat de València. Accessed October 28, 2013.

Gobierno de España. Ministerio de Trabajo e Inmigración. *Extranjeros Residentes en España a 30 de septiembre de 2011. Principales Resultados. Anexo de Tablas.* Madrid: Observatorio Permanente de la Inmigración, November 2011. Accessed March 13, 2013.

Gómez Ciriano, Emilio José. "Ecuatorianos en España." *Ecuatorianos en España: Una aproximación sociológica.* Madrid: Ministerio de Trabajo y Asuntos Sociales, 2007. 8–94.

Herrera, Lizardo. "La Churona y la réplica neobarroca: cartografías de un Ecuador transatlántico." *Archivos de la filmoteca. Cine e hibridaciones: avatares de la era digital.* 72 (2013): 63–78.

Jokisch, Brad. "Ecuador: Diversity in Migration." *Migration Information Source.* Migration Policy Institute, February 2007. Accessed December 27, 2014.

"La Churona." *Ecuador para largo.com.* Ecuador para largo, Accessed December 20, 2013.

"'La Churona' regresa a las salas de cine en Quito." Agencia Pública de Noticias del Ecuador y Suramérica ANDES, June 25, 2011. Accessed December 20, 2013.

Lefebvre, Henri. *The Production of Space.* Oxford: Blackwell, 1991.

Mignolo, Walter D. *Local Histories/Global Designs: Coloniality, Subaltern Knowledges, and Border Thinking.* Princeton, NJ: Princeton University Press, 2000.

"Parroquia de la Virgen de la Paloma." Parroquia Virgen de la Paloma de San Pedro el Real. Accessed October 15, 2013.

Paz y Miño, Gabriela. "La Virgen 'Churona' recibió un homenaje." *El Comercio.com.* Grupo El Comercio, September 9, 2007. Accessed October 30, 2013.

Pérez, Orlando. "La Churona." *El Telégrafo.com.ec.* El Telégrafo, May 18, 2011. Accessed December 29, 2013.

Prakash, Gyan. Introduction. *The Spaces of the Modern City: Imaginaries, Politics, and Everyday Life.* Eds. Gyan Prakash and Kevin M. Kruse. Princeton, NJ: Princeton University Press, 2008. 1–17.

Puga Álvarez, Valeria. "'La Churona' feliz estreno en los EDOC." *Blogspot.com.* May 16, 2011. Accessed December 29, 2013.

Rodríguez Hidalgo, Claudia. "Virgen de El Cisne venerada en Madrid." *UTPL.* Universidad Técnica Particular de Loja, July 27, 2006. Accessed October 24, 2013.

"Romería a Loja." Fundación Viva el Ecuador. Accessed September 9, 2013.

Sánchez, Daniel. "La patrona de Ecuador ya tiene casa en Lavapiés." *El País.com.* Ediciones El País, S.L., September 12, 2005. Accessed October 31, 2013.

Villarruel, Patricia. "'La Churona', historia de la identidad." *El Universo.com.* El Universo, September 27, 2011. Accessed December 19, 2013.

Chapter Nine

Rural Repopulation and the Fabrication of a Global Village: The Case of Aguaviva

Sohyun Lee

The "municipio (municipality)," equivalent to city or town, is "la unidad administrativa [the administrative unit]" (Pillet) of Spain. Even though town and city are similar concepts, unlike the *town*, the idea of *city* has been linked to a larger territory and a bigger population, with metropolitan and/or cosmopolitan attributes that have contributed to circulating or reinforcing its image as *global space*. Nevertheless, administratively, city and town are concepts at the same level in Spain, and both entities are affected by processes of globalization. The ambiguous and ubiquitous phenomena of globalization is not a process exclusive to big cosmopolitan centers, and planetary spaces or global cities may be formulated anywhere. Such is the case of Aguaviva de Bergantes, a small rural municipality located in the Province of Teruel, in Aragón, Spain. Aguaviva has existed for almost a millennium, mostly as an agrarian community, but rural migration to urban areas started affecting its population beginning in the 1960s.[1] In the 1990s the town depopulation reached alarming figures, declining to almost five hundred inhabitants, and those residents in the town were reaching old age. Both factors put in danger the continuity of Aguaviva as an administrative unit, and in year 2000 the town mayor, Luis Bricio, launched a project of repopulation and rejuvenation by importing residents from abroad, in spite of increasing border and immigration control.[2] The 2012 census of the Instituto Nacional de Estadística [National Statistics Institute of Spain] counts no more than seven hundred residents in Aguaviva.[3] The development of the repopulation enterprise was documented by director Ariadna Pujol in her film *Aguaviva* (2006), shot on location a few years following the implementation of Bricio's project.[4] By

the time the filming crew visits Aguaviva, the town had received a consider-
able number of immigrants from South America (Argentina), as well as from
Eastern Europe (Romania).[5]

Using various conventions of the documentary genre,[6] the film *Aguaviva*
attempts to project an impersonal and multidirectional perspective of the
demographic configuration of the rural town. Through a textual analysis of
the film's cinematic approach to space and local/global identities, this chapter demonstrates that the repopulation and the construction of a *global village*
in rural Spain is a complex process that defies strategic predictions. I examine how the film (re)presents social, cultural, and ethnic differences and/or
affinities that come into play in the process of (re)configuration of Aguaviva
as a local global space. The film foregrounds a narrative and a mise-en-scène
that exemplify planetary urban processes, breaking commonly held divisions
between rural/urban, global/local, and foreign/national citizenship. This suggests that global cities may be articulated anywhere around the planet, and
the effects of globalization reach local and marginal spaces regardless of
their size.[7] In fact, globalization imposes itself not as an entirely new spatial
order, but rather because it facilitates—via advancements in technology—
and accelerates existing configuration and reconfiguration mechanics of human habitat. In this way, the level or the magnitude of the globalization
process may not be measured or compared from one urban space to another
in one single linear scale, since multiple and complex factors interact in
particular ways in each particular space.[8] Thus the repopulation process of
Aguaviva may serve as reference case for other globalizing projects, but not
as an easily generalizable model due to its local specificities. Also, the situation of Aguaviva suggests that urban processes do not always obey their
designed agenda, regardless of its meticulously calculated measures.

Globalization, a slippery concept introduced in the mid-1960s,[9] has been
considered an imminent process for the past few decades. The concept of
globalization is controversial "whose definition is unclear" (Marcuse and
Van Kempen 261), and is approached from as many disciplines and perspectives as there are, hence "no single definition exists" (Murray 13). In the
meantime, it is also a process still in progress, and "we are therefore living in
a *globalizing* world" (Murray 14, emphasis added). By general usage, globalization is understood as a series of processes that promote increased mobility
and multidirectional flow of capital, people, practices, and products (including cultural products). According to Marcuse and Van Kempen, the global
tendencies in economic, political, social, and cultural practices and transac-
tions may have caused "spatial changes within cities" (5), where a new
spatial order has been observed starting in the 1970s (3).

This new spatial order tends to be more visible and more accelerated in
big urban areas, thus non-urban centers have been studied as different spaces
that contrast from cosmopolitan cities. Such is the study of demographic

evolution in rural areas presented by Roquer and Blay (2008), in which they classify Spanish *municipios* for their population size.[10] According to this study, the demographic profile in rural centers from 1996 to 2006 shows a polarization in growth patterns depending on the size of their initial number of residents. Demographic growth in rural Spain depends heavily on the influx of immigrants. However, rural zones with populations below two thousand show a continuous decrease of inhabitants. Two things call attention in Roquer and Blay's approach to population change in certain areas of Spain: First, their identification and classification of *municipios* as *rural areas* is based on figure of dwellers, since *non-urban zones* are those with fewer than ten thousand inhabitants. Their classification does not take into account production patterns in those areas, disregarding the agricultural aspect conventionally associated with rural communities. Second, their study reveals that incoming migration contributed to population growth only in *municipios* that had more than two thousand people, and smaller rural towns did not benefit from immigration flow, especially in the first five years following 1996.[11] Both of these observations apply to the demographic situation of Aguaviva.

Considering that present rural areas are not what they used to be, since "urbanism is everywhere today" (Zenner 413), "a distinction between agricultural/pastoral rural communities and industrial urban centers is no longer as sharp as it once was" (Zenner 415). Since economic activities do not distinguish rural from urban centers, often times the population size of a community is used as an indicator. Bayona and Gil Alonso[12] point out that counter-urbanization has created "new labour niches" (28) and occupations in rural areas of Spain are not "restricted to agriculture" (28) due to "economic restructuring" (30). [13] Thus they use the same classification, identifying as "rural municipalities" those which have a small number of inhabitants (29). For its population size, Aguaviva falls well into the category of *rural town* described in both studies, and alterations in economic production pattern are also applicable to this small town. Regarding the correlation between immigration settlement and original population size, Bayona and Gil Alonso's study comes to the same conclusion as Roquer and Blay's research. Demographic growth was positively influenced by incoming migration only in towns with larger populations, since "whereas most of metropolitan and coastal municipalities increased their population very significantly [rural municipalities] continued to show negative growth rates" (34). Nevertheless, Bayona and Gil Alonso's analysis relates, interestingly, not only to the number of initial population with immigration, but also with agrarian occupation. Rural towns tend to be smaller the more they engage in agricultural activities, and this, in turn, affects negatively immigration flow and settlement patterns. According to their findings, this was especially so for "Latin-Americans . . . as their proportion in the smaller villages is significantly low and increases as municipality size does" (35), whereas municipality size is greatly dependent on the proportion of agricultural activities, for "the higher the amount of people working in agriculture, the more demographically regressive a municipality is" (41).

The case of Aguaviva differs partially from the observations drawn from both sets of research, since immigration flow and settlement in Aguaviva have been artificially and systematically manipulated according to Bricio's project, while demographic change in small rural towns in Roquer and Blay's and Bayona and Gil Alonso's studies is left to spontaneous development. Over time an agrarian form of economic production did affect Aguaviva's immigrant population size, since many of the invited families tend to leave the rural town once their required settlement period is fulfilled, "because foreign workers leave agriculture too as their conditions improve [and] they turn towards more rentable and less *hard* sectors" (Éltető 71). Nevertheless, the fact that incoming migration was strictly controlled and supervised in Aguaviva does not allow a simple comparison with immigrants' dwelling patterns in other rural areas. Bricio's project requires that immigrants reside in Aguaviva for a certain amount of time and contribute to economic and demographic growth of the community in exchange for a placement package.[14] This condition assures immigrants' residency in Aguaviva, at least for a period of time, while assimilation and integration processes may potentially lead to their permanent residency.

Pujol's documentary unveils that Bricio's project did not necessarily develop according to expectations. The beginning of *Aguaviva* presents images of a town in a quiet winter morning, without any information about its location or its size. At this point, the film does not unveil Aguaviva's location in Spain, although this detail is not necessarily crucial in a film distribution system where the audience gets more than enough pre-screening information. Even so, and if we consider the text independently from its circulation background, the opening scene of *Aguaviva* works to (re)present Aguaviva as a nonspecific space. The heavy Argentinean accent of the voice-over dialogue that follows may suggest Aguaviva's location in Argentina, but the couple engaged in the dialogue do not know "cuándo comienza la primavera acá" [when the spring starts here], indicating that they are not in Argentina. After showing that Argentineans have been displaced from their home country, the screen provides information about the depopulation in Aguaviva, suggesting that the voice-over couple may be members of "invited immigrant families." The information regarding demographic crisis in Aguaviva classifies the town as a *rural setting* according to population size, while various shots of a restaurant and local scenery may situate Aguaviva in any geographical context. In fact, the audience does not learn that Aguaviva is located in Spain until Graciela, the Argentinean woman, holds a conversation with Agustina, a local woman. If we understand globalization as a process of homogenization,[15] among other processes, by which location specifics are diluted and all spaces share the same appearance, this introductory sequence sets, from the start, a configuration of the *municipio* of Aguaviva as local and global space.

The introduction establishes a frame of multiple factors to be considered in understanding the spatial nature of Aguaviva. From there the film visualizes Aguaviva as a *globalizing town*, while presenting also aspects particularly specific to this rural village in Teruel. Examples of the former are mainly conversations among immigrants about their new environment, or among locals about the newcomers. The added diversity to the demographic profile of Aguaviva, although by means of an artificial and controlled process, contributes by default to its globalization.[16] The film grants visibility mostly to immigrants from Argentina, while the effects of globalization are intensified in that some of the *Argentineans* are displaced Chileans who migrated to Argentina and were recruited from there to repopulate Aguaviva. The newcomers talk about their experiences of settling in Aguaviva: integration to a new community, adaptation to alternative cultural practices, coping with linguistic differences, searching for a way of life in a new economic and social environment. But they also express nostalgia for their homeland, food, customs, and family. The local residents discuss the changes in Aguaviva such as new cultural practices and a rejuvenated ambience. At the same time, old residents spend much time savoring their nostalgia for a common past. Memories of old local residents are represented on screen as the history of Aguaviva, suggesting that the cultural identity of the town is strongly rooted in its past, as opposed to the influx of different national symbols that the newcomers embrace.

Interaction among different groups is limited, since immigrants' occupation and usage of town space are clearly divided from the spaces occupied by original residents. Groups gather separately, not only by national origin, but also by age and gender, presenting various levels or dimensions of social interaction comparable to what Marcus and Van Kempen call "layered city" (265). The fact that national origin is not the only deciding factor for social grouping patterns in Aguaviva, as in any other community, suggests that globalization is not an exclusive social and spatial division force in a city. Globalization is, then, an "extension of forces already present over a much longer period of time" (Marcus and Van Kempen 262), and not an entirely new human dynamics. Moreover, the film shows that "the divisions of space are not only the product of divisions in society; they help to create those divisions" (Marcuse and Van Kempen 250), creating situations in which "opinions are only formed by stereotypes and decisions are made on the basis of uninformed preconceptions" (Marcuse and Van Kempen 251). Immigrants gather among them and locals do the same, excluding nonfamiliar groups. Argentineans complain that locals do not visit their shops, and Aguavivanos point out that Argentineans do not mingle with natives in local bars. Conver-

sations during these segregated gatherings are based on rumors or circum-
stantial impressions. Newcomers condemn discrimination and xenophobia
they have experienced, judging from the lack of clientele in their restaurant
or bullying of their child at school. Although ethnic discrimination may
cause these phenomena, other sociocultural variables may not be discarded.
In a different scene, a group of middle-aged male Aguavivanos say Argentineans are not hard workers—and by extension all "sudamericanos" (South
Americans)—in contrast to industrious Romanian settlers. Their comments
lack objective evidence, and their negative disposition toward Argentinean
immigrants is mainly due to resentment to the impression that Argentineans
live in Aguaviva obligated by their settlement package, while Romanians
came to populate the town by their free will and without any conditions. But
the misconception of the "other" and the reinforcement of that misconception
are not directed only toward immigrants, as pointed out by one Aguavivano
who mentions the apparently uncomfortable relationship between Aguaviva
and Ginebrosa, a neighboring rural town. This sequence portrays that they
are aware that isolation and lack of an open-minded interaction create prejudice. Therefore, spatial and symbolic common grounds are significant, and
the film shows encounters at various levels between locals and newcomers in
public spaces such as the church, the market, the plaza, the streets, and the
school. These places are transition spaces that allow contact among people of
different groups, acting symbolically as thresholds between an old and a new
spatial order. Especially, schools are represented as transitional spaces, and
the two sequences in the local classrooms exemplify that, through the institutionalized processes of mutual exploring, learning, sharing, and integration,
these children will probably be more inclusive Aguavivanos of tomorrow.

At times, the film tries to capture empathy between groups during difficult and deeply emotional moments such as the death of a relative that
Graciela had in Argentina. Nevertheless, this sequence shows that Graciela's
pain comes from events abroad, and she must also find consolation outside of
her current physical location. This exemplifies how "local forms of social
solidarity become less important" because immigrants have an "international
orientation and become less dependent" (Marcuse and Van Kempen 6)[17] on
local human networks. In fact, immigrants engage in long distance communication with family and friends back in their home countries for moral support. The documentary opens with an international phone call, and immigrants of all ages are frequently shown talking on the phone. One of such
sequences displays a series of phone calls in various languages throughout
the night. The documentary shows that "thanks to technology . . . they [are]
never entirely in Spain, or at least, not *only* in Spain" (Richardson 3). This
scene states also that "global culture can only be global media culture"
(Aneesh, Hall, and Petro 6). The transnational affective connections of immigrants are evident, but its portrayal on film is not exhaustive since the accel-

erated advance of media technology surely enables them to be better connected with their homeland than what *Aguaviva* was able to grasp from a public telephone booth in 2005. Local community is not their main source of affective support, and immigrants rely heavily on transnational human ties, available in their subjective emotive space. Nevertheless, the physicality and the correlation between human body and spatial context may not be disregarded, for space is "something experienced, produced, imagined, and understood through everyday living" (Richardson 19). In this way, despite areas that are "socially and spatially disconnected, fragmented and polarized" (Marcuse and Van Kempen 7), sharing of the same physical space allows emotional proximity, partial as it may be, as depicted when Graciela seeks consolation from the local priest, who later will ask town people to pray for her loss. Other spaces of convergence and mutual recognition between immigrants and locals are festive occasions such as traditional religious rituals. The Catholic festival *Cristo Rey* (Christ King) is an opportunity to proudly display global linkage and minimize physical distance among town dwellers. Festive events, Salzbrunn claims, act as "platforms for the negotiation of the inclusion and exclusion of newcomers and the transformation processes experienced by both the migrants and the cities" (166). As a ritual linked to a common religion, Aguaviva's Christ King Festival serves to (re)invent a sense of community and belonging through human interaction, enacting precisely what the town priest urges the population to do. The active participation in the festival preparation allows "migrants [to] become actors in both the restructuring and rescaling" (Salzbrunn 167) of Aguaviva as a global village.

Another globalizing aspect of Aguaviva as a nontraditional rural town is the economic production pattern dissociated from agriculture. Local women remember a past when agriculture was the primary activity in Aguaviva, but the documentary shows immigrants working in the service industry, since "ya nadie trabaja la tierra" [nobody works the land anymore]. Shifts in production patterns imply a transition of Aguaviva toward an urban or urbanizing process triggered by incoming migrants. As noted, immigrants tend to settle in areas with access to occupations in the tertiary sector, and have opted for nonagrarian enterprises for their living, often disregarding their viability in an unpopulated rural setting. Discrepancy between immigrants' expectations and Aguaviva's economic dynamics explain why the town was unsuccessful at retaining all incoming migration. Bayona and Gil Alonso affirm that "foreign immigration has not been the solution to rural depopulation" in most of rural Spain (45), and the population in Aguaviva has barely increased after ten years of its first flow of invited immigration. Nevertheless, judging the results of the Aguaviva repopulation project solely by the numbers may be misleading. Considering the average age of Aguaviva's inhabitants by 1990s, the maintenance of its population size for over a decade may well be evaluated as success.

For Marcuse and Van Kempen the city is not a whole organic entity, since "a city does not prosper or decline, particular groups in it do" (265), and they argue that seeing the city as an actor is a perspective that "does not hold today" (265). However, their approach to the city as a mere spatial container does not apply when the city itself was in danger of disappearing, as is the case of Aguaviva. Although their "metaphor of a layered city" (265) properly reflects the fragmented and divided spatial disposition of the newer Aguaviva, the town as a background—as multiple and layered as it may be—of human action is possible only as long as the town continues existing as an administrative unit. From this point of view, *Aguaviva* is the kind of "city film" where "the city becomes a protagonist" (Nowell-Smith 104). This is so not simply because of the method of location shooting, conventionally used in documentary filming; or because the "physicality of the setting, as much as the life within it . . . provides [an] initial inspiration" (105) for the film. In *Aguaviva*, the town is not merely a spatial context where people interact, and Aguaviva is placed as protagonist at the forefront of the documentary to enable the cinematic narrative. The city is no longer relegated to only providing the background or the mise-en-scène where the action takes place. The use of space in the documentary *Aguaviva* provides a different approach to the town as entity, pulling it up front as the main character of the film. Consider that the social dynamics in this documentary occur the way they are captured by the film precisely because of the local and global positioning of Aguaviva, including its complex historical and geographical trajectory. Note, in fact, the title of the film is simply *Aguaviva*, and this invites to conceive the town as an organic combination of space and time bound to a continuous alteration processes, well apropos of its meaning *Living Water*. The film suggests that globalization is at the core of such processes, and as "global cities are increasingly decoupled from the nation-state" (Glick Schiller and Çağlar 71), Aguaviva is gradually divorcing itself from the conventional "Spanish" national identity. The incoming migration is replacing Aguaviva's population both in actual bodies and in the introduction of new cultural practices and social dynamics that contribute to a substantial change of existing traditions and social norms. Then *el pueblo de Aguaviva* continues being *el pueblo de Aguaviva*, and its increasing separation from the nation-state may simply be considered symptomatic of the globalization process. On the other hand, in the particular case of Aguaviva, the new prospering group (young immigrants) that takes the place of a former group of inhabitants (old local dwellers) implies an exhaustive transmutation of the town by which *el pueblo de Aguaviva* is no longer the same *pueblo de Aguaviva*, especially when considering that the Spanish word *pueblo* not only means *town* but also *people*. From this point of view, the documentary *Aguaviva* depicts the town of Aguaviva as an active entity and not mere backdrop.

According to David Harvey, the "distinction between the geographical and the sociological imagination is artificial," and "the way space is fashioned can have a profound effect upon social processes" (24). Influence can go both directions where the spatial acts on social processes and, likewise, social practices can affect spatial structuring. Both dimensions are deeply related, but their interaction is complex and not always predictable. Harvey warns that modifying the spatial form of a city will not mold desired social processes, and that institutional constraints on social processes alone will not be enough to achieve necessary social goals (26), emphasizing that geographical and sociological imaginations are hardly distinguishable and act together in the (re)configuration of the city. The unforeseen development of Aguaviva's repopulation as a process of fabrication of a global village can be examined from this perspective. The invited immigration, although very carefully planned and backed up with strong historical rationale, was an a priori social planning that did not consider the rural town's spatial configuration, and it did not result in the specific social outcome that Bricio had expected.

Although intimately related, social processes or "social space" as Harvey calls them, "is complex, non-homogeneous . . . discontinuous and almost certainly different from physical space" (35). Therefore, "different culture groups develop totally different styles of representing spatial relationships, and these styles may, in themselves, be directly related to social processes and norms" (36) that, in turn, will affect spatial configuration in a never-ending loop. The idea that "cognitive processes" of spaces—real and imagined—have "complex impact upon behaviour" (Harvey 36) goes along the line of "constructive realism" (Aneesh, Hall, and Petro 2) that proposes that "constructions are real and the real is constructed" (3) in an ongoing cycle. Nevertheless, it must be considered that representation of spatial-social relationships is not always generalizable by groups—culture group is, in fact, a problematic concept—and the construction of the spatial imaginary is a much subjective process. Harvey mentions individual variations, but he notes, more importantly, that "social space . . . is also variable over time" (Harvey 36). Given that, the film *Aguaviva* depicts an Aguaviva that remains a rural town in Spain; but at the same time this town is no longer Aguaviva, and no longer entirely in Spain. Immigrants relocated in Aguaviva claim to be struggling for a sense of belonging, while they are, inadvertently, altering the *Spanishness* of Aguaviva and relocating the town in a new global map. The unsettling local and global disposition of Aguaviva is due to changes and (re)configurations of its spatial and social order facilitated and accelerated by migration, but not indebted solely to migratory flow. Globalization is a formidable and ubiquitous force, but certainly not the only force that govern human consciousness and experience, and its expansion does not necessarily depend on massive mobilization of people. As an ongoing process, the extension and evolution of globalization are part of numerous variables interacting on the axis of time. The passing of time that inevitably transforms the town, and repositions its locality in the global arena, is visualized in the film by the changing scenery of Aguaviva in different seasons, the renovation of street signs, and mostly by the shifting of its population, which implies a redefinition of *el pueblo de Aguaviva*. The ending sequence of a long, sad, and tired gaze of an old local man over a vibrant and playful group of young immigrants is an impressive cinematic description of the complex transition process of the town of Aguaviva, easily transferrable to other depopulated/ repopulated Spanish glocal rural towns in the new century.

NOTES

1. To see the chronological census of Aguaviva from 1842 to 2001 refer to the database of INE   http://www.ine.es/intercensal/intercensal.do?search=1&cmbTipoBusq=0&textoMunicipio=aguaviva&btnBuscarDenom=Submit+selection.

2. Further information on Aguaviva's repopulation within the context of Europe's tightened border and restrictive migration policies can be found in "Invited Migration from Argentina, *Hispanidad*, and Spain's Tightened Borders: Ariadna Pujol's Documentary, *Aguaviva* (2006)" by Lee. "Immigrants in Spain—Their Role in the Economy and the Effects of the Crisis" by Éltető (75–76) also discusses various border regulations of the Spanish government, including the "Plan Greco," based on the year 2000 law.

3. http://www.ine.es/jaxi/tabla.do?type=pcaxis&path=/t20/e260/a2012/l0/&file=mun44.px

4. The strategy of invited migration was adapted later by other small towns of Spain to solve rural depopulation. Éltető mentions that depopulation in 22 rural provinces of Spain "slowed down significantly due to the settlement of immigrants" by year 2010, noting that "certain villages attracted Latin-American people with special programs in order to avoid depopulation" (69), just like the project in Aguaviva.

5. Marcu and Gómez Nieto note that the Instituto Nacional de Estadística started including Romanians among "main immigrants" from year 2000. This coincides with the repopulation project of Aguaviva.

6. My previous article on *Aguaviva* presents an ample analysis of (re)usage of traditional documentary conventions and strategies in Pujol's film, which will not be discussed here. The cinematic techniques of the nonfiction genre in *Aguaviva* are also analyzed in Michelle Shepherd's "Documenting Domesticity in *Aguaviva* and *Extranjeras*." Kathleen M. Vernon presents a brief history of the documentary cinema in Spain and its rebirth in the twenty-first century (120–21).

7. I do not seek to disregard or devalue the differences in local and global urban scales. The issue of local and global scales affected and altered by migration is well discussed and analyzed from different perspectives through all chapters in Nina Glick Schiller and Ayşe Çağlar's *Locating Migration. Rescaling Cities and Migrants*.

8. Comparative studies between different global spaces and/or local spaces must take into account that cities cannot be "measured on a linear scale of more or less globalized . . . ignoring the way in which it is integrated into globalization processes" (Marcuse and Van Kempen 268).

9. According to *Merriam-Webster*, the first known usage of the term globalization was in 1951. The *Stanford Encyclopedia of Philosophy* (http://plato.stanford.edu/entries/globalization/) states the concept was applied as sociocultural idea in the 1960s by Marshall McLuhan's development of the image of "global village." From the beginning, there have been as many

definitions of globalization as theorists and commentators on the idea, but the consistent key-words are technology and space/time compression.

10. Based on data from national census and the Padrón de habitantes (local official register), published annually by the Instituto Nacional de Estadística.

11. Note that Partido Popular, led by José María Aznar, takes office in 1996. This meant reinforcement of anti-immigration measures.

12. Although their study is restricted to Catalan rural municipalities, their conclusions are relevant to Aguaviva, for rural depopulation and repopulation show similar patterns nation-wide.

13. "Counterurbanisation and New Social Class in Rural Spain: The Environmental and Rural Dimension Revisited" by Paniagua discusses the increasing exodus of urbanites to rural settings in Spain, triggered by changes in life style and the accessibility of economic activities from multiple locations.

14. For selection criteria of invited immigrants to Aguaviva, and details of the settlement package, refer to page 364 of my previous article. This article analyzes the political, historical, religious, administrative, and cultural background of the process of preselection or prefiltering of immigrants based on a romanticized idea of *Hispanidad*, designed to facilitate and accelerate assimilation of incoming population in Aguaviva, as represented by Pujol's documentary. The romantic notion of *Hispanidad* is "often fueled by governmental and economic policies at-tempting to legislate and legitimate the return of Spain's historical relationship with its former colonial periphery, namely Latin America" (Van Liew), and is precisely the administrative rationale behind Aguaviva's repopulation program.

15. It is important to note that homogeneity does not automatically mean equality or even-ness, in the same line that, as Shiel suggests, "unevenness" should not be confused with "heterogeneity" or "difference" with "resistance" (13).

16. Judith Goode's "global cities" are so in the proportion of foreign-born residents, and examples of such cities are big metropolis with over 30 percent of immigrants that may provide potential "global linkage" (146, 163).

17. Marcuse and Van Kempen discuss international networking mainly from the perspective of commodified services, not necessarily applicable to the context of Aguaviva where spatial order due to class division is less visible, at least as represented in this documentary.

WORKS CITED

Aneesh, A., Lane Hall, and Patrice Petro. *Beyond Globalization. Making New Worlds in Media, Art, and Social Practices*. New Brunswick, NJ: Rutgers University Press, 2012.

Bayona-i-Carrasco, Jordi, and Fernando Gil-Alonso. "Is Foreign Immigration the Solution to Rural Depopulation? The Case of Catalonia (1996–2009)." *Sociologia Ruralis* 53(1) (2013): 26–50.

Éltető, Andrea. "Immigrants in Spain—Their Role in the Economy and the Effects of the Crisis." *Romanian Journal of European Affairs* 11(2) (2011): 66–81.

Goode, Judith. "The Campaign for New Immigrants in Urban Regeneration: Imagining Pos-sibilities and Confronting Realities." *Locating Migration. Rescaling Cities and Migrants.* Eds. Nina Glick Schiller and Ayşe Çağlar. Ithaca, NY: Cornell University Press, 2011, 143–65.

Harvey, David. *Social Justice and the City*. Athens: University of Georgia Press, 2009.

Lee, Sohyun. "Invited Migration from Argentina, *Hispanidad*, and Spain's Tightened Borders: Ariadja Pujol's Documentary, *Aguaviva* (2006)." *Comparative American Studies* 9(4) (2011): 360–75.

Marcu, Silvia, and Israel Gómez Nieto. "La movilidad de los inmigrantes rumanos en la comunidad de Madrid: Pautas de asentamiento y retorno." *Scripta Nova* 15(341) (2010). Accessed November 18, 2013, http://www.ub.edu/geocrit/sn/sn-341.htm.

Marcuse, Peter, and Ronald Van Kempen. *Globalizing Cities: A New Spatial Order?* Hoboken, NJ: Blackwell, 2000.

Murray, Warwick, E. *Geographies of Globalization*. New York: Routledge, 2006.

Paniagua, Angel. "Counterurbanisation and New Social Class in Rural Spain: The Environmental and Rural Dimension Revisited." *Scottish Geographical Journal.* 118(1) (2002): 1–18.

Pillet Capdepón, Félix. "Las escalas del espacio: desde lo global a lo local." *Scripta Nova.* 12(270) (5). (2008). Accessed November 18, 2013, http://www.ub.edu/geocrit/sn/sn-270/sn-270-5.htm.

Pujol, Ariadna. Dir. *Aguaviva.* (España) ALEA Docs and Films. 2006. DVD.

Richardson, Nathan. "Spanish Territories, Global Geographies. Exploring Space and Place in a New Spain." *Constructing Spain. The Re-imagination of Space and Place in Fiction and Film, 1953 – 2003.* Lanham, MD: Bucknell University Press, 2012, 1–29.

Roquer, Santiago, and Jordi Blay. "Del éxodo rural a la inmigración extranjera: el papel de la población extranjera en la recuperación demográfica de las zonas rurales españolas (1996–2006)." *Scripta Nova* 12(270) (129). (2008). Accessed November 18, 2013.

Salzbrunn, Monika. "Rescaling Processes in Two "Global" Cities. Festive Events as Pathways of Migrant Incorporation." *Locating Migration. Rescaling Cities and Migrants.* Eds. Nina Glick Schiller and Ayşe Çağlar. Ithaca, NY: Cornell University Press, 2011, 166–89.

Schiller, Nina Glick, and Ayşe Çağlar, eds. *Locating Migration. Rescaling Cities and Migrants.* Ithaca, NY: Cornell University Press, 2011.

Shepherd, N. Michelle. "Documenting Domesticity in *Aguaviva* and *Extranjeras.*" *Crossings: Journal of Migration and Culture* 3(1) (2012): 103–17.

Shiel, Mark. "Cinema and the City in History and Theory." *Cinema and the City: Film and Urban Societies in a Global Context.* Eds. Mark Shiel and Tony Fitzmaurice. Oxford: Blackwell, 2001, 1–18.

Van Liew, Maria. "New Modernity, Transnational Women, and Spanish Cinema." *CLCWeb: Comparative Literature and Culture* 12(2) (2010). Accessed November 20, 2013.

Vernon, Kathleen M. "*Un instante en la vida ajena/A Glimpse of Other Lives* (José Luis López-Linares, 2003): domesticating the documentary archive." *Spanish Cinema 1973 – 2010. Auteurism, politics, landscape and memory.* Eds. María M. Delgado and Robin Fiddian. Manchester: Manchester University Press, 2013, 117–32.

Zenner, Walter P. "Beyond Urban and Rural Communities in the 21st Century." *Urban Life. Reading in the Anthropology of the City.* Eds. George Gmelch, Robert V. Kemper, and Walter P. Zenner. Long Grove: Waveland Press, 2010, 413–20.

Another Look at Immigration

La guerra del golf (The Golf War) *by Lucía Sánchez*

Thomas Deveny

Almost all of the films on immigration to Spain deal with immigrants from Africa or Latin America, and often they are irregular migrants and those who are marginalized by Spanish society.[1] As of 2012, Romanians and Moroccans are the two largest groups of immigrants, but the third largest is from Great Britain. The documentary film *La guerra del golf* (*The Golf War*, 2011) by Lucía Sánchez reveals the impact of this group on the region of Murcia. With this influx of affluent immigrants, developers build golf courses and luxury resorts to house the foreigners, which in turn has an important impact on both the economy (including Moroccan immigrant labor) and the ecology of land and water usage. In many ways, Murcia represents an extreme case of what is happening in all of Spain: questions about water usage, over-construction of housing, foreign tourism and immigration, corruption, the economic crisis, and broken dreams are all themes in this documentary that makes audiences consider what type of future they want for Murcia and for Spain. Although all of these issues are intertwined, the most important one at both the local and global level—for Murcia, for Spain, and for everyone on the planet—is water usage.

Given the myriad social and ecological ramifications of this topic, it is not surprising that Lucía Sánchez decided to film a documentary on golf tourism and its impact. Following the categories by David Bordwell and Kristin Thompson, *La guerra del golf* is a synthetic documentary with a rhetorical form: it combines interviews with material filmed as "direct cinema" and it "presents a persuasive argument." (130, 140). Bill Nichols concurs: "Documentaries seek to persuade or convince us: by the strength of their argument or point of view and the appeal, or power, of their voice" (43). Furthermore,

Patricia Aufderheide notes that the documentary genre is "defined by the tension between the claim to truthfulness and the need to select and represent the reality one wants to share. Documentaries are a set of choices—about subject matter, about the forms of expression, about the point of view, about the story line, about the target audience" (127). In addition to the interviews and "direct cinema" techniques, Sánchez uses artwork and voice-over narrative to inform the audience of facts and create a "story line" regarding the social issues that the film addresses. Sánchez's film is an example of "eco-cinema," which as Paula Willoquet-Maricondi defines it, consists of "films that overtly engage with environmental concerns . . . by exploring specific environmental justice issues . . . [and] that actively seek to inform viewers about, as well as engage their participation in, addressing issues of ecological import." ("Introduction" 9–10).The film makes us consider what is the relationship between *murcianos*—and by extension, not only all Spaniards, but all of us—and the earth?

The influx of affluent immigrants to Murcia is the root cause for the problems manifested in the film. Between 2001 and 2011, the number of British immigrants grew from 94,860 ("La población") to 365.596 ("Extranjeros"), making them the third largest immigrant group in Spain. According to Joaquín Rábago, Spain is the "country preferred by the British for a change of life."[2] Many of the new British immigrants reside in Murcia, and quite often they are attracted to the region because of the possibility of playing golf. Indeed, Francisco Feo Parrondo observes, "The majority (62 percent) of foreigners who play golf in Spain are British" (61). Writing in 2001, he notes the benefits and costs of the golf industry in Murcia: "the elevated costs of the golf courses and related installations are compensated for by the high economic benefits that they generate" (61), although he concedes that "from an ecological point of view, one of the greatest problems of golf courses is their high consumption of water: the 160 courses in existence in Spain in 1994 consumed as much water as three million residents of Madrid" (63).

Both the regional and national press wrote about this seemingly exorbitant water usage. In 2010, M. Sánchez, writing in the regional newspaper from Murcia, *La Verdad* [The Truth], informed the public, "The 17 golf courses constructed in the middle of a drought in the regional community of Murcia need between 15 and 22 cubic hectometers of water annually, which is practically the equivalent of what the city of Albacete [172 thousand inhabitants] consumes in two years." According to an article in Madrid's newspaper, *La Nueva Tribuna* [The New Tribune]:

> We should be aware that the amount of water consumed by a tourist is double what a local inhabitant consumes. The tourist activity that consumes the most water is golf. It is evident that this tourism is expensive, and it provides

important economic benefits. In 2007, it generated some 2,673,000,000 euros. . . . This amounts to an increase of 480 percent between 1997 and 2007.
Golf tourists generate four times as much income as a normal tourist, and
twice the amount of a Spanish golf player ("El agua").

Although these data make the influx of foreign golf tourists seem like overwhelmingly positive economic news, the editorial expresses a caveat: "The
environmental impact of golf courses is evident" and it notes the "excessive
use," "loss of quality of subterranean water," the "misuse of fertilizers," and
the problem of pesticides resulting in "an intense deterioration of the aqui-
fers " ("El agua"). Given these ecological problems, the newspaper takes an
editorial stance to improve the situation: "Therefore, we should demand,
first, a cessation of new golf course construction, and second, the golf
courses now in existence should comply with all the hydrological and environmental regulations contained in our national legislation and that of the
European Union" ("El agua").

The shots of airplanes arriving at the Murcia airport from northern Europe
(Ryanair, JetairFly, Norwegian Air) indicate the origin of the tourists who
vacation or have second homes in that region. The following sequences
underscore the importance of the British in this new phenomenon: there is an
announcement in voice-over by a woman who welcomes passengers in English and declares that Murcia enjoys "300 days of sunshine per year;" and a
man leaving the airport carrying a bag and his golf clubs walks in front of a
large billboard that advertises in English, "Your home on the golf course."[3]

Interviews are an important component of documentary cinema, and
Sánchez and her team question several of the groups involved in these vital
issues. One important group interviewed throughout the film is farmers, since
land for the construction of houses was previously dedicated to agriculture,
and a golf course employee notes that where the course now stands, they
used to grow melons. The first farming couple grows figs, and the man states
that although the resorts recycle water, their water usage increases propor-
tionately with the number of resorts built: "If there is not enough, they take it
from me." He notes that "the law is on their side" since it allows contractors
to appropriate land "for public works," and the resorts are considered "works
of social interest." He adds, "According to the law, that is progress, that is
prosperity, and if those people want to construct, they have the right to do it."
His most telling words, however, are, "You can't eat houses," a phrase he
repeats for emphasis. The close-up of a golf ball in a fig tree is a strong visual
image that achieves its intended rhetorical effect.

The director also interviews English residents in Murcia to determine
their relationship to their adopted land. None of these Englishmen are young;
presumably they are retirees. We first see a series of interview questions
written on green note cards, which we later see in the hands of some of the

interviewees. The note cards are often placed next to or interspersed with objects that hint at possible answers, thus shaping the "story line." The card asking, "What's your main reason for coming here?" is next to hors d'oeuvres prongs with golf ball motifs; containers of Cross and Blackwell marmalade, Worcestershire Sauce, and Heinz Beanz precede the question, "What kind of contact do you have with the Spanish people?" As Thomas Wilson observes, "food and drink" are "signifiers of group culture and identity" (12), and in particular, "eating and drinking . . . [are] constituent elements in the creation and reproduction of local, regional and national cultures and identities in Europe" (11). These products are culinary markers of English identity, and their availability in Murcia connotes a lack of cultural assimilation. The final note card with the question, "What do you know about the problems we have with water?," is placed in a sink; drops of water falling on it symbolize both the scarcity of water and its implicit waste. The interviewees answer forthrightly, and there is no sense that they are "set up" in any negative way. One woman declares, "I just love the climate, I love everything about it. I love the people. I love the slow way people live.... I like the food. I like the cheap cost of living. I think I like everything about Spain." A man states, "The main reason I came here with my wife is because we're retired, and we find it nice, and warm, and friendly." However, some of their answers raise ethical questions regarding the relationship between host countries and new residents. As a point of comparison, the "Code of Ethics for Education Abroad," formulated by the Forum on Education Abroad, indicates guidelines regarding "Relationships with Host Societies."

> While engaging with host societies, "organizations should demonstrate: sensitivity to and respect for differences between local cultural norms and those of the home culture; awareness of the program's impact on the local community, a commitment to creating sustainable local relationships that are mutually beneficial, and an effort to minimize any negative effects on the host society." Should not the same criteria apply to tourists and immigrants?

The immigrants often seem oblivious to both the natural and social context of their new home. Throughout the film, the constant shots of arid hills contrast with the green areas of the golf courses and resort areas. In this visual context, when a woman comments, "Well, I don't really know what was here before, but I imagine it was really nice," it shows a lack of awareness on her part. The same is true of a man who admits his lack of knowledge of Spanish: "I'm not very good at Spanish. 'Hola,' 'un poco más,' which means 'a little more.' 'The bill,' I forget now." When asked if she can name five famous Spanish people, a woman can only name Franco. Since immigrants' impact on water usage is a main theme of the film, this is also part of the interview process. A man states, "There is a problem here with water, mainly due to the hot climate. ... if we had the arid conditions in England like we have here, we'd be absolutely grounded [sic] to a halt. I think they manage here very, very well." That there is only one interviewee with this awareness constitutes a negative portrait of this immigration. The average expatriate in this film seeks fun in the sun while not making an effort to assimilate and is oblivious to the impact he or she has on the local ecology.

The interview of a Spaniard who works at a golf course provides a positive perspective on the industry, and his presence in the film shows the non-Manichaean element of the documentary.[4] He claims that "people tend to complain" about water usage for golf courses, but without correct information. The comparison he makes is telling: "In Spain, the surface area of golf courses is 1.7 percent of that of soccer fields that there are in Spain. What should we do, eliminate the golf courses or the soccer fields? What creates more jobs, golf courses or soccer fields?" After noting the number of vacant houses near the golf course, he declares, "We have to promote golf because we don't have enough players to support all the courses that we have. So we live mainly off of foreign players who come to play. So we have to promote golf in our country." Although the fallacious reasoning and circular logic should not convince any viewers, the information this golf course employee offers echoes that of the press releases on the part of the industry. In contrast to the statistic that in Spain, agriculture is the "main consumer of water with over 75 percent of the total" (D. Chico and A. Garrido 76), the golf industry maintains that golf courses use only 1 percent of the water that agriculture does (Club Murcia). However, some of the statistics are a bit deceptive: the article notes that "One hectare (10,000 square meters) of golf course needs about 4,000 m3 of water per year" (Club Murcia). Furthermore, one must take into account that the average 18-hole golf course covers 45 to 77 hectares (110 to 190 acres) (Crownove). Pepe Jover, president of the Golfing Federation, Murcia, also notes that since 2001, "Murcia is the only autonomy in Spain that requires courses to be irrigated with recycled water." One can only ask: is he bragging or complaining? Why are not all golf courses in Spain required to do so?

In addition to interviews, Sánchez uses "direct-cinema" in the film, and the best example is footage of a demonstration in Murcia against further housing development. It begins with close-ups of demonstrators chaining themselves together in solidarity. The demonstration includes chants, "Murcia no se vende" [Murcia is not for sale], as the camera pans the group of chained demonstrators, as well as signs that read, "El consumerismo no te hará feliz" ["Consumerism will not make you happy"] and "La tierra no es nuestra. Nosotros somos de la tierra" ["The land is not ours. We are of the land"]. These signs strike at the heart of the issue: is development, which supposedly brings prosperity, what the people of Murcia want?

The style of the documentary takes a sharp turn away from "direct-cinema" as the director uses artistic cutouts of new houses and their residents together with a voice-over that gives the impression of a newscaster giving headlines in order to inform the viewer of the cycle of housing boom and bust in Spain: "In Spain, 600,000 homes are constructed each year, more than in France, Germany, and the United Kingdom combined," but with an 8.6 percent drop in construction, a hand knocks the cutout homes down. As the "newscaster" continues with more headlines—"40 percent fewer apartments sold than the previous year," "Numerous families cannot pay their mortgages"—the shots of idle construction cranes and half-built houses underscore the stark reality of the crisis. Speculation and greed are the underlying factors for the Spanish housing bubble, and in Murcia, this was fueled by the presence of foreign (British) expatriates with a level of affluence to afford the homes in the golf resorts.

The economic crisis prompted by the housing bubble affected not only affluent British expatriates, however, but another group of immigrants as well: Moroccans who worked in the construction industry. Director Sánchez again opts for "direct-cinema" style, as she films two immigrants as they go about their daily lives trying to cope with the situation. The first scene involves a Moroccan immigrant in a *locutorio* or small business that provides telephones.[5] The poignant conversation in Arabic with subtitles informs the audience of his difficult situation: he would like to go home, but he is unemployed and has no money for the trip. The hand-held camera tracks the two men as they walk down the street, and we "overhear" their conversation about how difficult their economic situation is. When they go to an employment center, the camera pans down close-ups of offers, but the immigrants lament that the jobs all require experience that they do not have.

Another interview on an abandoned construction site informs us of the massive plans that now stand paralyzed: a *murciano* explains that developers were going to build 4,220 homes, a shopping mall, and a swimming pool for retired Norwegians, but now there is no money. Money, again, is at the heart of the matter: "the worst part of this is that the public administrations sometimes supported all this development because it moves a lot of money." This *murciano* does not hold back on his questioning and criticism of such policy, stating that these developments

> "require services, and how are they paid for? By raising taxes on those of us who live in the municipality. I don't understand how a municipality with six thousand inhabitants can go from one day to the next to having fifty or sixty thousand... This mess is what has caused the country to be in the shape it's in. The agricultural sector was abandoned . . ."

As this *murciano* goes to a restaurant where he watches television, the TV newscast adds to the information regarding money and corruption in the housing sector: in the municipality of Librilla, a civil servant is charged with having earned seven million euros in bribery and corruption.[6]

Although the important social issues of over-construction and water usage form the crux of the film, the director does not forget that there are individuals whose dreams of a leisurely retirement have been broken. As an elderly English couple walks around an abandoned construction site, this theme of broken dreams comes to foreground. The husband and wife both seem incredulous as they walk among empty buildings with broken windows; he comments, "all these were completed properties," and his sigh as he looks at his wife is telling. His incredulity ("What happened here?") is based on their previous experience ("People were so, so professional"). The shot of broken glass and his comment, "in less than year's time, I was expecting to be playing golf," make this scene very poignant. Yet there is also a desire for justice, as the wife comments that she wishes they could "get them to admit what they've done." The shots of abandoned trucks and heavy machinery as well as tattered flags of the development waving in the wind underscore the couple's hopelessness.

Englishmen were not the only affluent immigrants who suffered in the housing collapse; Spaniards and Latin Americans lament their situation as well. The latter seems to manifest a certain ingenuousness, however, as a man tells of his opinion about Spain: "You have to invest here, because this is a first-world country where immorality does not exist. . . . We have been swindled. The man had a Ferrari. He was swimming in money." Shots of half-built abandoned homes again underscore his testimony. Spaniards also note how they were lured to invest because of the easy money offered them, and another panning shot of arid hills is a constant visual thread that subverts the notion of constant construction in the area. The presence of a billboard in Spanish confirms that foreigners were not the only ones targeted by developers. The rhetoric of the advertisement includes claims of excellent quality— "En precio y calidad Número 1" ["Number 1 in Price and Quality"]--and invocations using the familiar "tú" form—"Fíjate en los demás y compra" [Check out everybody else and buy]—exhorting to compare, or perhaps subtly to "keep up with the Joneses." This combines with the subconscious associations with the company name "Grupo Trampolín" [Trampoline Group] of jumping higher and the visual design of the billboard (the "o" in the company name is in the shape of a golf ball) to convince prospective buyers. But Sánchez reveals the corruption of this developer by including both newspaper headlines and testimony by interviewees that underscore the dimensions of graft. The interviewees complain that the mayor practically installed a real estate office in city hall, and the headlines call the Trampolín case "a swindle of European dimensions."

Director Sánchez uses artistic cut-outs of homes to underscore the dimensions of corruption, with the newscaster-type voice-over together with note cards that contain the headlines, so the viewer is given the information in two "channels of information" so as to give it more gravity. [7]

> Torre Pacheco. The mayor is accused of embezzlement of public funds and corruption.
> Totana: Six persons arrested in a rezoning scheme.
> Mazarrón: The mayor pays 33,000 euros to a city council member who allowed the rezoning of forty-two million square meters of rural land.
> Cieza: The mayor had envisioned building five thousand homes and a golf course that would have benefited his daughter-in-law (owner of the majority of the land).

The identification of one town after another, with a repetition of similar charges of corruption, emphasizes the widespread nature of this problem.

Given this problem of corruption, the female interviewer of the documentary seeks out the mayor. Although she starts by naming "La Tercia, your town," "La Tercia" is really the name of the golf resort in Sucina. The mayor's reaction—"Very beautiful"—puts a positive spin on the situation, but her follow-up comment, "Lots of uninhabited houses," puts him on the defensive, and he tries to justify himself with wishful thinking: "Right now there are a lot of homes that have not been sold ... but if it were at 100 percent, there would be an important boost." The camera circles them during the interview, and when it stops, in the background between the mayor and the interviewer, a sign reads, "Se vende". [For sale], underscoring the depth of the economic crisis. The interviewer's question, "Do you think that it has enriched the town?", elicits answers that justify the "building mentality" and the "get rich quick" mentality: "The land was not worth much . . . and all this progress and the resorts came, they sold their land really well . . . with substantial profits." The underlying theme of water also is part of the interview, as the mayor declares,

> "Everything that people say . . . that we are using drinking water for the golf courses, that we are wasting water, it's a lie. In Murcia we know about the use of water, which is life. Everything here is because there was water. Because other regions have been generous. Giving us this water to subsist, because these people have to drink water, we have to be realistic."

Nevertheless, these statements on water usage rest on the premise that having a huge increase in population is a good thing; if the immigrant population were not there, it obviously would not need water. The montage of long shots in which Sánchez juxtaposes images of swimming pools with the dry surrounding land is an example of the assertive nature of the documentary. [8]

Toward the end of the film, two farmers joke with typical Spanish black humor. When one states that people believe that agriculture should be for northern Africa, and Murcia should be the residential zone of Europe, he also quips, "We are going to be the old folks' home of Europe" to which his companion retorts, "We're going to learn to give shots now." One opinion reflects the vox populi regarding a major theme in the film—corruption: "I think they've laundered a lot of money with this." And the return to humor indicates a certain resignation regarding a situation beyond their control: "I think, Amancio, that the last farmers are going to be you and I." Although he laughs at his own joke, it is black humor indeed, but how else can local farmers react to the influx of foreigners and the greed of local builders and politicians that threaten their lifestyle?

Throughout the film, a British golfer gives "tips" on how to play, which provide another type of humor of the film: he advises never to swear or throw your club, yet he moves the ball after pointing out an airplane. Mark Minster (29), in his analysis of David Guggenheim's *An Inconvenient Truth*, follows Aristotle's theories on rhetoric to show how humor can play an important function in ecocinema: pathos is a key element of persuasion, and the Greek philosopher notes, "Our judgments when we are pleased and friendly are not the same as when we are pained and hostile" (I.2.3). Minster believes that humor in Guggenheim's film is important, since "we are persuaded by likeable characters we can trust and maybe even emulate. We are persuaded by humor and believable emotion . . ." (26). In Sánchez's film, the golf coach's humor puts the viewer at ease, but it does not establish the empathetic relationship with a protagonist as Guggenheim does with Al Gore.

The assertive nature of the documentary in portraying the social and ecological problems in Murcia takes a new twist in some of the final sequences of the film, where there is a change in tone. The voice-over narrative now turns sarcastic, and the jerky hand-held camera images of house numbers or shots of "idyllic" views from your hypothetical new home of near-by apartment buildings underscore the absurdity of the situation:

> In the region of Murcia, we have 18,000 homes for you to choose from. Come and get to know us . . . Homes equipped with air conditioning and heating so that nobody will live in them. . . Enjoy your terrace with a view of the building in front of you . . . Be the first inhabitant in a resort with 144 homes. Advantages: turn on loud music, and you won't bother anybody. Go around in the nude, and nobody will see you. Live like Adam and Eve in a new paradise.

The irony in the film, which develops into biting satire here, is an important trope, because as Michael Zryd observes, "irony challenges documentary film's favoured modes of sincerity and 'sobriety,' . . . [and] can furthermore construct a powerful, supple, and complex *ethos* (where *ethos* is understood as the persuasive appeal of the documentary 'voice') (1–2). This satirical sequence here would make British viewers think twice about living in such a "paradise."

The final segments of the film tie in several of the themes: corruption (the close-up of a headline indicates a police investigation), the impact of the economic crisis on immigration (the Moroccan immigrant takes a train to leave Murcia), and most importantly, water. Ironically, in the final shots, it rains as a car travels down the almost flooded streets of the city.

International studies on water policy note the difficult situation in Spain. Marq De Villiers observes that while "Europe has, on the whole, plenty of water, about 4,000 cubic metres per person per year . . . the situation in Spain, however, is much more dire, at an average of 2,800 cubic metres, and much lower in the east and south [i. e. Murcia], where consumption is passing critical levels" (34). And Velma Grover observes, "In Spain water scarcity is dominating the agenda for water management," and she explains that national policy consists of "the construction of large hydraulic infrastructures transferring water between river basins, [and] there are few experiences in which the traditional approach has been replaced by a new one in which rationality of water use is a guiding principle" (247). She emphasizes, "The National Hydrological Plan of 2001 is firmly based on huge inter-basin transfers of water as a way of redistributing water on Spanish territory. In this way, the plan does not face the scarcity problem by adopting efficiency criteria based on the rationalisation of its use" (248). Geologist José Antonio García Ayala notes that the water situation in Murcia received television coverage in 2002, which resulted in a change in national legislation, with the National Hydrological Plan "expressly prohibiting the use of water from the Ebro River for watering golf courses."

The situation regarding water usage in Murcia garnered international press attention: Elizabeth Rozenthal, writing for the *New York Times* in 2008, noted how when a local journalist, Chema Gil, exposed a scandal involving building permits, he received death threats, but continues to draw attention to this vital issue: "'The model of Murcia is completely unsustainable,' Mr. Gil said. 'We consume two and a half times more water than the system can recover. So where do you get it? Import it from elsewhere? Dry up the aquifer? With climate change we're heading into a cul-de-sac. All the water we're using to water lettuce and golf courses will be needed just to drink.'" And sometimes justice on this issue moves slowly: in an article in September 2013, Inmaculada De la Vega reported in the most important Spanish national press (*El País*) that Pascual Carrión, a shepherd who took a developer to court in 2006 over a plan to build fifteen thousand homes on his land, had won his case.[9]

Documentary films almost never do well at the ticket office, but new technology gives them other opportunities. *La Guerra del Golf* is a Spanish-French co-production that unfortunately has not had commercial distribution on the big screen, but it deserves to be seen in DVD format. Hopefully, this analysis will bring attention to the documentary; as Cheryll Glotfelty notes, "ecocritical work shares a common motivation: the troubling awareness that we have reached the age of environmental limits, a time when the consequences of human actions are damaging the planet's basic life support systems" (xx). The public needs to be informed about the issues that the film explores regarding immigration and its subsequent repercussions so as to formulate policy that will make for a better future in Spain. Can a balance be achieved between the economic benefits from the influx of affluent immigrants and the need to preserve our planet's most precious natural resource? After viewing this film, both Spanish and foreign audiences will hopefully reflect and act on these issues. Paula Willoquet-Maricondi believes "ecocinema overtly strives to inspire personal and political action on the part of viewers, stimulating our thinking so as to bring about concrete changes in societies, locally and globally" (Shifting Paradigms 45). In that regard, *La guerra del golf* should take its place at the front lines of ecocinema in Spain.

NOTES

1. See the chapter on Spain in Thomas Deveny's *Migration in Contemporary Hispanic Cinema*.
2. All translations, unless otherwise noted, are my own.
3. The film exists in two versions, one of 70 minutes and one of 52 minutes. The longer version, which was shown at film festivals in Spain, begins with a voice-over narrative setting the context of Murcia and its dry climate. The short version has been shown on television (RTBF, TVtours, YLE, and France 3). It was also shown at film festivals such as the Seminci (Valladolid), Fipa (Biarritz), and the Women's Film Festival in Brussels (Sánchez, Message).
4. Documentaries, by their very nature, sometimes advocate for a certain social cause, and therefore can be said to be unbalanced. But as Patricia Aufderheide notes, "Edward R. Murrow once said, 'Anyone who believes that every individual film must represent a "balanced" picture knows nothing about either balance or pictures'" (2).
5. The *locutorio* is a common motif in migration cinema, providing a link to home and family that was more difficult in days gone by. Multiple examples of migration films with *locutorios* include Fernando León de Aranoa's *Princesas*, Pedro Pérez Rosado's *Agua con sal*, Helena Taberna's *Extranjeras* , David Riker's *La ciudad,* and Sandra Gugliotta's *Un día de suerte*. See Thomas Deveny, *Migration in Contemporary Hispanic Cinema.*
6. The longer version of the film contains an interview with an ecologist who explains how activists stopped a development in Sierra de Alpenar, and that arrests were made in conjunction with corruption regarding the proposed development.
7. Heath notes that Metz's five channels of communication in cinema are moving "photographic image, recorded phonetic sound, recorded noises, recorded musical sound, and writing" (218).
8. As Carl Plantinga notes, non-fiction films are those that assert that the states of affairs they present occur(red) in the actual world" (18) and non-fiction films "are *about* something, and make *claims* and *assertions* about extrafilmic reality" (43).
9. However, the developer may appeal the case.

WORKS CITED

"El Agua y los campos de golf españoles." *Nueva Tribuna.* February 16, 2011. Accessed March 15, 2013.

Aristotle. *Rhetoric*. Trans. W. Rhys Roberts. *Internet Classics Archive*. Accessed October 26, 2013.

"Extranjeros en la UE y en España." *Boletín informativo del Instituto Nacional de Estadística*. Accessed September 19, 2013.

"La Población extranjera en España." Instituto Nacional de Estadística. Accessed September 19, 2013.

Aufderheide, Patricia. *Documentary Film. A Very Short Introduction*. New York: Oxford University Press, 2007.

Bordwell, David and Thompson, Kristin. *Film Art: An Introduction*. 7th ed. New York: McGraw-Hill, 2004.

Chico, D. and A. Garrido. "Overview of the extended water footprint in Spain: The importance of agricultural water consumption in the Spanish economy." *Water, Agriculture and the Environment in Spain: can we square the circle?* Eds. Lucia De Stefano, M. Ramón Llamas. Leiden, The Netherlands: CRC Press/Balkema, 2012.

Club Murcia. "Water and Golf: The Facts." October 30, 2006. Accessed October 30, 2013.

"Code of Ethics for Education Abroad." The Forum on Education Abroad. Accessed May 22, 2013.

Crownove, Matt. "How Many Acres Are Needed for an 18 Hole Golf Course?" *Golfsmith*. Accessed September 27, 2013.

De la Vega, Inmaculada. "El pastor de Jumilla que frenó 15.000 chalés salva sus terrenos de la piqueta." *El País*. September 18, 2013. Accessed September 18, 2013.

Deveny, Thomas. *Migration in Contemporary Hispanic Cinema*. Lanham, MD: Scarecrow Press, 2012.

De Villiers, Marq. *Water. The Fate of Our Most Precious Resource*. Rev. Ed. Toronto: McClelland and Stewart, 2003.

Feo Parrondo, F. "Los campos de golf en España y sus repercusiones en el sector turístico"; *Cuadernos de Turismo* 7 (2001): 55–66. Accessed March 20, 2013.

García Ayala, José Antonio. "Agua y golf en la región de Murcia." Accessed March 15, 2013.

Glotfelty, Cheryll. "Introduction." *The Ecocriticism Reader. Landmarks in Literary Ecology*. Eds. Cheryll Glotfelty and Harold Fromm. Athens and London: U Georgia P, 1996: xv–xxvii.

Grover, Velma I. *Global Common and Global Problems* . Enfield, NH: Science Publishers, 2006.

Heath, S. "Metz's Semiology: A Short Glossary." *Screen* 14.(1–2) (1973): 214–226. Accessed January 31, 2012.

Jover, Pepe. "Golf Courses." Club Murcia. April 3, 2006. Accessed March 15, 2013.

Nichols, Bill. *Introduction to Documentary*. Bloomington: Indiana University Press, 2010.

Plantinga, Carl. *Rhetoric and Representation in Nonfiction Film*. Cambridge: Cambridge University Press, 1997.

Rábago, Joaquín. "España, el país preferido por los británicos para cambiar de vida." August 24, 2007. Accessed March 15, 2013.

Rosenthal, Elizabeth. "In Spain, Water Is a New Battleground." *New York Times*. June 6, 2008. Accessed August 26, 2013.

Sánchez, Lucía. *La guerra del golf*. Madrid: Alokatu, S.L., Les Films D'Ici, 2011. DVD.

Sánchez, Lucía. "Re: Necesito su permiso." Message to the author. March, 22 2014. Email.

Sánchez, M. "Los 17 campos de golf de Murcia gastan la misma agua que Albacete en dos años." *La Verdad*. March 26, 2010. Accessed March 15, 2013.

Willoquet-Maricondi, Paula. "Introduction: From Literary to Cinematic Ecocriticism." *Framing the World: Explorations in Ecocriticism and Film*. Ed. Paula Willoquet-Maricondi: Charlottesville: University of Virginia Press, 2010: 1–22.

——. "Shifting Paradigms: From Environmentalist Films to Ecocinema." *Framing the World: Explorations in Ecocriticism and Film*. Ed. Paula Willoquet-Maricondi: Charlottesville and London: U Virginia P, 2010: 43-61.

Wilson, Thomas. "Introduction: Food, Drink and Identity in Europe: Consumption and the Construction of Local, National and Cosmopolitan Culture. " *European Studies* 22 (2006): 11–29. Accessed October 31, 2013.

Zyrd, Michael. *Irony in Documentary Film: Ethics, Forms, and Functions.* Diss. New York University, 1999.

III

Multicultural Encounters in Local Spaces: Cinematic Depictions

Chapter Eleven

Spaces Occupied, Literal and Metaphorical, in Contemporary Spanish Fiction and Film: 1997–2011

Donna Gillespie

In 2013, the Instituto Nacional de Estadística (INE) placed the total foreign population in Spain at 5,520.133 (11.7 percent of the total population) (ine.es). Women comprise 48.5 percent of the total registered foreign population for this year compared to men, a 0.4 percent increase from 2012 (48.1 percent). The proportion of female to male immigrants varies enormously by region of origin. Women constitute 61.4 percent of the Central American and Caribbean immigrant population, 48.2 percent of the EU 27, 57.1 percent of other European countries, 55.9 percent of the South Americans, 55.6 percent of the North Americans, 41.3 percent of the Asian immigrant population, and 38.7 percent of the Africans (ine.es). There was a steady rise in the immigrant population for years, and although the census has shown a decrease in the total registered foreign population for 2012 and 2013, the percentage of female compared to male immigrants continues to rise. The recently published second "Plan Estratégico de Ciudadanía e Integración 2011–2014" discusses the new phenomenon of the "proceso de feminización de la inmigración en España" [process of the feminization of immigration to Spain] and reiterates that there has been an 18 percent increase in female immigrants in the past fifteen years. The Plan affirms that these women have developed a more autonomous role and have begun to initiate the migratory process rather than simply taking part in it (248).

With the sharp increase in immigration to Spain in the late twentieth and early twenty-first centuries, not only has cultural production begun to explore the identity (and often ambivalent nature) of the woman immigrant as "other," but also the spaces occupied by these women in their adopted country.

139

Zygmunt Bauman problematizes the issue of overpopulation in today's globalized world and its effects on the "outcasts" that inhabit it. In his book,
Wasted Lives: Modernity and Its Outcasts, the epigraph to the chapter titled,
"Are There Too Many of Them?" reads: "There are always too many of
them. 'Them' are the fellows of whom there should be fewer—or better still
none at all. And there are never enough of us. 'Us' are the folks of whom
there should be more" (34). He reinforces the idea that the persistent "images
of 'economic migrants' and of 'asylum seekers' both stand for 'wasted humans' . . ." (58); they evoke resentment and work to uphold the division
"between the 'inside' and the 'outside' in a globalizing world that pays it
little respect and routinely violates it" (58). This chapter explores the spaces
occupied by migrant "outcasts" and the subcommunities they form in Spanish written and cinematographic texts as they negotiate between *inside* and
outside positions in contemporary Spanish society. I will present the physical
and metaphorical spaces occupied by women immigrants in twenty-first century Spanish narratives by women writers and directors, drawing from concepts developed by Dolores Juliano and Josefina Ludmer, among others. In
discussing physical spaces, I will refer to personal and professional spaces. I
also present metaphorical spaces designated as "islas urbanas" by Ludmer to
demonstrate a new sense of "sub"-community among the immigrants.

The integration of the immigrant population into Spanish society has been
prominent in governmental studies and media news. The aforementioned
PECI II affirms that integration is a primary goal; the blueprint is significantly more ambitious than that of the previous PECI 2007–2010, seeking "el
paso de un nivel satisfactorio de coexistencia—una coincidencia en tiempo y
espacio de carácter pacífico—a un nivel óptimo de convivencia, la cual su-
pone la interacción y relación armoniosas" [the shift from a satisfactory level
of coexistence—a pacific synchronization in time and space—to an optimal
level of coexistence, one that leads to harmonious interaction and relations].[1]
Terms such as "ciudadanía, interculturalidad y democracia" [citizenship,
interculturality, and democracy] further define the objective of the Plan (ex-
tranjeros.mtin.es). It is in this sociopolitical context that women writers and
filmmakers in Spain have undertaken to represent their newly multicultural
environment and the challenges it presents in Spanish society.[2]

At a conference held at Casa América, "La Mujer Inmigrante en los
Medios de Comunicación" in 2008, Peio Aierbe shows that a biased portrayal of the woman immigrant in the media has not escaped notice. She reports,
based on news articles published for a period of fifty days prior to the conference, that 53 percent of the news dedicated to women immigrants deals with
domestic violence, 30 percent with trafficking and prostitution, and 22 percent with employment issues (amecopress.net). Clearly there is little opportunity for other representations; as long as the news reports primarily on such
issues among women immigrants, the public will continue to envision these

women as victims or pariahs, lacking individuality and voice, rather than as active participants in their communities.

Some writers and directors strive to problematize this portrayal in their works. Earlier narratives by women writers and directors (1997–2000) clearly show women immigrants as victims, whether of a shipwreck or of a loss ultimately leading to suicide (Lourdes Ortiz's *Fátima de los naufragios*) or of the need to secure legal status in Spain (Iciar Bollaín's *Flores de otro mundo*). More recent texts by women (2001–2011) portray the subtle transition that has taken place in the past several decades as women immigrants arrive of their own volition, begin to occupy mainstream jobs (although many are still portrayed in service-oriented jobs), receive education and become active in their communities (Najat El Hachmi's *Jo també sóc catalana*).

The marginal positioning is seen particularly in the earlier works: *Háblame musa, de aquel varón* (Chacón 1998), *Fátima de los naufragios* (Ortiz 1998), *Flores de otro mundo* (Bollaín 1999), and "Al'Yaza'ir" (García Benito 2000).[3] The more recent narratives, in contrast, place the characters in urban areas (although some continue in marginal positions): *Salsa* (Obligado 2002), *Extranjeras* (Taberna 2003), *Jo també sóc catalana* (El Hachmi 2004), *Si nos dejan* (Torres 2004), *Aguaviva* (Pujol 2006), and *Cosmofobia* (Extebarria 2007).[4]

In "Fátima de los naufragios," Fátima dwells at the water's edge, never leaving her spot on the outskirts of the small fishing village. She eventually becomes part of the landscape: "aquella estatua hecha de arena y sufrimiento que de algún modo perturbaba el paisaje y ponía una nota oscura en el horizonte" [that statue made of sand and suffering that somehow perturbed the landscape and left a dark impression on the horizon] (10). She is in a fixed position, literally and metaphorically, and becomes one with her surroundings. At the end she is enveloped by the sea; her permanent marginal presence is never compromised.

Another example of a woman immigrant who remains fixed on the perimeter of society is the eponymous protagonist of "La piel de Marcelinda"; a young Jamaican prostitute who works in the Casa de Campo, a park located on the outskirts of Madrid. Marcelinda's character is never depicted outside of this environment; she lives and dies (by suicide just as Fátima does) there. Aisha in Dulce Chacón's novel also resides on the perimeter of her living and working space; she and her husband are caretakers at a secluded ranch in southern Spain, "Pedro y Aisha se encontraban en la casita de los guardeses, una pequeña vivienda aislada del edificio central" [Pedro and Aisha could be found at the tiny guard house, a small dwelling isolated from the main building] (70). They are not only marginalized in their living and working space, but also in the community; they frequently go into town to attend gatherings in abandoned homes to interact with other immigrants searching for missing friends and family members.

Nieves Garcia Benito's "Al-Yaza'ir" portrays a seventeen-year-old Moroccan who is summoned by her father to join him and her brothers in Murcia. This first-person narrative depicts the isolation and despair of an immigrant woman who is marginalized first by her own family and customs (she is blamed the death of her mother who suffered complications after her birth and ultimately died), and subsequently by the autochthonous population and her family in her adopted country. She makes the treacherous crossing on a *patera* alone, and finds no one waiting for her on the "other" side. Her father finds her (pregnant), negotiates her release from her "dueño" [owner], and physically abuses her "sin piedad" [without mercy] (167). She narrates her story from the confines of her current "home" in Spain: "Mi padre me encerró aquí, donde ahora estoy, en una habitación de su casa, sin luz y sin ventanas, esperando que él nazca vivo o muerto y oliendo a humedad sin una lágrima" [My dad locked me up here, where I reside now, in a room in his house, without light or windows, waiting for him to be born alive or dead, smelling of dampness and without a tear] (167). She lives on a plantation and is kept locked up while the men are working. She tells her story of physical and emotional isolation, certain that death awaits her as soon as the baby is born. She finds consolation in talking to the walls that surround her, walls that literally and metaphorically keep her in a tightly sealed and contained space, far from any true interaction or integration into society.

In the film, *Flores de otro mundo*, Patricia moves from Madrid to rural Santa Eulalia, in hopes of meeting a local man to marry and thus secure her residency in Spain. Shortly after her arrival, she marries Damián and stays in town to begin a family with him; this secluded and abandoned environment strips her of her occupation as a beautician and of her ties to friends and family (her cultural identity). Her occupation as a housewife keeps her in a marginal role at home. Patricia's servant-like role at home has her running errands, taking care of the animals, and cleaning the house. In one scene, her aunt and friends come from Madrid to visit and as they come through the main entrance of the home where the animals are kept, they joke that she not only cares for but lives with the animals. Patricia's role, like the others we have seen, highlights the invisibility of immigrant women. In their study of female migrations in Spain, Carlota Solé and Sònia Parella note: "Social marginalization of migrant women involves their invisibility, both in the work sphere (given the kind of job carried out and the conditions accepted) and in the socioeconomic sphere (they are not considered as social actors or agents who decide and/or participate in public life)" (73).

In the more recent narratives of the corpus, women continue to inhabit the margins, but some have moved into new spaces as well. Graciela in *Aguaviva* is an example of the persistent peripheral positioning of the woman immigrant: she and her husband live in town, but the restaurant they are given to run is an isolated locale on the outskirts of the community. The first image of this space is an old, rusted sign, and the establishment sits behind a pad-locked gate; images of abandonment, entrapment, and seclusion underline the marginalization she encounters in her new surroundings. As they prepare for the opening of the restaurant, we hear Graciela speaking with her husband while the camera scans the layout of the kitchen of "El Quesito." In the final scene of this segment, the camera focuses on a window through which we view Aguaviva at a distance. Graciela is physically removed from the town center in an abandoned restaurant that she now runs.

Ana Torres's interview documentary *Si nos dejan* also portrays the soci-oeconomic marginalization of women immigrants, focusing on Barcelona.[5] Juanita, an Ecuadorian who migrated to Spain alone, sells drinks on the beach out of a portable cooler; she works to send money to her family in Ecuador. She confirms that she is an illegal immigrant and comments that her roots are in Ecuador where she was raised, married, had children, and was divorced. Despite her commentary, she is portrayed walking up and down the beach—literally the margins of the country— smiling and singing to some of her clients. In a haunting and beautiful voice, she sings "Si nos dejan," a love song full of hope in which the lyrics anticipate a brighter future for its protagonists, yet the "new world" that Juanita has found has not fulfilled the dreams associated with it. Spectators identify with this immigrant woman, singing about hope and the future, yet visibly struggling to make ends meet. Juanita's peripheral positioning as an illegal "street" salesperson is indicative of her marginal socioeconomic status and suggests her emotional isolation; she states that her only hope is to be able to return home someday to her family and children.

Ana Torres inserts herself into the documentary; we hear her voice on occasion, see her reflection, or see the shadow of her bike as she rides through the streets of Barcelona (using a point of view camera shot) looking for work and making her film. At the end of the film we see a side shot of the director seated at her computer working on the documentary. Written text is displayed onscreen that informs the viewer what the interviewees are current-ly doing: Torres still does not have her work papers, but instead of cleaning houses as she was doing in one of the earlier segments, she is working on this documentary. She is also marginalized in her new surroundings, and even in her own film. She chooses to include herself, but using a technique that does not allow us to see a close-up shot of her as we do the other immigrants; she places and maintains herself at the periphery. This deliberate placement dem-onstrates Torres's identification with a marginal status as she is an immigrant herself facing daily challenges in her new surroundings.

Although some of the newer films show women immigrants in marginal personal and professional spaces, several of the more recent narratives also portray them in new spaces and roles. The women of Helena Taberna's documentary film *Extranjeras* (2003), Lucía Extebarria's novel *Cosmofobia* (2007), and Clara Obligado's novel *Salsa* (2002) all occupy metropolitan loci; they reside in Madrid.[6] In speaking about urban spaces, Chambers affirms that there is a "shifting, mixing, contaminating, experimenting, revisiting and recomposing that the wider horizons and the inter- and trans-cultural networks of the city both permit and encourage" (94). For example, the diverse groups of women presented in *Extranjeras* occupy jobs ranging from illegal street vendors to business owners. Susana, a second-generation immigrant whose parents are from Guinea, works at a corporate clothing store in *Cosmofobia*, and Viviana is an Argentinian writer in *Salsa*. Clara Obligado's *Salsa* is an example of self-representation that offers a unique perspective on the life stories of women immigrants in Spain. The works mentioned here successfully blur the center/periphery boundaries by presenting marginalized characters who assume agency and occupy a place of resistance.

In an article that explores the conceptualization of space, Doreen Massey affirms: "precisely because it *is* the sphere of the potential juxtaposition of different narratives, of the potential forging of new relations, spatiality is also a source of the production of *new* trajectories, *new* stories. It is a source of the production of new spaces, new identities, new relations and differences" (38). The narratives selected show a change in "spatiality" as women immigrants acquire new agency and new relations in their shift from peripheral to central spaces, both literal and metaphoric, between earlier and more recent texts. Massey asserts that "multiplicity" is necessary for there to be "space," and this, in turn, allows for the existence of more than one voice in that space (28). This multiplicity is primarily evident in more recent narratives and serves to present a certain resistance to the sociocultural norm.

Some of the newer narratives portray a multicultural group of women immigrants pursuing a different sense of community. This was impossible for characters in earlier works who lived in isolating circumstances. I will denote these new groupings as subcommunities as they are formed outside the dominant culture, and are shown to be single-, multi- or inter-cultural. These groups coalesce and function in the city, yet very seldom mix with the autochthonous population and therefore remain outside the hegemonic culture. In her book, *Las que saben: subculturas de mujeres*, Dolores Juliano examines the concept of a "subcultura femenina" [feminine subculture] and maintains that undervalued groups question the hegemonic culture and subvert the conceptual categories that define them by creating their own interpretations of the world (18).

As we shall see, the differences portrayed in these narratives contribute to the discourse of multiculturalism and cultural "mestizaje" by incorporating the formation of new multicultural subcommunities. Each community demonstrates resistance to the dominant culture by affirming difference in public spaces. These collectives permit the expression of native religious and soci-ocultural practices in their adopted country and function as what Josefina Ludmer calls an "isla urbana" 'urban island': "Están afuera y adentro al mismo tiempo: afuera de la sociedad, en la isla, y a la vez adentro de la ciudad, que es lo social, donde se demarcan nítidamente los niveles y ocurre la historia y también 'la subversión'. . . . Esa es su posición exterior-interior de la ciudad (la sociedad, la nación, la ley, la historia o la razón)" [They are outside and inside at the same time: outside society, on the island, and inside the city, that which is social, where levels are sharply accentuated and the story occurs, as well as 'the subversion'. . . . That is their outside-inside position in the city (society, nation, law, history, or reason)] (131). I will provide a more in-depth analysis of *Extranjeras*, *Cosmofobia*, and *Salsa* as compared to the aforementioned texts in order to demonstrate the concept of subcommunities in the newer narratives.

Extranjeras portrays one of the most diverse groups of women in a single narrative. Filmed as a series of interviews, it presents images and voices from a multicultural group of women (Ecuador, Peru, Poland, Romania, Senegal, China, etc). The majority of the women interact (or speak of doing so) solely with other members of their ethnic group, or with other minority commu-nities, such as the "Cocina Intercultural" that brings together women from Venezuela, Colombia, the Dominican Republic, and so on, in Alcobendas to share recipes and stories with each other as they build trust and gain aware-ness of their differences and similarities. The Colombian Ángela Botero introduces the organization and discusses the need for this type of intercultu-ral space: "Que estar en la cocina nos junta, es un ritual. Más que llenarnos es alimentarnos de los saberes y de la compañía de mujeres que vienen de otros países, y que la mejor manera para comenzar a confiar y a creer en las otras es haciendo cosas juntas y hacer un plato de cocina entre todas" [Being in the kitchen unites us, it is a ritual. More than fill us up, it nourishes us with knowledge and the company of women from other countries, and the best way to begin to trust and believe in others is doing things together and making a dish all together] (*Extranjeras*). These women find a space to affirm their identities, form an intercultural group, and express their differ-ences.

The camera also follows a couple of young immigrant women from Ecua-dor (Paulina and Andrea) as they attend their weekly Sunday gathering with other Ecuadorians in the Retiro Park. This single cultural group socializes together: they cook a feast of typical Ecuadorian food and play games. They also work together cutting hair, selling drinks to tourists, and performing as musicians for onlookers. Some work illegally to make ends meet in a defined space clearly set apart to express their cultural traditions and affirm their ethnicity. Paulina and Andrea sit at the park and discuss these gatherings as a "réplica" of what they might find in Ecuador and one comments: "Me siento muy identificada" [I identify] (*Extranjeras*). They see the purpose of these weekly meetings to allow them to feel connected and organized. Chambers discusses the disruptive quality of the metropolitan migrant's visibility:

> For the modern metropolitan figure is the migrant: she and he are the active formulators of metropolitan aesthetics and life styles, reinventing the languages and appropriating the streets of the master. This presence disturbs a previous order. Such an interruption enlarges the potential as the urban script is rewritten and an earlier social order and cultural authority is now turned inside out and dispersed. (23)

The immigrant women portrayed represent communities from all over the world, each with sociocultural differences that are shown to perpetuate their marginal position in Spanish society. The Chinese women are the first group in Helena Taberna's documentary; they are a united and cohesive band that seeks to maintain their culture by continuing to speak their own language. The Chinese women discuss ties to their culture of origin and the importance of passing on their customs and traditions to future generations. *Extranjeras* also presents a group of Polish and Ukrainian women. Through their experiences and stories, the spectator views another intercultural community in Madrid. The camera follows Joanna, a Polish lawyer who came to Madrid to join her boyfriend, to the neighborhood of Aluche where there is a weekly open air market; a space for them to converse with each other, make connections, send and receive packages, and buy magazines or newspapers from "home" each Sunday.

All of these examples in *Extranjeras* demonstrate a lack of interaction with the autochthonous population. Taberna comments on this in her *Guía didáctica*; she discusses the "guetos" that are formed in countries with an influx of immigrants that both impede the process of integration and provide immigrants with a refuge that permits them to maintain their language and cultural customs (51). *Extranjeras* illustrates the existence of subcommunities that form and function outside/inside Spanish society.

There is new subject positioning in the documentary *Extranjeras*; the women are owners of restaurants, hair salons, and "locutorios." They are teachers, they attend the University, form part of musical groups such as "Africa Lisanga," and they perform in clubs. It is noteworthy that these characters occupy spaces in central Madrid and they are seen frequenting very visible public places. This constitutes a subversive strategy that challenges the homogenizing norm of the dominant culture.[7] Taberna's criteria for selecting her subjects parallel those of the other women authors and directors of the more recent narratives; few portray women prostitutes or the vicissitudes of crossing to Spain on a *patera*. Their works challenge the predominant images in the media and offer an intimate view of the daily life, struggles, and concerns of women immigrants, thus offering the public an alternate vision of this population. The women portrayed or interviewed are more like Bauman's "us" and less like "them," a strategy that attempts to obviate the persistent binary oppositions that grip societies beset by globalization.

There are a few narratives that portray immigrants developing a sense of community with Spaniards. When this occurs, however, it is because the locals are "escaping" to these subcommunities or are marginalized for emotional or physical reasons. *Cosmofobia* intertwines the stories of Spanish and immigrant women who come together at an activity sponsored by the Comunidad de Madrid's social services, the "taller de autoayuda." The narrative is presented as a series of interviews and the reader determines the objective of the interviews when Amina, one of the immigrant women at the Center, tells her interviewer that although she doesn't feel that she would be useful in telling the story about the neighborhood, she will collaborate. Amina voices her trust in the interviewer: "Sí, ya sé que usted no juzga y que no lo contará nunca, que es como si se lo contara a un médico . . . Además, usted es mujer, es diferente, claro" [Yes, I know that you won't judge me or tell anyone about it, it is as if I am talking to a doctor. . . . Furthermore, you are a woman, of course, it is different] (169). The women are no longer speaking to their male psychologist, Isaac, at the Center; they are clearly aware of the difference in sharing their stories with a woman. The author chooses to present these women with a voice of their own as they share their trials in first-person narrative.

The intercultural gathering at the "Centro de Autoayuda" in *Cosmofobia* is an example of a Spanish and immigrant subcommunity. The various characters in the novel present different perspectives on life and relationships in Madrid. Much of the action centers around friendships and connections that are formed at the "Caserón Grande" whose services include: support for women and older adults, Spanish language classes for immigrants, transcultural mental health, immigration and law services, workshops, daycare, and the like. No character is given more importance than another and the novel portrays the development of relationships between them: Spaniards and immigrants, wealthy and poor, artists and working professionals, and so on. Etxebarria's novel illustrates Ella Shohat and Robert Stam's concept of polycentric multiculturalism by presenting both Spanish and immigrant characters (without developing one more than the other) and by interweaving their life stories and demonstrating connections between them all. One of the women asserts that profound relationships are formed there and although they are always told they shouldn't see each other outside the center, no one abides by that rule (160).

The women immigrants in *Cosmofobia* all live in Lavapiés, the oldest and most centrally located "barrio" in Madrid. Valero-Costa finds that in *Cosmofobia*: "Los españoles quieren recuperar el barrio de Lavapiés pero se quedan en la periferia" [The Spaniards want to reclaim the Lavapiés neighborhood, but they remain on the periphery] (37), corroborating that at least part of the immigrant population in Madrid lives inside the traditional city center in this novel. Miriam, a Spaniard who lives in the barrio, takes her children to a park outside of the neighborhood, in a more affluent area where all the children are white. The invisible walls that divide the Spaniards from the "rest" within this city center is clearly outlined in the text. One of the women states that on one side of the street there are the tourist bars, designer lofts, theaters, and hotels, and on the other side the immigrants, Social Services children, drunks, gangs, and drug dealers (94). The immigrants are grouped together with delinquents and drug users. The multicultural groups coexist in the heart of the city, forced to confront their fear of the "other" (in the workplace, on the streets, and in the Centro Social).

In the novel, the center/periphery boundaries blur, but the parallel portrayal of the lack of a *truly* intercultural environment outside the Center reinforces the divisions that persist in Spanish society. This subcommunity of women is positioned outside the dominant culture because of the circumstances of their personal and professional encounters; all confront either emotional or physical abuse or problems that bring them to the Center for help. Their circumstances bring them together as they share their stories on the inside, yet they are not encouraged to maintain these relationships with the group on the outside. One of the interviewees comments: "Si es lo que dice la Claudia, que es la novia de Isaac, que este es un barrio multicultural, pero no intercultural" [That is what Claudia says, Isaac's girlfriend, that this is a multicultural neighborhood, but not intercultural] (176). On the "inside," their lives intertwine and the women form friendships and develop a sense of community, immigrants and Spaniards alike. Yet, on the "outside," their differences predominate and limit the possibility of a truly intercultural environment.

Obligado's *Salsa* portrays another intercultural subcommunity; it gathers at a Salsa club located in Madrid, Los Bongoseros de Bratislava. This locale unites the protagonists in the narrative: Omara, Ulises, Viviana, Jamaica, Marga, Gloria, and Jotabé. Both immigrants and Spaniards frequent the establishment to escape from their lives on the *outside*. Ludmer discusses a different sense of territory portrayed in the Latin American novel she studies, developing the idea of the "urban island" as a space where binary divisions are blurred. This space: "iguala a sus habitantes porque los une por rasgos preindividuales, biológicos, postsubjetivos; por un fondo 'natural' como la sangre, el sexo, la edad, las enfermedades o la muerte" [equalizes its inhabitants because preindividual, biologic, and postsubjective characteristics unite them; with a natural essence like blood, sex, age, illness or death] (133). This underground Salsa Club invites all classes and races to interact within the confines of the club's walls and forget about their lives on the outside: "En esos pasadizos que recorren los subsuelos hay una plaza tomada por la población oscura que de día se busca la vida y de noche se junta para bailar" [There is a plaza in the underground passage ways overtaken by an obscure population, that by day makes ends meet and by night gathers to dance] (80).

The subcommunity is formed where most of the action takes place, a night club hidden in the underground of Azca in Madrid. This space welcomes a multicultural group where clients can easily forget about their differences. When Gloria and Ulises take to the dance floor, the natural element that ties them together is exemplified as they dance together, "las lenguas se empinan y luchan como dos animales marinos de vientre azul, encrespadas, ápice contra ápice, él recorre el paladar y su bóveda" [their tongues tip up and fight like two blue-bellied animals, agitated, tip to tip, he traverses the palate of her cavern] (81). Desire and passion reign in this "tugurio" [hovel] that those on the outside call "super under" (75).

What unites this group is the "natural essence' that Ludmer proposes, but in this case it is desire and the sensual Salsa dance that binds them together and eliminates the differences so evident on the outside. In this space, prebiologic tendencies reign: desire and passion. Just as Ludmer found in the "urban islands" of her narratives, in Los Bongoseros de Bratislava:

> Los habitantes de la isla . . . parecen haber perdido la sociedad o algo que la representa en la forma de familia, clase, trabajo, razón y ley, y a veces nación. Se definen en plural y forman una comunidad que no es la familia ni la del trabajo ni tampoco la de la clase social, sino algo diferente que puede incluir todas esas categorías al mismo tiempo, en sincro y en fusión. [The island inhabitants . . . appear to have lost society or something that represents it in the form of family, class, work, reason and law, and sometimes nation. They are defined in plural and form a community that is neither family nor work nor social class, but rather something different that can include all of these categories at the same time, in synch and in fusion.] (131)

This synchronization, much like dance, allows them to experience a retreat, even if it is for a brief period of time, and break away from the dominant culture that *otherizes* them in their outside lives. Here their differences are negligible; their lives are temporarily fused into one common denominator, their rhythm and dance, in their harmonious urban island.

All of these communities represent novel spaces being occupied in more recent narratives; like those loci presented by Ludmer, they have strict boundaries defined as an exterior/interior zone that are territories at the same time inside and outside the city (and society) (131).

As the selected novels demonstrate, more recent works portray women immigrants in more central and urban positions and spaces. There is a transition from a homogeneous representation of the immigrant "other" in earlier texts to heterogeneous portrayals of a diverse group of immigrant women in newer narratives. Yet even though more central spaces are occupied, the women still remain outside the dominant culture. The subcommunities that they form with each other, with other ethnic groups, and on occasion with Spaniards, can be viewed as subversive insofar as these associations allow the immigrants to assert their ethnicity and practice their traditional customs in very visible, public spaces. Bhabha maintains:

> Political empowerment, and the enlargement of the multiculturalist cause, come from posing questions of solidarity and community from the interstitial perspective. Social differences are not simply given to experience through an already authenticated cultural tradition; they are the signs of the emergence of community envisaged as a project. (3)

The immigrant women portrayed in these narratives are empowered in these interstitial spaces; although they are persistently marginalized, their agency is portrayed in a variety of personal and professional spaces, and in their subcommunities, which not only increase their visibility, but in some cases, diffuse their differences (as in *Salsa*). Fiction and film of the new millennium question binary classifications, such that the division between center and periphery begins to blur as Ludmer observes: "después de 1990 se ven nítidamente otros territorios y sujetos, otras temporalidades y configura- ciones narrativas: otros mundos que no reconocen los moldes bipolares tradi- cionales. Que absorben, contaminan y desdiferencian lo separado y opuesto y trazan otras fronteras" [after 1990 other territories and subjects can be clearly seen, other temporalities and narrative configurations: other worlds that do not recognize the traditional bipolar molds. That absorb, contaminate, differ- entiate what is opposite and separate and trace new frontiers] (127). Bauman corroborates this "contamination" in his study and proposes: "The planet is now full" (69), and since the "wasted humans" can no longer be disposed of out of site, they must be "sealed off in tightly closed containers" (85). These "containers" that limit their integration into Spanish society, these subcom- munities that the women immigrants form in their adopted country, are places of agency and resistance permitting the forging of new attitudes and cultural expressions within the dominant culture that persistently margi- nalizes them.

NOTES

1. Unless otherwise indicated, the Spanish to English translations are mine.
2. In a "preliminary study" in Ana Rueda's book on "hispano-marroquí" literature, Sandra Martín explains the often ambiguous and overlapping terms, multiculturalism, and pluralism. She states that Giovanni Sartori clarifies the concepts by defining multiculturalism as closed homogenous communities of different and separate cultures whereas pluralism is defined as open communities that integrate various cultures and tolerate difference (qtd. in Rueda, 43–44,

note 24). Accordingly, I will use the term multicultural to describe the Spanish society presented in my works, since none of my narratives presents a pluralistic society.

3. In their "Introduction: Women on the Move in Southern Europe," Floya Anthias and Gabriella Lazaridis discuss "the notion of 'periphractic' space (from the Greek 'fencing in'), to denote the spatial dimensions of marginalization and social exclusion" (7–8).

4. For additional narratives by women writers and directors that portray women immigrants to Spain, please see the following: "América Colón" (1997) by Juana Salabert, *Las otras vidas* (2005) by Clara Obligado, "Cartas a Nora" in *Invisibles* (2007) by Isabel Coixet, *Un novio para Yasmina* (2008) by Irene Cardona, *Retorno a Hansala* (2009) by Chus Guitérrez, and *Ojos de gato* (2011) by Lourdes Ortiz.

5. Jose Monterde includes Ana Torres's documentary in his extensive review of migration film. He affirms that the Argentinean director, an illegal immigrant herself, gives voice to immigrants in the city of Barcelona as they confront their new life in Spain (87). Torres's documentary is a valuable contribution to my corpus as it is the only film produced and directed by an immigrant woman.

6. The four regions in Spain with the highest representation of women immigrants are: Cataluña with 553,293 women, the Comunidad de Madrid with 537,546, the Communitat Valenciana with 423,210, and Andalucía with 336,000 (II PECI, 31). The majority of the immigrant population resides in urban centers, with women constituting almost half of their total number.

7. Martinez-Carazo offers an excellent analysis of the spaces occupied by women immigrants in *Extranjeras*. She states that there is a "resignificación" of these emblematic and public spaces such as Cibeles, Atocha, and Retiro, whose symbolism is reformulated by the presence of the other. (269).

WORKS CITED

Aguaviva. Dir. Ariadna Pujol. Cameo Media S.L., 2006. DVD.

Anthias, Floya, and Gabriella Lazaridis. *Gender and Migration in Southern Europe: Women on the Move*. Oxford: Berg, 2000.

Bauman, Zygmunt. *Wasted Lives: Modernity and Its Outcasts*. Oxford: Polity, 2004.

Bhabha, Homi. *The Location of Culture*. New York: Routledge, 1994.

Chacón, Dulce. *Hablame musa, de aquel varón*. Madrid: Punto de Lectura, 2007.

Chambers, Iain. *Migrancy, Culture, Identity*. London: Routledge, 1994.

El Hachmi, Najat. *Jo també soc catalana*. Barcelona: Columna, 2004.

Etxebarria, Lucia. *Cosmofobia*. Barcelona: Destino, 2008.

Extranjeras. Dir. Helena Taberna. Lamia Producciones Audiovisuales, 2003. DVD.

Flores de otro mundo. Dir. Iciar Bollaín. Alta Films, S.A., 1999. DVD.

García Benito, Nieves (2000). "Al-Yaza'ir." *El retorno/el reencuentro: la inmigración en la literatura hispano-marroquí*. Ed. Ana Rueda. Madrid: Iberoamericana Editorial Vervuert, 2010, 159–67.

Instituto Nacional de Estadística. "Avance de la estadística del Padrón continuo a 1 de enero de 2013" Notas de Prensa, April 22, 2013. Accessed December 14, 2013.

Invisibles. "Cartas a Nora." Dir. Isabel Coixet, et al. Pinguin films, 2007. Online video clip. *Youtube*. May 27, 2007. Accessed August 15, 2012.

Juliano, Dolores. "La inmigración sospechosa y las mujeres globalizadas." *Mujeres de un solo mundo: globalización y multiculturalismo*. Eds. Carmen Gregorio Gil and Belén Agrela Romero. Granada: Universidad de Granada, 2002, 123–34.

———. *Las que saben: subculturas de mujeres*. Madrid: Horas y Horas, 1998.

Ludmer, Josefina. *Aqui América Latina: una especulación*. Buenos Aires: Eterna Cadencia, 2010.

Martínez-Carazo, Cristina. "Cine e inmigración: Madrid como espacio de encuentro/desencuentro y su representación en *Extranjeras* de Helena Taberna." *Hispanic Research Journal: Iberian and Latin American Studies* 6(3) (2005): 265–75.

Massey, Doreen. *Power-Geometries and the Politics of Space-Time: Hettner-Lecture 1998.* Heidelberg: University of Heidelberg, 1999.

Monterde, José. *El sueño de Europa: cine y migraciones desde el sur.* Madrid: Ocho y Medio, 2008.

Obligado, Clara. *Las otras vidas.* Madrid: Páginas de Espuma, 2005.

———. *Salsa.* Barcelona: Plaza & Janés Editores, 2002.

Ortiz, Lourdes. *Fátima de los naufragios.* Barcelona: Planeta, 1998.

———. *Ojos de gato.* Madrid: Irreverentes, 2011.

"Plan Estratégico de Ciudadanía e Integración 2011–2014." *Gobierno de España: Ministerio de Trabajo e Inmigración.* Accessed November 4, 2011. *Retorno a Hansala.* Dir. Chus Gutiérrez. Cameo Media S.L., 2009. DVD.

Rodríguez, Bonnie. "Peio Aibe: la mujer inmigrante es invisibilizada en los medios de comunicación." *AmecoPress,* April 4, 2008. Accessed November 12, 2011.

Rueda, Ana, and Sandra Martín. *El retorno, el reencuentro: la inmigración en la literatura hispano-marroquí.* Madrid: Vervuert, 2010.

Salabert, Juana. "América Colón." *Páginas amarillas.* Eds. Antonio Álamo and Sabas Martín. Madrid: Lengua de Trapo, 1997, 397–404.

Shohat, Ella, and Robert Stam. *Unthinking Eurocentrism: Multiculturalism and the Media.* New York: Routledge, 1994.

Solé, Carlota, and Sònia Parella. "Migrant Women in Spain: Class, Gender and Ethnicity." *Gender and Ethnicity in Contemporary Europe.* Ed. Jacqueline Andall. Oxford: Berg, 2003, 61–76.

Taberna, Helena. *Guía didáctica: Extranjeras.* 2nd ed. Pamplona: Lamia Producciones Audiovisuales, 2006.

Torres, Ana. "Si nos dejan." Online video clip. *Youtube.* May 14, 2008. Accessed August 15, 2012.

Chapter Twelve

The City I Live In: Almodóvar Reshapes Madrid as Spain Goes *Glocal*

María R. Matz and Carole Salmon

In 1992, British sociologist Roland Robertson defined and popularized the concept of globalization in the English-speaking world as "the compression of the world and the intensification of the consciousness of the world as a whole" (8). Richard Giulianotti and Roland Robertson took it a step further in their 2004 article "The Globalization of Football: A Study in the Glocalization of the 'Serious Life,'" arguing that "globalization is marked culturally by processes of 'glocalization', whereby local cultures adapt and redefine any global cultural product to suit their particular needs, beliefs and customs" (546). The portmanteau word "glocalization" blends the sounds and the meanings of its two components: the interaction of the global and the local.

Originally referring to the economic market that was becoming global in the 1980s, the social and cultural effects of globalization consequently became a topic of study for scholars of various fields in the Humanities and Social Sciences. It is impossible to understand glocalization without first understanding globalization, as it appeared in reaction to the unification movement that globalization implies. At a 1997 conference on "Globalization and Indigenous Culture," Robertson stated that glocalization "means the simultaneity—the co-presence—of both universalizing and particularizing tendencies." By extension, the concept of glocalization can refer to anything that undergoes an alteration or a transformation in order to better suit the needs or the desires of local consumers. For obvious reasons, this trend best applies to cultural products accessible via the Internet, which potentially reaches out to almost everyone regardless of social class, economic status, and geographic location, but it is also observed by means of any form of visual media such as television and cinema. Indeed, movies travel worldwide and can reach viewers virtually anywhere, even in the most remote parts of the world via the Internet. In that respect, any "glocal" film contributes to cultural heterogenization, as a counterpart of the cultural homogenization that Americanization—and American cinema—have also spread.

In this chapter, we analyze how Pedro Almodóvar's cinema is an example of the concept of glocalization in Spain at the cultural level. Since the end of the dictatorship in 1975, Spain has constructed a new national discourse still promoting its cultural uniqueness within the new global perspective in which all European countries were reinventing their national images. Certain cultural elements considered as stereotypes of Spain until then (flamenco, gazpacho, bullfighting, Spanish flag, etc.) have been revamped in order to gain a positive value on the international scene. Indeed, Pedro Almodóvar's worldwide recognition as a filmmaker has allowed him to highlight some very specific elements of the Spanish identity embedded in the geography of its cosmopolitan capital city, Madrid. In his films, key elements representing the Spanishness of the capital are often intertwined with the characteristics of glocalization. As we will explain, not only do Almodóvar's films translate the dynamics and interactions between people within the city, but also between people and the urban space, and lately between national and transnational spaces.

ALMODÓVAR AND THE CITY: LOCAL SPACE(S) IN A GLOBAL WORLD

Pedro Almodóvar arrived in Madrid in the late 1960s and even though the city he encountered was not what he expected, he quickly became aware of its many possibilities. As stated in his film *Laberinto de pasiones* (Labyrinth of Passions, 1982), Madrid is "la ciudad más divertida del mundo" [the most fun city in the world].[1] In this way, since the beginning of his career, Almodóvar has adopted Madrid as the backdrop for most of his films. Indeed, his love affair with the big city has only been broken a few times; even when the plots took place in different locations across the Spanish geography such as Barcelona, Valencia, the Canary Islands, Toledo, or Santiago de Compostela, Almodóvar always returned to his forgiving city. For him, Madrid is more than a city where his characters live and interact with each other; it is a character in itself. Moreover, as Marvin D'Lugo has stated, "the city is regularly imaged as a cultural force, producing forms of expression and action that challenge traditional values by tearing down and rebuilding the moral institutions of Spanish life" (47). This relationship creates an organic dynamic in which the urban space is not just a background, but also an active participant in the story, and where everything within and around the city is in constant movement. His fondness for filming his characters in emblematic places and monuments traces back to his first 1974 short film, *Film político* (Political Film), and still continues in his last feature, *Los amantes pasajeros* (I am so Excited, 2013).

For many decades, Almodóvar and the city have shaped each other, to the point that both fiction and reality witness the reconfiguration of many of the capital's neighborhoods. As the director and the city have merged their paths, viewers have witnessed several waves of the many changes that are constant-ly contracting, expanding, growing, and flowing in Madrid. The underlying humanity of the city is constantly portrayed in his films, which examine how characters interact within the "social and physical dimensions of their urban spaces and . . . their urban lives are shaped by the material and emotional conditions of their lives in the city" (Foster 45). The people who live there are shaped by their surroundings and the newcomers have to adapt or they become isolated in this urban space.

The "other" is portrayed in many Spanish films of the dictatorship era as a stereotypical poor and uneducated national migrant who typically comes to Madrid in hopes of a better life. In 1970, under martial law, Madrid was a standardized cultural space where regional differences were not tolerated. Almodóvar's lens captures this stereotype and the opening scene of *Carne Trémula* (Live Flesh, 1997) takes us to a brothel's room where a young woman, Isabel (Penélope Cruz), is about to give birth. The "Madam" Doña Centro (Pilar Bardem) is at her side and through the screaming, we realize because of her accent that this young prostitute is from the South of Spain (Andalusia). A few scenes later, in a city bus, Isabel gives birth to a baby boy, Victor (Liberto Rabal). Madrid at night during Christmas time is de-serted because of the curfew. Isabel is one of the many examples of the stereotypical "other": she is not from Madrid, she is a prostitute, and she cannot even count her due date as Doña Centro states: "¡Ay! La incultura que mala es" [Oh my God! What a horrible thing is the lack of education!]. At the end of the film, in an endlessly repetitive cycle allowing a new beginning, a grown-up Victor tells his newborn son that twenty years ago, at the time of his own birth, people were scared and locked up in their houses, and that now, "Por suerte para ti, hijo mío, hace mucho tiempo que en España hemos perdido el miedo" [luckily for you, my son, in Spain, we stopped being afraid a long time ago]. In Victor's lifetime, Madrid has witnessed a profound political, social, and cultural change and, even though he is the son of a migrant, he has fully become part of the city. This film gathers a large quantity of images from the city, thus creating the connection between spaces and historical periods. Through the use of different shots filmed from the windows of moving city buses, the viewer goes from the old city to the new neighborhoods, and vice versa, which symbolizes the rebirth and expansion of the city for a new generation of Spaniards.

The traditional Madrid mixes with the contemporary one and, as Almodóvar has recognized on several occasions, the city has always provided him with the perfect scenery and suitable fauna (sassy and ideal) for each and every one of his films.[2] A plethora of marginal characters, such as prostitutes, transsexuals, transvestites, thieves, rapists, etc. have always populated the Almodovarian universe. As early as 1980, in *Pepi Luci Bom y otras chicas del montón* (Pepi, Luci, Bom and Other Girls of the Heap), Almodóvar brings a high number of these eccentric and underground characters to the big screen. Most of the time, they are not fully developed but function as stereotypes of *la movida madrileña*'s typical crowd: drug addicts, artists, singers, gays, bisexuals, etc. [3] Intertwining fiction and reality, many of these individuals are not originally from Madrid but from other regions of Spain such as La Mancha and Andalusia, for example. The city, at that time, was a magnet attracting people from all horizons and social classes in their search for newly acquired freedom.

Around that time, Spain also opened up its borders to foreigners from countries under political turmoil and as a result, political refugees are present in several of Almodóvar's films such as *Laberinto de pasiones* and *Todo sobre mi madre* (All About My Mother, 1999); but it is not until *Volver* in 2006 that immigrants are fully integrated into the daily lives of the lead Spanish characters. In this later film, we recognize the stereotypical character of the Latin American prostitute who lives in a blue-collar Madrilenian neighborhood built in the early 1950s on the outskirts of the city. Besides the fact that she practices one of the oldest professions of the world, Regina (Maria Isabel Díaz) is presented as a socially integrated and financially independent woman; moreover, with Regina's material help and moral support, the main character of the film, Raimunda (Penélope Cruz), a migrant from a small village in La Mancha, is able to open her own restaurant and to reach financial independence and social recognition.

The director shot many scenes of his films in the centric Plaza the Callao and the Gran Vía street, an area well known in Madrid for drug dealing and prostitution, activities that mainly involve immigrants from Latin America. However, Almodóvar's films never portray these specific problematic areas of Madrid as such. On the contrary, he establishes them as the heart of the capital. This is not the case of Barcelona's nightlife in *Todo sobre mi madre* whose image is tainted by a shocking scene of prostitution and violence. Almodóvar's choice to show immigrants as a more established presence in his filmic universe by the late 1990s is not random. It reflects a sociopolitical and economical reality in modern-day Madrid and, by extension, in Spain; where the growing importance of Latin American immigration became an integral part of the Spanish working force and of Spanish daily life.

In a reverse movement, *¿Qué he hecho yo para merecer esto?* (What have I done to Deserve this? 1984) takes us back to the Spanish emigration wave of the 1960s toward Europe, mainly France, Germany, and Switzerland. In this film, Gloria's (Carmen Maura) abusive husband worked in Germany as a driver before returning to Spain to become a taxi driver. They live in the eastern Madrilenian suburb of Concepción, "a setting which combines the crowed alienation of the big city with the anxious solitude of the periphery" (Smith 55). A few years later, *Tacones lejanos* (High Heels, 1991) shows another migratory movement: the return to Spain as a motherland. When singer Becky del Páramo (Marisa Paredes) returns from Mexico, she has to face her past in Madrid, a city that she decided to abandon fifteen years before. The media publicize her return and, as she mentions, the city she finds is completely different from the one she left and remembered. It is interesting to note that, even though she is an immigrant returning to her home country after many years, the director addresses neither the reasons for her return nor where Del Páramo truly belongs. Her character's identity is solidly established from the moment she lands in Madrid's Barajas airport, and she never doubts this identity as a public figure: the great Spanish singer Becky del Páramo.

The process of internal Spanish migration from the rural to the urban space or vice versa—or local versus global—is equally represented in Almodóvar's films. The reasons for these movements are opposed: the hope of getting a better life or escaping the hardship of another. The melodramatic film *¿Qué he hecho yo para merecer esto?* gives a clear vision of the shadowy lives of many migrants from their Spanish villages to the big city. The grandmother character (Chus Lampreave) functions as the stereotypical grandmother from the village who moved to the city in search of a better life. She is an illiterate older woman unable to adapt nor to adjust to the demands and standards of the urban life. Eventually, she returns to her roots in the village and takes one of her grandsons with her.

As the German website *Focus Migration* states in reference to Spain "while immigration has become a key political and social issue in public debate, discussion over what it will mean for Spain and the Spanish self-image in the future is only starting to get off the ground." As foreigners and rural migrants alike are quickly assimilated into the Almodovarian urban space, their own cultural identity is never fully presented, and their roots are never clearly explained. It seems to us as if Almodovarian immigrant characters share a lack of definition of their origins, as if they were not an essential part of what defines their reshaped identity as Spanish (or Madrilenian) residents. Maybe it is because cosmopolitanism, through globalization and glocalization, is essentially geared toward what we are becoming rather than where we come from.

SPACE VERSUS PLACE AND THE CONCEPT OF NON-PLACES

If, for us, "space" refers to vast landscapes with undefined limits, such as the sea, the sky, or the night, "place" designates some locations that are easily identifiable and precisely localized. In other words, "places" constitute a delimited portion of the physical "space" such as an apartment, a town or a city, a hospital, a shop, a bedroom, or an airport (Bessy and Salmon).

It is, however, important to distinguish between intimate places belonging to the private space, and more depersonalized places belonging to the public space. The city, as a whole, can be very impersonal; but, if we look into each neighborhood, we find specific public places in which the characters meet and interact with each other, and we can also find warmth and humanity. Following Henri Lefebvre's spatial theory as presented in *The Production of Space* (1991), bars are the best example of such public places in urban life, as they reflect the social and cultural diversity among neighborhoods and are the intersection of the social and economic structures of the area in which they are located. Moreover, Edward Soja in *Thirdspace: Journeys to Los Angeles and Other Real and Imagined Spaces* (1996) goes one step further and combines spatiality with sociality, adding the historical component to this mix. Consequently, according to Soja's terminology, bars can be considered as micro-geographies reflecting the daily life of specific groups established throughout the macro-geography of Madrid as a whole. To get an accurate and nuanced image of the capital, it is crucial to consider these two geographies as equally important.

In Almodóvar's films, bars are places of interaction and socialization while they are a space for personal reflection and growth—being at the heart of different neighborhoods, they offer a safe haven for the characters to interact with each other. Among the many Almodovarian cosmopolitan places in *Laberinto de pasiones*, (Labyrinth of Passions, 1982), the viewer sees in its opening scene, *Bar Wooster* at San Millán 3, where the two main characters meet. In this bar, formerly called *La Bobia*, Almodóvar and his crowd used to hang out on Sunday morning during *la movida*. In other scenes and movies, the *Museo Chicote* bar is where Judit (Blanca Portillo) reveals her big secret in *Los abrazos rotos* (Broken Embraces, 2009); at the *Círculo de Bellas Artes*, Alcala 42, Andrea Caracortada (Victoria Abril) and Nicholas (Peter Coyote) discuss a script in *Kika* (1993); in *Bar Cock*, Reina 16, DJ Diego (Tamar Navas) plays music in *Los abrazos rotos* and, last but not least, in *La flor de mi secreto* (The Flower of My Secret, 1995) at Gravina 11, in the tavern *Angel Sierra*, the main character Leo Macias (Marisa Paredes), drinks a *carajillo* [coffee and cognac] after her suicide attempt. The director's decision to choose bars with a long historical presence in Madrid's social scene reinforces the identity of the city as a character, as they constitute social and cultural landmarks for Madrilenians. Through the local memories associated with these places, Almodóvar emphasizes a social structure, an economic life and, more importantly, he underlines some important cultural values embedded in the places themselves. In a way, Almodóvar's tendency to film these symbolic bars has captured more than glocalization. It is what several scholars have been calling "rooted cosmopolitanism." Will Kymlicka and Kathryn Walker have defined this concept as one in which "human beings often combine profound local, ethnic, religious, or national attachments with a commitment to cosmopolitan values and principles that transcend those more local boundaries." Almodóvar's bars materialize the very essence of local rootedness that "requires and involves the very roots it claims to transcend" (Kymlicka and Walker 1).

The Almodovarian urban geography is both unique and symbolic of the capital city. Following French ethnologist Marc Augé, inspired by Michel Foucault's theory of *Hétérotopies*, we can apply the concept of "non-places" to this analysis of Almodovarian Madrid (Bessy and Salmon). Augé defines "non-places" in the city as "installations necessary to the fast-paced circulation of people and goods (express roads, connectors, airports) as well as means of transportation themselves, or gigantic malls" (Augé 48). One of the main consequences of globalization is the intensification of people's geographic mobility across the planet. In his latest production, *Los amantes pasajeros*, Almodóvar has taken the concepts of space and place (or non-place) to a whole new level, as the film happens almost entirely in the air between Madrid and Toledo, on a Peninsula Airlines plane that was supposed to go to Mexico City. Instead, it flies in circles before eventually landing in a deserted and unused airport in La Mancha. The plot develops itself within two spaces: the almost surreal, disconnected, and circular air space in which the plane flies and idles, and the city of Madrid where the rest of reality is happening. All of the characters/passengers are prisoners in the plane, which is experienced as a space without place—a non-place.

The profusion of non-places in our society, such as Augé defines them, automatically complicates the anchoring of identity and the people's sense of belonging to a place. According to him, "the traveler's space would be an archetype of the non-place" (Augé 110), a place of passage that is temporary, a necessary sojourn for people's circulation, and, for immigrants, an essential element of their voyage. According to Augé, a plane is *par excellence* a non-place, because it is never designed for settling down. It is a transitory tool, the sole purpose of which is to allow people to travel from one point to another. However, in *Los amantes pasajeros*, when the crew discovers that the plane will never be able to reach its destination, and that everyone is in danger of dying, the dynamics among the passengers drastically change, and everything ends in a sex orgy, as if social norms did not apply anymore in this near-death situation. Almodóvar is able to connect the non-place of the plane with Madrid through the cabin phone. Several scenes in the film portray a counter shot in the plane where different passengers make private phone calls through the broken cabin phone; and, as a consequence, everyone's privacy is violated, as everyone listens to, and even participates in, the conversations. Furthermore, when Madrid appears on the screen, we see a woman on the top of a bridge, *El Viaducto*, ready to commit suicide. Bridges are also

non-places, as people are only supposed to cross them. In literature, bridges are traditionally places of passage and transition (both literally and figuratively) between different worlds or spaces and, as such, they play a symbolic role in any story in which they appear, whether it be in oral tradition or written or cinematic works. In Madrid, *El Viaducto* has an intense overpowering presence, both spatially and symbolically, especially for those who live in the city, as this landmark symbolizes a place of death and transition and is a sadly famous location for suicides. Besides its symbolic meaning, this specific bridge appears in two of the director's films, so that Almodovarian fans viewing *Los amantes pasajeros* can remember its appearance in *Matador* (1986) and retroactively appreciate the changes the city has undergone.

All of these non-places assume the role they are supposed to play in our global society; but, in this particular film, they also allow some characters to be saved, which reintroduces some degree of humanity and emotions throughout the urban space that is by definition dehumanized and emotionless. Through the process of glocalization, even non-places can become places, just as cosmopolitanism can be rooted.

WHAT CITY DO I LIVE IN? GLOBAL, GLOCAL, OR RETURNING TO THE ROOTS?

Within the Almodovarian universe, rooted attachments contain in their core the seeds for more cosmopolitan commitments. Viewers are able to recognize these local elements and to analyze them as part of their own glocal universe. Throughout a cathartic process, the audience is able to relate personally to the many colorful characters who populate Almodóvar's films. The Almodovarian auto-intertextuality in his own *oeuvre* is also an essential part of this personal identification and catharsis. Through this evolution, the viewer as well as the characters are transformed into loyal citizens of Madrid who (re)create their roots in this cosmopolitan city. Meanwhile, as Almodóvar's last films suggest, the world is getting more global than ever at a very fast pace. These changes have brought a feeling of global uncertainty to these latest films; nevertheless, thanks to the director's chosen portrayal of the city, Madrid is a place where we can still clearly identify many glocal elements of today's Spanish identity.

Following the general trend of globalization and multiculturalism, *Los amantes pasajeros* reflects the process of internationalization that European countries are experiencing nowadays. As a direct consequence, Madrid is shown as a cosmopolitan city and the new visible immigrant population is now included in the Almodovarian universe. A warning at the beginning of the film explains that there is no connection with reality, but it is because none of the passengers are sober or clean, not necessarily because there is no connection between this fiction and the reality of today's Spain. Here, Almodóvar clearly addresses the current immigration situation that the country is facing. Through this *mise en scène*, the strong multiculturalism of today's Spain is underlined. However, the director makes a clear distinction among the various immigrant populations who live in Spain, denouncing the social inequalities between first-class and second-class newcomers. Translated in terms of traveling, this social and economical reality is materialized in the sedation of the entire economic class including the flight attendants by the first-class crew in order to avoid a general panic as the plane has a technical problem that prevents it from flying to Mexico City, consequently putting everyone's life in danger.

From the beginning of the film, the nationalities of the alert protagonists are clearly stated and dialogues are filled with stereotypes. This voyage can be seen as a metaphoric contemporary interpretation of the first encounter between the Old World and the New World, Spain and Latin America. In a surreal dialogue, actor Ricardo Galán (Guillermo Toledo) asks another passenger: "you're from South America?" and he replies "No, I'm from Mexico," to which Ricardo comments "that is even worse!" Almodóvar exploits the cliché of Mexico as a violent country full of drugs cartels and murderers. Bruna (Lola Dueñas), a Spaniard, is a psychic who has been hired to find the bodies of several Spaniards murdered in Guadalajara, México. They were involved in the drug cartels that will help her find their corpses; Norma Boss (Cecilia Roth) is a Latin American immigrant who arrived in Spain in the 1970s during the time of the *Destape*.[4] With no connections or money, she became a famous dominatrix and "Madam." As another example of the role of visible immigration, economic class passenger Nasser (Nasser Saleh) has a key role in the life of first-class passenger Bruna since, while in his sleep, he helped her lose her virginity. His first name and physical appearance suggest that he is from North Africa but this is never mentioned. He represents masculinity, virility, and sexiness for Bruna. If we take this idea to the next level, since she can foresee the future, does this mean that the future of Spain is tied to immigration in terms of fertility rates? Also, it is a sign of cultural mixing and interracial alliances. Is the other/the foreigner/the immigrant the salvation of the aging Old World?

Through the lens of his camera and in a palimpsestic manner, Almodóvar narrates the deep transformation that Spain has undergone since the 1970s, and most of his characters have mirrored society and its evolution. Pepi, Luci, and Bom could have never lived in another place but the 1970s Madrid of *la movida*, and the same can be said about the characters of *Laberinto de pasiones* who lived in the Madrid of the 1980s. At the turn of a new century, the Almodovarian Madrid has transformed itself as new waves of immigrants have fed the glocality, creating a multicultural reconfiguration of the city and of Spain. We wonder if Almodóvar's next productions will focus on visible immigration in Spain, or if he will go a step further and will relocate his plots and characters outside of the motherland.

NOTES

1. All translations are ours unless otherwise specified.
2. By "suitable fauna," we mean characters who are considered as eccentrics, literally outside of the center, and figuratively non-mainstream, outside of the common moral and social norms of their time.
3. *La movida madrileña* (Madrilenian Scene) was a countercultural movement that appeared in 1975 during the transition period after the fall of Franco's dictatorship.
4. Literally meaning "undressed," it was a movement of sexual liberation that emerged in Spain after Franco's death in 1975. In films it was characterized by a display of erotic and sexual images.

WORKS CITED

All about My Mother (*Todo sobre mi madre*). Dir. Pedro Almodóvar. 1999. Sony Pictures, 2000. DVD.
Augé Marc. *Non-Lieux. Introduction à une anthropologie de la surmodernité*. Paris: Seuil, 1992.
Bessy, Marianne, and Carole Salmon. "Tour d'horizon des représentations de la migration dans le cinéma français depuis 2006: histoire(s), lieux, ancrages." 2013. TS. Unpublished essay.
Broken Embraces (*Los abrazos rotos*). Dir. Pedro Almodóvar. 2009. Sony Pictures, 2010. DVD.
D'Lugo, Marvin. "Almodóvar's City of Desire." *Quarterly Review of Film and Video* 13(4) (1991): 47–65.
"Spain" *Focus Migration*. August 2008. Accessed January 30, 2014. http://focus-migration.hwwi.de/Spain-Update-08-200.5420.0.html?&L=1.
Foster, David William. *Mexico City in Contemporary Mexican Cinema*. Austin: University of Texas Press, 2002.
Foucault Michel. "Des Espaces autres" in *Dits et écrits*, vol. 4, Paris: Gallimard, 1994, 752–62.
Giulianotti, Richard, and Roland Robertson. "The Globalization of Football: A Study in the Glocalization of the 'Serious Life'." *British Journal of Sociology* 55(4) (2004): 545–68.
High Heels (*Tacones lejanos*). Dir. Pedro Almodóvar. El Deseo S.A., 1991. Film.
I Am So Excited (*Los amantes pasajeros*). Dir. Pedro Almodóvar. Sony Pictures, 2013. Film.
Kika. Dir. Pedro Almodóvar. 1993. Vidmark Entertainment, 1994. Videocassette.
Kymlicka, Will, and Kathryn Walker. Introduction. *Rooted Cosmopolitanism: Canada and the World*. Ed. Kymlicka, Will and Kathryn Walker. Vancouver: University of British Columbia Press, 2012, 1–27.
Labyrinth of Passion (*Laberinto de pasiones*). Dir. Pedro Almodóvar. Alphaville, 1982. Film.
Law of Desire (*La ley del deseo*). Dir. Pedro Almodóvar. 1987. Sony Pictures, 2009. DVD.
Lefebvre, Henri. *The Production of Space*. Oxford: Basil Blackwell, 1991.
Live Flesh (*Carne trémula*) Dir. Pedro Almodóvar. 1997. Samuel Goldwyn Films, 1998. Film.

Matador. Dir. Pedro Almodóvar. Sony Pictures, 1986. Film.

Pepi, Luci, Bom and Other Girls of the Heap/ Pepi, Luci, Bom and Other Girls Like Mom (*Pepi, Luci, Bom y otras chicas del montón*). Dir. Pedro Almodóvar. 1980. Cinevista, 1992. Videocassette.

Political Film (Film político). Dir. Pedro Almodóvar. 1974. Short Film.

Robertson, Roland. *Globalization*. London: Sage, 1992.

Rouse, Margaret. "Glocalization?" *WhatIs.com*. May 2013. Accessed September 20, 2013. http://whatis.techtarget.com/search/query?q= glocalization.

Smith, Paul Julian. *Desire Unlimited: The Cinema of Pedro Almodóvar*. 2nd ed. London: Verso, 2000.

Soja, Edward. *The Thirdspace: Journeys to Los Angeles and Other Real and Imagined Spaces*. Cambridge, MA: Blackwell, 1996.

The Flower of My Secret (La flor de mi secreto). Dir. Pedro Almodóvar. 1995. Sony Pictures, 2008. DVD.

Volver. Dir. Pedro Almodóvar. 2006. Sony Pictures, 2007. DVD.

What Have I Done to Deserve This? (¿Qué he hecho yo para merecer esto?). Dir. Pedro Almodóvar. 1984. Genius Products, 2002. DVD.

Women on the Verge of a Nervous Breakdown (Mujeres al borde de un ataque de nervios). Dir. Pedro Almodóvar. 1988. Sony Pictures, 2009. DVD.

Chapter Thirteen

Geography of Capital: Torremolinos, Modernity, and the Art of Consumption in Spanish Film

William J. Nichols

In the summer of 2006, headlines in newspapers throughout Spain revealed the culmination of an investigation begun in November 2005 into instances of "corrupción urbanística" along the Costa del Sol, but primarily in Marbella. Known as *Operación Malaya*, the investigation conducted by the Ministry of the Interior has led to charges of bribery, misuse of public funds, violation of public office, price fixing, trafficking of influences, tax fraud, money laundering, and more against municipal officials in Marbella (including the mayor, tax assessor, and former police chief), private lawyers who worked as "go-betweens," and directors of some of the largest construction companies in Andalucía. Payments were made to political officials in exchange for facilitating permits, granting licenses, and awarding bids for construction projects for various hotel, aquatic, and recreational sites. In what *El País* called in an editorial (June 28, 2006) the "perfecta simbiosis entre política y construcción" [the perfect symbiosis between politics and construction], this scandal and dozens of others throughout the peninsula implicate the spectrum of political parties to expose an endemic corruption within the fiscal, juridical, and political institutions that guide modernization and urbanization projects in Spain. Ultimately, what Operación Malaya reveals is the endgame of Spain's contemporary narrative of modernity which began with the "desarrollismo" [developmentism] of the 1960s, when a small, picturesque fishing village named Torremolinos was transformed into the epicenter of Spain's tourism industry and an emblem for urban development.[1]

In *The Urban Experience*, David Harvey describes urban spaces as texts whose configuration, framed by the demands of and desires for capital, articulates systems of power, reinforces the established order, and reproduces social hierarchies. Fetishized urban spaces, when read and interpreted "correctly," impose a narrative that upholds the dominance of capital accumulation through urban development projects. Harvey refers to the imposition and inculcation of this narrative as "urbanization of consciousness" (249) in which the symbolic order of the city infiltrates both individual and collective awareness. Often referred to as the Las Vegas of Spain, Torremolinos best exemplifies a fetishized urban space where leisure masks the machinations of capital with a ludic narrative and accentuates the effects of capital on cultural identity during the years of Spain's "desarrollismo" in the 1960s.[2] A remote fishing village in the 1950s, Torremolinos became the epicenter of the Spanish tourism industry in the 1960s and 1970s with the famous slogan "¡España es diferente!" [Spain is different!] that marketed Spain and Spanish culture as an exotic "other" to northern European vacationers.[3] Torremolinos seemingly learned from Las Vegas, to echo Robin Venturi's now classic examination of the titular city, through the interpenetration of local and global that transformed the virgin beaches of the Costa del Sol into an archetypical city designed to attract the consumptive gaze of the tourist throught a superimposition of "elements of a supranational scale on the local fabric" (Venturi 18). The commodification of cultural identity (through the images of flamenco dancers, bullfighters, guitars, and other "typically" Spanish markers) to attract international capital converted Torremolinos into a "non-place" as defined by Marc Augé. Characterized by contractual exchange and individuals' transitory presence in a ludic space, Augé's conception—exemplified by highways and train rails designed for the circulation of people and goods, airports and hotels, large shopping malls, and, of course, amusement parks— is characteristic of what he calls "supermodernity," in which history is supplanted by spectacle that transforms the subject's gaze by destabilizing it and assimilating it into conformity. A commodified "non-place," Torremolinos is emblematic of the early years of Spain's tourism industry. Torremolinos, along with other cities along the Costa del Sol like Benalmádena, Marbella, and Puerto Banús, continues to attract hundreds of thousands of tourists a year from northern Europe, and has become a model for unbridled construction and consumption in Spain.[4]

This chapter seeks to examine the critique of the "narrative of development" in Spain by looking at cinematic representations of Torremolinos. By juxtaposing images from films from the era of "desarrollismo" in the late Franco years to recent depictions of development along the Costa del Sol, I explore a perceived arc of modernization in Spain. In many films, Torremolinos serves as a destination to which the protagonists hope to arrive and acts, therefore, to reify the tenets of consumer culture and free market capitalism that may be seen as metaphorical for Spain's road to modernity. I argue that a logical trajectory in the critique of Spanish modernity extends from such early films as *El turismo es un gran invento* (1968),[5] *Los días de viejo color* (1968), *Verano 70* (1969), *El hombre abominable de la Costa del Sol* (1970), *Una vez al año ser hippy no hace daño* (1969), *Los días de Cabirio* (1971), *Manolo la nuit* (1973), *El puente* (1977), and the documentary short *Crónica, Torremolinos Invierno* (1965) to more recent titles like *Hola, ¿estás sola?* (1995), *Caja 507* (2002), *Torremolinos 73* (2003), *Carreteras secundarias* (1997),[6] TVE's documentary titled *Concrete Coasts* (2005), and even the very

low-budget zombie b-movie *Karate a muerte en Torremolinos* (2003), and the very big-budget blockbuster sequel *Torrente 2: Misión en Marbella* (2001). Here I will focus on two films: Pedro Lazaga's 1968 film *El turismo es un gran invento* and Pablo Berger's *Torremolinos 73* from 2003. These two films can be contemplated as bookends in which the former that offers a seemingly prophetic critique of the redefinition of space and identity during the age of "desarrollismo" and the latter engages the viewer's nostalgic gaze with irony to frame the early years of Spanish tourism within the country's current economic reality.

El turismo es un gran invento opens with a close-up of the British, French, German, and Spanish flags and pulls back to a panoramic shot of some undetermined tourist locale where a line of cars arrive to "Puerta de España" [Port of Spain] and "Aduana" [Customs].[7] A montage of images follow that define this destination as a ludic space framed by capital and leisure—beaches with throngs of sunbathers and swimmers, high-rise hotels along the coastline, speedboats with waterskiers, people playing tennis, cranes looming over hotels, and signs directing tourists to money exchanges and restaurants. As the images flow over the viewer in a series of quick cuts, a pop song offers this "place" ironically as somewhere people go to lose themselves, "Me gusta hacer turismo/es algo estimulante/es una emocionante manera de viajar / Olvide sus problemas / no piense en los negocios / y déjele a su socio / el deber y el haber/ Relájese en la arena / consígase un flirteo / y sienta el cosquilleo / del sol sobre su piel. / Y luego por la noche / con un whisky delante / descanse en el sedante sillón de un buen hotel" [I like to do tourism / it is something very stimulating/ it is an exciting way to travel. / Forget your problems / don't think about work / and let your colleagues / take care of business. / Relax in the sand / Flirt a little bit / Feel the caress / of the sun on your skin / and later at night / with a whiskey in hand / lounge in the comfortable armchair of a high-class hotel]. As the song concludes and cedes to a fast-talking voiceover, the viewer is left with an image of the skeleton of a hotel under construction with a large crane looming over the coastline, "Turismo, turismo, turismo" [Tourism, Tourism, Tourism], booms the narrator, "Una palabra mágica que está en boca de todo el mundo. Y que ayer, aunque estaba en el diccionario, nadie sabía lo que significaba" [A magic word that is on everyone's lips. And that yesterday, althought it was in the dictionary, nobody knew what it meant]. The rhythm of the narrator's voice coupled with the rapid succession of images evokes the sense of vibrancy and vitality that tourism is perceived to inject into Spanish society. He urges, "¡Viajar, viajar, viajar! En coche, en avión, en barco, como sea, a pie si es necesario. Conocer cosas nuevas, comer paella" [Travel, travel, travel! ¡By car, by plane, by ship, however, by foot if necessary. Get to know new things and eat paella!]. The Costa del Sol, a geographic location for tourists and a metaphorical destination for Spanish modernity, offers leisure and culture as equally valued commodities subsumed by and consumed within the logic of global capitalism. This opening scene concludes with a montage of quick cut still shots of signs for money exchanges, parking lots, and restaurants that finish with close-ups of hotels that quickly pan out and cut from one to another producing a sense of velocity and vertigo. A close-up on car license plates from other European countries through another series of quick edits celebrates a new Spain whose porous borders invite foreign consumption, in sharp contrast with the autarquic policies of the first half of the dictatorship. Torremolinos, then, exemplifies Spain's incursion into mass media global capitalism as what Tatjana Pavlovic has called a "mobile nation" (1) in which the modern values of mobility, technology, and capital have supplanted the previous patriarchal, conservative, traditional values now considered backward.[8] In contrast to the immobilization of the autarquic principles that framed the political, economic, and social policies of the first half of the Franco regime, Pavlovic argues that the technocratic economic apertura of the 1960s "was marked by new social and sexual mores and consumer habits of a society of leisure" (15). The so-called Spanish Miracle that refers to the economic resurgence of Spain in the latter half of the Franco dictatorship likewise brought a sense of social mobility and agency through consumption, values that acquired a metaphorical manifestation in the automobile, specifically the SEAT 600.

The ludic, Dionysian disorientation of the opening scene shifts to a quiet, empty field in Aragón where a group of men survey the area and the mayor (Paco Martínez Soria) argues that the pueblo Valdemorillo needs to embrace the model set by the Costa del Sol to revitalize the life of the town. The mayor exemplifies Harvey's urbanization of consciousness as he fully assimilates the ideology behind the narrative of development, "Estamos olvidados. Y lo que es peor, atrasados. Lo que hay que hacer es cambiarlo todo, ponerse al día, y hacer aquí la Costa de Valdemorillo" [We are forgotten. And even worse, we are behind the times. What we need to do is to change everything, get with the times, and create here a Costa de Valdemorillo]. As they walk the town, he points out the need for modernization and the town assessor (José Luis López Vázquez) takes notes. Local customs must be redefined within the logic of global flows of capital and the demands of international tourism, he asserts. The stream where women wash clothes should be converted to a coastline, the decaying seventeenth century fonda replaced with a parador, a "supermercado" constructed where townspeople can sell their "melocotones" [peaches] and "higos" [figs], and finally, Spanish customs perceived to be inconsistent with a modern identity must be eliminated, "Hay que acabar con el dominó, con el tute, y con el mus. Es un atraso. Hay que echarlo todo abajo" [We need to get rid of dominos, tute and mus. It is backward. We need to get rid of it all].

Nevertheless, one major obstacle stands in the way of their desire to attract tourists and, more importantly, the capital they would bring to the town. When the assessor informs the mayor that to undertake such a large scale urban renewal project would require a lot of money ("un dineral"), the mayor's response announces the kind of public/private collusion that was rampant in the Operación Malaya. At the local bank, after an employee denies the mayor the funds he requests and instead tells him to take out a line of credit, the mayor replies indignantly, "¿Para qué si es para el beneficio del pueblo? ¿O quieres que todo siga igual? Aquí la gente o se muere de aburrimiento o se muere de hambre" [What for if it is for the benefit of the town? Or do you want everything to stay the same? Here either people die from boredom or they die from hunger]. The mayor later solves this problem by establishing a "suscripción popular" [public cuota] in the town that is both "voluntaria y obligatoria" [voluntary and obligatory] to raise the funds needed to travel to the Costa del Sol and begin the cycle of what Harvey calls "flexible accumulation" (256), using capital to earn capital. Once in the Costa del Sol, the mayor and the once reticent assessor become enthralled with the luxury of the high-rise hotels, the leisurely lifestyle on the beach, and the open sexuality of scantily clad Scandinavian women, especially a dancing group named "Las BubyGirls," whom they later invite to Valdemorillo.[9] Yet, as their money dwindles, they convince the town to send more funds not with the promise of progress for the town but by tantalizing them with the fulfillment of their individual desires for prestige, power, and sexual prowess. Postcards convey, or better yet market, visions of how their lives might improve.

At the conclusion of "El turismo es un gran invento," Lazaga ironically underscores the fleeting flexibility behind "flexible accumulation" when the town celebrates a letter received from the Ministry of the Interior granting the mayor a hearing within four months. Under a billboard boasting the upcoming inauguration of the Parador de Turismo de Valdemorillo (despite the fact that no plans for construction exist or have even been approved), townspeople dance a traditional Aragonese jota.[10] Not only does the dance contrast with the sexualized spectacle offered by "Las Bubygirls," when they perform in the town, but it leaves the viewer with lingering doubts about the survival of authentic local customs as they are reconstructed and reconfigured within the capitalist framework of global tourism.

While Lazaga's *El turismo es un gran invento* captures the contradictions of Spain's initial incursion into global capitalism, Pablo Berger's *Torremolinos 73* (2003), set in the waning days of the Franco dictatorship, ironically engages the viewer's nostalgic gaze to revisit Spain of the early 1970s. While the characters in both films possess a certain innocence about the economic, urban and media transitions that accompany the political changes in Spanish society during the late 1960s and early 1970s, the contemporary audience of Berger's film is keenly aware of the path that Spanish modernity followed in the decades after Franco's death. In *Torremolinos 73* capital defines the lives of Alfredo López (Javier Cámara) and his wife, Carmen (Candela Peña) well before they ever realize it. One of the remaining four employees, reduced from a team of forty at Montoya Publishers, Alfredo, a dying breed of salesmen, travels door-to-door enticing housewives to purchase the leather-bound collection of the Enciclopedia de la Historia de la Guerra Civil Española with a "free" bust of el Caudillo, el generalísimo Franco.[11] After a series of cutbacks at Montoya Publishers, Alfredo's boss, don Carlos (Juan Diego) informs him that the company would be restructuring in order to introduce a "nuevo producto revolucionario y secreto" [new secret and revolutionary product], and invites him to the 1er Congreso de la Editorial Montoya [The First Conference of Montoya Publishing] to share in the company's future business endeavor because, don Carlos states (seemingly echoing the words of the mayor in *El turismo es un gran invento*), their only options are "renovarse o morir" [change or die]. At the conference, don Carlos projects a film in which Dr. Johansen from the Instituto de Sexología de Copenhagen [Sexology Institute of Copenhagen] proposes a collaboration with Montoya Publishers to produce an Enciclopedia Audiovisual de la Reproducción [Audiovisual Encyclopedia of Reproduction] in which the "reproductive rituals and customs" of Spain would be documented on film as part of an "educational" series to be distributed in Scandinavia.

The film-within-film technique dismantles Dr. Johansen's supposed scientific discourse and apparent educational purpose by allowing the viewer to become aware of his or her own gaze and not only to contemplate the narrative construction that masks the doctor's intentions but also to view the film itself as a material object that may be defined by the purpose of its message, be it academic, scientific, educational, commercial, or artistic. When don Carlos clarifies, after the film has ended, that the employees who wish to participate would receive 50,000 pesetas plus a commission for each of the films they shoot in their homes "mientras copulan" [while they copulate], the viewer senses the Dr. Johansen's interests are less educational or scientific and more commercial (and pornographic as we later learn). Moreover, the use of film-within-film suggests another kind of transition complementary to the change in social mores and political attitudes of the time in which the film is set. The communication of Dr. Johansen through visual images and the move of Montoya Publishing from print to audiovisual technology suggests an incursion into the realm of simulacra, symptomatic of Spain's future postmodernity. It epitomizes the technological transition that accompanies the political transition and leads, argues Richard Maxwell in *The Spectacle of Democracy*, to the dominance of transnational conglomerates, principally North American, in the landscape of privatized mass media, primarily television, in Spain (26–29).

The tension between "art" and "commerce" emerges when Alfredo learns that the Danish supervisor of the collection, Erik Molander, was once an assistant to Ingmar Bergman, and he obsessively devours all things Bergman—his biography, books on his film techniques, and his films, especially "The Seventh Seal"—in order to master the art of cinema. That Bergman becomes Alfredo's cinematic model and creative inspiration adds a new facet to the perceived dichotomy between "art" and "commerce" in which Alfredo seeks to transcend the frivolous, commercially popular national cinema of Spain exemplified by the likes of *No desearás al vecino del quinto* (1970), *Adiós Cigüeña, Adiós* (1971), or *Lo verde empieza en los Pirineos* (1973) (all of which are mentioned specifically in the film). Alfredo's hope is to surpass the "national" and touch on "universal" themes with his serious Bergman-esque existentialist drama in black and white about a widowed millionairess who returns to the hotel in Torremolinos, where she and her late husband spent their honeymoon, and there meets a mysterious man dressed in black who looks remarkably similar to her dead spouse. The choice of Spain's Costa del Sol as the setting for Alfredo's film, ironically titled "Torremolinos 73," further underscores the perceived opposition between "art" and "commerce" while problematizing the distinction between the "national" and "international" in a global free market.

The film-within-film technique of *Torremolinos 73*, first with Dr. Johansen's visual message and especially with Alfredo's film, creates a mise-en-abyme that allows the spectator not only to become aware of the film's construction but also its commodification. That Alfredo's film carries the same title as the film the spectator views confuses, moreover, the distinction between "art" and "commerce" and intertwines the black-and-white existentialist drama Alfredo creates with the commercial sexual comedy that we as spectators watch (and consume). Such confusion problematizes the easy dichotomies between "art" (or "culture") and "commerce" or "national" and "international" (or "universal"). The confusion between "art" and "commerce" or "national" and "international" is blurred in an earlier scene when a tall, blond star-struck Scandinavian man follows Carmen through Galerías Preciados repeating "Carmen, guapa" [Carmen, pretty] and begging for her to autograph an advertisement for her "films" in a Danish skin magazine. Alfredo realizes that the films he and Carmen had made were marketed in northern Europe not for educational purposes but as part of a lucrative porn industry. While the Spanish men in *El turismo es un gran invento* yearn for the open sexuality of Swedish women like "Las Bubygirls," in *Torremolinos 73* Carmen becomes an exoticized Spanish porn goddess to be consumed by the male gaze in Scandinavia. In both examples, instances of authentic local identity, in this case gender, are exported as mediated cultural commodities that are redefined within the transational exchanges of a global market.

After they arrive to Torremolinos to begin shooting the film, a taxi drives Alfredo and Carmen through a barren landscape of looming high-rise hotels, abandoned beaches, and closed restaurants characteristic of February on the Costa del Sol while the Formula V, a famous pop group of the late 1960s, sings "Eva María se fue buscando el sol en la playa / con su maleta de piel y su bikini de rayas" [Eva María left looking for sun at the beach / with her leather bag and her striped bikini]. The contrast between summer leisure and cold reality parallels the discordant perceptions of the purpose of cinema expressed by the taxi driver and Alfredo. After Alfredo proudly and thoughtfully explains the plot of his film and its artistic contribution to cinema, the taxi driver, in an excited Andalusian accent, replies, "Pues, a mí las que me gustan son las Bud Spencer and Terrence Hill donde terminan pim pam pam . . . ¡Ay, qué bueno!" [I love the movies with Bud Spencer and Terrence Hill where they end bam bam bam. So good!]. The taxi driver is referring to a series of approximately eighteen films, many of which were shot in southern Spain between Málaga and Almería, known as Spaghetti Westerns, starring Terrence Hill and Bud Spencer. Some of the more familiar titles of these two actors include *They Call Me Trinity* (1970) and *Trinity Is Still My Name* (1971). Though often disparaged, as Alfredo does in this scene when he looks away ignoring the taxi driver, the low funds and cross-cultural collaborations of the Spaghetti Westerns actually contributed to a demythification and reinvention of the accepted conventions of the Western genre. The low-budget quality, minimalist aesthetic, and gratuitous violence of the Spaghetti Westerns described by the taxi driver contrasts greatly with the highly stylized, avant-garde vision Alfredo hopes to achieve with his art-house film. As the taxi driver flails his hands about, wildly imitating a gunslinger handling a pistol, Formula V sings, "¿Qué voy a hacer? ¿Qué voy a hacer?" [What am I going to do?], while Alfredo smiles patronizingly at the taxi driver and disinterestedly contemplates the coastal city through the lens of his Super 8 camera. The scene not only differentiates the popular tastes of the mainstream movie-going public from Alfredo's artistic vision, but likewise emphasizes the latter's unawareness of the influence the perception of market demands will exert on his film later.[12] The carnavalesque atmosphere and the orgiastic ecstasy of the tourism industry in Lazaga's film contrasts strongly with the winter wasteland of Torremolinos in *Torremolinos 73.* Yet, both views of Torremolinos accentuate the accumulation of spectacles that endow the city with an inauthentic, mediated identity characterized by, as Dean

McCannell states in "Cultural Tourism," "a mélange of markers of Spanish fishing village traditions,

working-class fantasies of jet set luxury and Spanish versions of British fish and chips cuisine. The Spanish fishermen, or their children, are now integrated into the global economy as service workers for transnational tourism" (2).

As they begin to film in February, the desolate beach landscape of Torremolinos and Tivoli World, empty of tourists, accentuates the town's status as a ludic non-place, in Augé's terms, defined by leisure and capital while serving as a metaphor for the protagonist's existential vacuity in Alfredo's film. The viewer suffers the same destabilizing effects as Alfredo's film by confronting the internal contradictions of the film-within-a-film that is at once frivolous and existential. The protagonist enjoys typical tourist activities with the figure of Death (a personification that evokes Bergman's *The Seventh Seal*) in scenes at the hotel pool, eating paella on the beach, walking along the coast at sunset, dancing in an empty night club and drifting in the Mediterranean on a pedal-boat. The scenes of tourism culminate in an absurd Fellini-esque dream sequence at Tivoli World, an amusement park in Torremolinos, where Carmen's character confronts her own death in a coffin dragged by dwarves dressed as flamenco dancers and bullfighters. The surreal spectacle of this scene in Alfredo's film exposes the inherent ritualized spectacle that defines the abandonded hotels and beaches of the Costa del Sol as what Dean MacCannell would call an "empty meeting ground" that is itself as an empty signifier, literally and figuratively, endowed with meaning by the gaze of the tourist. While the visual composition of Alfredo's film evokes the avant-garde techniques and surrealist imagery of Fellini, Bergman, and Buñuel, the costumed dwarves underscore the exoticized identity of Spanish cultural production and the loss of local authenticity within a global market.

Later, the dichotomy between Alfredo's artistic vision and the taxi driver's popular taste reasserts itself when the aspiring auteur must undertake an existentialist examination of his own conscience after don Carlos suggests some "pequeños cambios al guión" [small script changes]. A sex scene between Carmen and the handsome Danish leading man, Magnus, would, asserts don Carlos, make the film more marketable in Scandinavia and allow them to recoup the money invested in Alfredo's project. Faced with the decision either to adhere to his artistic integrity or cede to market demands, Alfredo ironically wanders the empty night-time Calle San Miguel, the main street in the Torremolinos shopping district, where he seems unaware of the presence of capital that permeates his surroundings. After he ends his walk on the beach, the Danish crew and actors appear and go skinny-dipping, dragging Alfredo into the water with them, a metaphoric display of the uncontrollable forces of capital that have co-opted his artistic vision.

After finishing the shoot of "Torremolinos 73," with the sex scene included, Alfredo abandons his frustrated cinematic dream for a seemingly more satisfying, or at least more autonomous, career of filming weddings and home videos. While Alfredo had envisioned that his "Torremolinos 73" would have transformed the landscape of Spanish cinema, a postscript at the end of Berger's film informs the viewer that the title of the film within a film had been changed to "Las aventuras y desaventuras de una viuda muy cachonda" [The adventures and misadventures of a very horny widow] for its subsequent, and very successful, international release in Scandinavia. Released in 1977 with its new title, the film received a "clasificación S" in Spain that, though applied to some films for violent content, was a classification used by and large to distinguish films that might be offensive because of their explicit, if softcore, sexual representation. Far more explicit than the Spanish bikini sex comedies of the late 1960s and early 1970s, the "S" movies, though, despite the stigma such a rating attached to the film, enjoyed the same mainstream distribution as any other feature film. Alfredo's film, after the title change and "S" rating, however, saw its domestic audience greatly reduced, limiting it, informs the postcript, to only 1,373 people who viewed the film in Spain. Subsumed into the logic of consumer capitalism, the philosophical weight of Alfredo's film, as well as any supposed local cultural authenticity, disintegrates and disappears under the global market demands for exotic Spanish porn.

Contemporary Spain, Vázquez Montalbán declares, is the land of "el Gran Consumidor" [Big Consumer], where an inundation of simulacra disintegrates meaning, mass media technology is omnipresent, consumption has become the primordial value that defines everyday life, and the logic of capital has established hegemony over cultural production. The ludic space of Torremolinos serves to reify the consumerist tendencies of Spanish society as the country opened itself politically and economically in the 1970s, embracing Constitutional values and free-market ideology as both inseparable and complementary. In both *El turismo es un gran invento* and *Torremolinos 73*, Torremolinos is presented as the figurative destination of Spanish modernity, a place where local customs are subsumed into the cultural logic of global capitalism and are rendered a mediated spectacle for the consumption of the tourist's gaze. Yet, if this is true, then one must wonder if Spain's current economic crisis is the end of the road or just a stopping point on the way to another non-place.

NOTES

1. In "Unconstrained Growth: The Development of a Spanish Resort," John Pollard and Rafael Domínguez Rodríguez assert that development in Málaga has been characterized by a

laissez-faire approach since the early days of urbanization in the 1960s, an approach they describe as a "Third World mentality toward attracting capital no matter what the cost to "architectural style or violation of the landscape" (38).

2. In "The Linguistic Implications of Mass Tourism in the Gaeltacht Areas," Gearóid Denvir refers to Torremolinos as "plasticville" (27), whose populist, mass tourism contrasts with the supposed desire for cultural authenticity seen in elitist forms of tourism such as eco-travel. Similarly, Barke and France refer to the Costa del Sol as a "monolithic concentrarion of development (most say over-development), consisting of a continuous sprawl of concrete created by unconstrained land and property speculation" (265). Ironically, this point is made much earlier in a 1972 Monty Python sketch in which a man named Mr. Smokestoomuch (Eric Idle) enters a travel agency in search of an "adventure holiday" because he is tired of the tourist packages that take one to inauthentic and falsified places like Torremolinos.

3. Sasha Pack, in *Tourism and Dictatorship*, notes that this tourism propaganda formed part of a vast industry he calls "consumer diplomacy" and exemplifies a technocratic turn in Spanish politics where bureaucratic leaders demonstrated a wide range of backgrounds including languages, culture, social sciences, and economics (148–49).

4. *Costa Ibérica*, a book developed by students and professors at the Escuela Superior de Arquitectura (ESARQ) in Barcelona and based on studies performed during a three-week workshop in 1998, combines cartography, urban planning, population analysis, and graphic design to analyze the effects of the "sueño californiano" [California dream]. Urban development has sought and continues to seek, the authors argue, to combine gastronomy, leisure, nature, and construction, while disregarding their ecological impact, to increase population density while maximizing area in order to skyrocket land value and attract capital, making the Iberian coast the "equivalente europeo de California" [the European equivalent of California] (172–73).

5. Sally Faulkner has referred to the comedies of the 1960s in Spain as a "cinema of contradiction" in which the results of the politics of openness are change and conflict. In the "comedias de desarrollismo" [developmentalist comedies], social fears are manifested in which Spanish masculinity is threatened by the open, aggressive sexuality of foreign women (specifically Swedish women), Catholic values are subverted by a progressively more materialist society and a rapidly changing Church, and political stability is upended by the accelerated rhythm of technological transformations that introduce and extol the value of consumer capitalism within a mass media society.

6. In *Carreteras secundarias*, Torremolinos is a point of departure, not a destination, for the protagonists.

7. At the end of the opening credits, the viewer reads that the montage is composed of images from coastal cities throughout Spain, "Los exteriores de esta película se han rodado en Madrid—Marbella—Torremolinos—Torrelaguna—Valdemoro—Talamanca—Torremocha—Aigua Blava—Benidorm—Salou—La Junquera—Mazarrón—Tossa—Bagur—Tarragona—Barcelona—Alicante." That these locations are interchangeable emphasizes their status as non-places, spaces defined by capital and leisure where one goes to lose oneself.

8. An especially poignant example of Spain's desire for mobility and modernity may be found in Juan Antonio Bardem's 1976 film *El Puente* when Juan (Alfredo Landa) travels across half the country to reach Torremolinos. In one scene, he encounters two American women who leave him behind when his sputtering motorcycle is unable to keep up with their fast convertible.

9. While the political implications of the female body during the Franco years have been widely explored, especially within the context of the regime's Nationalist-Catholic ideology, both films analyzed in this chapter present the progressive commodification of gender as Spain assimilates the logic of market-driven capitalism and mass media technology. For more information on the "transitions" of the female body during the Franco regime, consult Aurora Morcillo's *Seduction of Modern Spain: The Female Body and the Francoist Body Politic*.

10. In *Destination Dictatorship*, Justin Crumbaugh explains the origins of the *Parador Nacional* hotels throughout Spain as a way to commodify Spain's patrimonial heritage and to render it a mediated spectacle through cultural tourism (54).

11. The opening scene foreshadows the interpenetration of space, capital, and urban development as the viewer follows Alfredo passing a billboard for housing in a new, modern development named "Mi paraíso" [My paradise].

12. The scene concludes with the taxi's arrival to the Hotel Cervantes, the same hotel that was the primary location in the Costa del Sol in Pedro Lazaga's *El turismo es un gran invento*.

WORKS CITED

Augé, Marc. *Non-Places: Introduction to an Anthropology of Supermodernity*. John Howe, Trans. London: Verso, 1995.

Barke, Michael, and France, Lesley A. "The Costa del Sol." *Tourism in Spain: Critical Issues*. Eds. Michael Barke, John Towner, and Michael T. Newton. Oxford, UK: CAB International, 1996, 265–308.

Crumbaugh, Justin. *Destination Dictatorship: The Spectacle of Spain's Tourist Boom and the Reinvention of Difference*. Albany: State University of New York Press, 2009.

Denvir, Gearóid. "The Linguistic Implications of Mass Tourism in the Gaeltacht Areas" *New Hibernia Review* 6(3) (Autumn 2002): 23–43.

Faulkner, Sally. *A Cinema of Contradiction: Spanish Film in the 1960s*. Edinburgh: Edinburgh University Press, 2006.

Harvey, David. The Urban Experience. Baltimore: Johns Hopkins University Press, 1989.

Maas, Winy, ed. *Costa Ibérica: Hacia una ciudad del ocio*. Barcelona: Actar Editorial, 2000.

MacCannell, Dean. "Cultural Tourism." Web. July 20, 2013.

———. *Empty Meeting Grounds: The Tourist Papers*. London, UK and New York: Routledge, 1992.

"Marbella, segundo acto." *El País* (June 28, 2006). Web. October 20, 2006.

Maxwell. Richard. *The Spectacle of Democracy: Spanish Television, Nationalism, and the Political Transition*. Minneapolis: Minnesota University Press, 1995.

Morcillo, Aurora G. *Seduction of Modern Spain: The Female Body and the Francoist Body Politic*. Lewisburg, PA: Bucknell University Press, 2010.

Pack, Sasha. *Tourism and Dictatorship: Europe's Peaceful Invasion of Franco's Spain*. New York: Palgrave Macmillan, 2006.

Pavlovic, Tatjana. *The Mobile Nation: España Cambia de Piel (1954–1964)*. London: Intellect, 2011.

Pollard, John, and Domínguez Rodríguez, Rafael. "Unconstrained Growth: The Development of a Spanish Resort." *Geography* 80(1) (1995): 33–44.

Torremolinos 73. Dir. Pablo Berger. Perfs. Javier Cámara, Candela Peña. Estudios Picasso, Mama Films, Nimbus Film Productions, Telespan 2000, 2003. Film.

El turismo es un gran invento. Dir. Pedro Lazaga. Paco Martínez Soria, José Luis López Vázquez. Pedro Masó Producciones Cinematográficas, 1968. Film.

Vázquez Montalbán, Manuel. *Panfleto desde el planeta de los simios*. Barcelona: Grijalbo, 1995.

Venturi, Robin, Brown, Denise Scott, and Izenour, Steven. *Learning from Las Vegas: The Forgotten Symbolism of Architectural Form*. 13th ed. Cambridge, MA: MIT Press, 1994.

Chapter Fourteen

Immigration and Spanish Subjectivity in *No habrá paz para los malvados*

Diana Norton

The 2011 film *No habrá paz para los malvados* (dir. Enrique Urbizu)[1] reimagines the circumstances leading up to and surrounding the kind of terrorist attack that occurred on March 11, 2004, when ten bombs exploded on Madrid's commuter trains, killing 191 and injuring 1,500 more.[2] The film emphasizes the problems of communication that plague Spanish state security agencies and thus allow terrorist activity to go undetected, while at the same time criticizing the ineffectiveness of the state in the face of global capitalist forces. The film does not, however, fully explore the racial and cultural confrontations underpinning such violence or problematize possible ideological motives for the attack. On the contrary, it falls into a neo-imperialist trap of stereotype and racism to locate violence on the margins of society, thus reimagining Spanish identity in the age of globalization in opposition to (foreign) terrorist and criminal threats. Indeed, I argue that *No habrá paz* reconstructs the geographic space of Spain as a borderland—that is, a contested territory characterized by violent racial conflict—even as it rejects the ethnic and racial complexity that characterizes the world's borderlands as part of Spanish identity. Despite the contemporary image of multiculturalism prevalent in Spain and Europe, the resistance to hybridity in *No habrá paz* illustrates a continued attachment to the idea of a hegemonic national identity as defined by racial attributes.

Though some scholars view interactions within borderlands as mutually beneficial (yet benign) cooperation, Latin American theorists such as Néstor García Canclini and Gloria Anzaldúa have long held the position that a borderland is an inherently creative geographic space where members of different cultures meet, mingle, and forge a hybrid culture. According to

García Canclini, this increased contact between peoples of different nationalities means that "today all cultures are border cultures" ("Hybrid Cultures"
261). *No habrá paz* represents Spain as a border culture through its setting of
multicultural Madrid. The opening scene of the film shows the protagonist,
Santos Trinidad, in a bar being attended by a Latin American waiter while a
news item regarding security preparations for a fictional G20 summit in
Madrid blares in the background. Urbizu uses this setting in a very superficial way, though, as all Latin American and African characters are one-
dimensional stereotypes, adding "local color" to Madrid's neighborhoods but
not contributing positively to the overall health of the nation. *No habrá paz*
rejects the possibility of a coexistence of immigrants and Spaniards, and it
insinuates that the hybridity that results from such multiculturalism is contradictory to an ideal "Spanish national identity." The term hybridity, however,
does not fully encapsulate the violence implicated in frontier cultural encounters. In fact, when discussing her own experience as the child of a borderland,
Gloria Anzaldúa labels the US-Mexico border an open wound "where the
Third World grates against the first and bleeds" (25). A similar violence
permeates *No habrá paz*, and one might surmise that the film allows for a
hybrid understanding of Spanish-ness, given that the Spain of the film is a
space of violent identity formation. Nevertheless, the concluding sequence
presents Spanish identity in the twenty-first century as staunchly European.

Though Anzaldúa's experience as a *chicana* is highly specific to the US-
Mexico border, her claims apply more broadly, even in Europe, as Anna
Triandafyllidou has explained: "It is the interaction between [immigrants and
Europeans] that might generate prejudice and conflict" (x). In fact, the concept of a borderless world relies upon racial difference as an invisible wall
separating Europeans from non-Europeans. As Alana Lentin remarks in her
article regarding the absence of racial discourse in Europe, race reinforces
the necessity of borders to demarcate geographical and national inclusion
and, most importantly, it "has established what it means to be both European
and non-European" (492). Thus, though race often goes unmentioned in
discussions of national identity, racism and the creation of racialized "others"
nonetheless form the backbone of such discourse. According to Achille
Mbembe, the racialization of the other forms the basis of nationalisms: "The
perception of the existence of the Other as an attempt on my life, as a mortal
threat or absolute danger whose biophysical elimination would strengthen
my potential to life and security . . . is one of the many imaginaries of
sovereignty characteristic of both early and late modernity itself" (18). We
perceive racial difference as threatening, and this justifies a lack of empathy
when foreigners die to serve the interests of the state, or even of a post-
nationalist conglomeration, such as the European Union.

As the southernmost member of the European Union, Spain is the contemporary   site   in   which   to   contest   Europe's   racial   identity.   A

(re)conceptualization of Spain as solely European denies the effects of being the gateway into Europe from Africa and the Americas. In her discussion of migration and the construction of national identity in Spain, Désirée Kleiner-Liebau notes that by the mid-1980s, migrants began to choose Spain due to "its geographical situation at the outer border of the European Union, a border which separates two regions with enormous differences in demographic and economic development" (80). The geographic space of Spain does not simply mark the edge of the First World, but it also forms a vast borderland across which potentially dangerous people, images, and ideas move. According to Parvati Nair, this space is one of hybridity, which "supposes a temporal layering since the term . . . implicitly connects Spain's former colonial relation to Morocco [and Latin America] with its multicultural present resulting from immigration, while also pointing to the future through its conception of identity as process" (75). A hybrid understanding of Spanish national identity would take into account not just its present multiculturalism, but also the long history of cultural encounters within the space of the Iberian Peninsula.

Despite its multicultural image, resistance to hybridity in Spain illustrates a continued attachment to the idea of a hegemonic national identity—problematic in a world of transnational migration, where immigrants retain their ties to their country of origin, even as they live and work elsewhere (Smith 4). Nair elaborates that immigration into Spain has created for migrants "an 'in-between' or interstitial position that is not that of Latin America, Morocco or Spain but the product of global displacements" (85). Thus immigrants to Spain are neither Spaniards nor still recognized completely as members of their home country. Rather, the ties that they forge across borders make them hybrid individuals, occupying a space that is not exactly a nation. Hybridity is particularly prevalent in *No habrá paz*,[3] as certain bodies are represented as raced and othered, in spite of their Spanish nationality. Yet the expendability of these 'foreign" bodies indicates the logic of the racial state, as the representation of Spain in the film is reinforced as white.

This othering happens by reducing Latin American and African characters within the film to dark skin and different accents. The plot summary of *No habrá paz* states that Santos Trinidad, a missing person's detective, "finds himself involved in a shooting". His involvement is not that of a casual bystander, however. Rather, he drunkenly shoots three Colombians and then methodically cleans up the evidence of his participation. The use of the passive "se" in the film's plot summary deflects responsibility for the shooting from Trinidad, and in so doing, lessens the import of the loss of these immigrant lives. One of the victims, Ingrid, is a naturalized Spanish citizen who Trinidad immediately identifies as Colombian because of her accent. In this scene, even being a naturalized Spanish citizen does not protect Ingrid from racism, or even violence, thanks to her country of origin. This stereotyping is embedded at all levels of the film, as the script calls for the madam to have a South American accent (as opposed to one from Eastern Europe or anywhere else), a linguistic trait retained in the Spanish language subtitles, though absent in the English ones.

All Latin American characters in the film are distinguished by their accents, which signals to the audience both that these characters are markedly different and that this difference contributes meaning to the story. In addition, the African characters speak to each other in Arabic, a linguistic decision unnecessarily marked in the film's subtitles. If ethnic identity and linguistic identity are indistinguishable, as Anzaldúa states, then discrimination based on linguistic differences (not only a foreign language, but also accented speech) is akin to discrimination based on ethnicity (81). Though Ingrid's death may be excused by Trinidad's need to leave no witnesses, it also demonstrates a necessity to maintain the racial integrity of the nation. In spite of her claims of legitimacy as a Spaniard, her Colombian origin automatically places her under suspicion by linking her with a country whose drug trade has wreaked havoc on Spanish security forces and funded terrorist attacks.[4] In the post-immigration world that Spain occupies, Ingrid remains suspiciously other and therefore needs no complexity added to her character. Her racialized body and accented speech are simply signifiers of foreignness, and her sudden presence and immediate departure in the film require no other explanation.

In addition to race and language, *No habrá paz* distinguishes foreigners by the types of violent acts that they employ and that are employed on them. For instance, the Colombians are heavily implicated in drug trafficking; the African terrorists inflict violence through disguised bombs (a choice that reinforces them as Islamist extremists, even though they never mention their justification for blowing up a mall); and Trinidad wields a pump-action shotgun readily, yet also engages in brutal hand-to-hand combat when directly threatened. Though guns pervade all three camps, these more stereotyped instances of aggression serve as signifiers for the viewer, identifying each criminal as foreign and justifying their demise. The occurrence of violence in *No habrá paz* arises out of the very existence of Spain as the borderland between the First and Third Worlds. Yet, the film's carnage also emphasizes the idea that a strictly demarcated and highly militarized border mechanism will somehow protect the First World from any Third World influence. The racially based aggression represented in *No habrá paz* reinforces the fallacy that specific types of violence are caused by specific types of people. In his sociological study of violence in the post-9/11 era, Michel Wieviorka points to its mercurial nature, stating, "It cannot be stabilized or controlled by its protagonist, who will be unable to establish a level or threshold at which its intensity can be regulated" (162). In spite of the perception that criminals incite violent behavior, violence itself actually generates criminality, thanks to its uncontrollability. By stereotyping bloodshed as being incited by foreign influences, the representations of violent acts in *No habrá paz* insinuate that Western societies can eradicate violence by somehow eliminating those who do not belong.

According to the representations in *No habrá paz*, those who do not belong in Spain are not just foreign nationals, but also any Spanish nationals whose characterizations might suggest hybridity. As a Colombian claiming Spanish nationality, Ingrid is one of three hybrid characters, including Trinidad and El Ceuti, the Muslim Spaniard from Ceuta and leader of an Islamist terrorist cell. Because of their hybridity, Trinidad and El Ceuti are able to effectively permeate all levels of Spanish society. Trinidad's Catholic name combines with the image of an American cowboy (pump-action shotgun, signature phrase of "roknrrol") to create a vigilante anti-hero.[5] Though Trinidad is a decorated Spanish soldier, his easy use of guns and fisticuffs identifies him with the cinematic tradition of the American vigilante, thus alienating him from the Spanish nation he dies trying to protect. As a policeman and former special operations soldier suffering from PTSD, Trinidad inhabits both the official government space and the criminal underbelly of Madrid, and thus, can cross the boundaries separating them. His crossing comes at a price, though, as his mimicry of the American vigilante distances him from a European Spanish ideal and validates his sacrifice.

In a similar manner, El Ceuti surrenders his life in the service of a higher order, but his hybridity is obscured by a Manichaean representation of an evil Islamist terrorist. Thanks to Western stereotypes of Islam under the War on Terror, the only identity available to El Ceuti is that of a religious fanatic. In fact, the sole explanation for his acceptance of a marginalized religious identity is that he "went crazy with religion,"[6] a phrase that highlights his one-dimensionality. In addition, El Ceuti's alleged mistreatment of his wife constructs him as an untrustworthy stereotype of repressive Islamic masculinity. When Trinidad asks El Ceuti's in-laws if he is Arab, the woman quickly defends him as not only Spanish, but also from a well-respected family. Her defense cannot overlook the fact that the photo that Trinidad examines contains an image of the ideal Muslim couple, not the ideal Spanish one.

In spite of his one-dimensionality, El Ceuti at first appears to be multiple people: the husband of a Madrilenian, Paloma García García, and at the same time, a Muslim so devoted to Islamic traditions that he would not associate with women; a nice man from a "good family" and yet, a nefarious criminal mastermind. In fact, this multiplicity of identities is precisely what defines El Ceuti's hybridity. Although Spanish by birth, he is represented as foreign both racially (he has dark skin) and linguistically (he speaks Arabic), and his death implies that the coexistence of these identities is impossible. In spite of his citizenship, his skin color and origin outside of the peninsula (close to Morocco) mark him as a terrorist. If we approach El Ceuti as a hybrid character, he ceases to be both villain and terrorist. Instead, he becomes a heroic rebel, fighting to maintain a complex identity denied to him as a citizen of the Spanish state.

El Ceuti's name reduces his character to a geographic location, even though the hybridity that defines Ceuta (a Spanish city on the African continent and the epitome of a bordered city in a borderless world) connotes a more complex individual than his moniker indicates. With regard to the Spanish border with Africa at Ceuta, Can Mutlu and Christopher Leite note that balancing economic flows and security fears "have resulted in the implementation of exceptional measures at the border" (21). These measures include extensive walls and barbed wire fences, along with surveillance cameras. However, the walls separating Spain from Morocco also allow a sort of selective permeability: favoring passage of Spanish citizens into Morocco, but heavily restricting passage into Ceuta (and thus, Spain and Europe). In fact, the inherent tension surrounding the selective permeability of borders in the era of Islamist terrorism has both expanded border cultures and made them more volatile in the twenty-first century. Though the border at Ceuta never explicitly appears in *No habrá paz*, the film portrays some of the exceptional measures employed there as having spread to more centralized urban areas such as Madrid, ostensibly to protect citizens in the occurrence of violent crime. As represented in *No habrá paz*, the division of Madrid's urban space into high-capital areas of whiteness and consumption and low-capital ghettoes spatially reconstructs the border within the city and reinforces this urban segregation through surveillance.

The internal reconstruction of the border means that Spanish territory is itself fragmented by capital and immigrant flows. In discussing a trend that he titles the new military urbanism, Stephen Graham labels "immigrant districts within the West's cities as 'backward' zones threatening the body politic of the Western city and nation" (16). Yet the isolation of immigrants to the First World into zones that retain Third World characteristics cannot prevent the hybridity that will still arise out of this close contact. Parvati Nair explains: "The tacit encounters of self with other that result from migratory movements across border zones both propel and disperse cultural identity in the act of social survival" (73). For immigrants to survive, their cultural identity must adapt to that of their new country. Yet at the same time, if immigrants are ever to be fully considered as residents (not just visitors) of their new country, then its culture must adapt and adopt pieces of their own, not just segregate them into ghettoes.

As a way of portraying the tensions wrought by immigration, *No habrá paz* spatially reconstructs the border at Ceuta within Madrid through racial and class segregation, specifically by portraying foreigners as occupying only the space of Lavapiés. Originally a Jewish settlement outside of the city walls of medieval Madrid, Lavapiés has since become a neighborhood for working-class Madrilenians. In the last thirty years, the population composition of Lavapiés has shifted with the influx of Latin American and African immigrants (Feinberg 6–7). The presence of these foreigners has changed the signification of this urban space in that not only is it a poor neighborhood, but now its poverty has also been racialized, such that what used to be a class division is now both a class and racial division. This conflation of class and race reconstructs inner-city Madrid as a colony within the heartland: "The projection of colonial tropes and security exemplars into post-colonial metropoles in capitalist heartlands is fuelled by a new 'inner-city Orientalism'" (Graham 16). In *No habrá paz*, this inner-city Orientalism manifests itself through violence toward all racialized others, even those who are actually Spanish citizens. This combination of racial difference and violence also illustrates the need to control immigrants through segregation and surveillance, implying that the immigrants are the cause, rather than the recipients, of said violence.

If foreigners are isolated to Lavapiés, then the consumption practices in the mall reveal the habitat of wealthy Spaniards. According to the representations in *No habrá paz*, the poor neighborhood of Lavapiés is not a shopping destination, but rather a site of foreign and suspicious activity. In contrast, the IslAzul mall is a space of recreation in the form of consumption. The white Spaniards who shop at the mall are innocent potential victims of religious fanaticism, rather than complicit participants in a corrupt system. In *La globalización imaginada*, García Canclini states that the combination of attractive design, security, and cleanliness, along with movie theaters and other entertainment venues, makes malls the preferred cultural centers for wealthy citizens (173). In spite of their commercial aims, malls have been converted into cultural spaces, in addition to spaces that both order and fragment the identities of the individuals who use them. As enclosed spaces, their walls reenact the borders that serve to regulate economic flows: those who occupy the space of the mall are those who have the money to do so. Daniela Vicherat Mattar theorizes that, as modern borders are dissolved through agreements such as the Schengen Agreement in Europe, "b/ordered spaces" arise to structure identity formation and establish desired behavior in a "borderless" world (78). If we take a mall to be an ordered space, bordered by walls, then these walls promote pure consumption as desirable behavior and restrict the access of those who lack the economic, and even racial, means to participate.[7]

Both in real life and in the film, the IslAzul mall serves as a structure that classifies people based on their consumption in a capitalist society and acculturates them into consumerist spending practices. In fact, El Ceuti's presence in the mall is another indicator of his hybridity: his access to both legal and illegal capital allows him to freely navigate both Lavapiés and the mall. Given how the representations in *No habrá paz* conflate class and race, any dark-skinned mall-goer seems out of place, as dark skin indicates poverty and thus an inability to participate in the world of consumption. For this reason, the image of El Ceuti and his cohorts shopping at the mall marks a transition in *No habrá paz*: Trinidad has found his witness but uncovered something much more sinister, only hinted at in the suspicious escape by the three would-be terrorists. At the end of the film, we discover that the mall is actually the site of the planned terrorist attack, a violent intervention that questions the space of consumption in Western culture. Though El Ceuti participates in the global capitalist system, the fears incited by his racial identity are reaffirmed in his attempt to destroy it. Trinidad's surveillance of the three men in the mall casts suspicion on them and signals their criminality, as if they were always-already felons by virtue of being watched.

Though Trinidad's observation in the mall may seem benign, the constant use of surveillance mechanisms within *No habrá paz* illustrates how completely the violence that the Western world used to contain at its edges has now come to infiltrate the center. Graham states: "Paradoxically, the imaginations of geography which underpin the new military urbanism tend to treat colonial frontiers and Western 'homelands' as fundamentally separate domains . . . even as the security, military and intelligence doctrine addressing both increasingly fuses" (15). The surveillance footage employed in *No habrá paz* illustrates the ways in which the other has fully penetrated the Spanish urban landscape, while also aiding in segregation. Surveillance does so by creating a wall between the observer and the observed, much like the cinematic camera creates a wall between the actors and the viewers. In fact, Urbizu uses supposedly objective security footage to construct a criminal subjectivity: though we all are recorded on security footage every day, we only appear as subjects within that footage once we are suspected perpetrators of some crime.

For instance, immediately after shooting Ingrid, Trinidad pauses to assess the scene of the crime and looks up. In a reverse shot, we see Trinidad standing, gun in hand in the middle of the club, dead bodies hidden out of frame. This shot is in black and white, static and distorted, and set at a slightly off-kilter angle, as if taken by a surveillance camera. The scene of the triple homicide is not the only time that Trinidad will appear on a security camera, and surveillance in the film serves to construct an invisible wall that separates criminals from their victims. That we see Trinidad through the lens of a surveillance camera multiple times in the film reminds us of his culpability: he is being watched because he is guilty. In addition, security footage visually links Trinidad to the criminality of his witness in the DVD stolen from the strip club. We watch the footage playing on Trinidad's television, and as Trinidad climbs the stairs in one frame, his witness exits the office in another. Nonetheless, even as Trinidad is watched and monitored, he observes the city, especially the immigrant neighborhood of Lavapiés, where his scrutiny recreates the (supposedly objective and detached) point of view of surveillance. Thanks to a subjective camera angle in this scene, the viewer also watches, participating in Trinidad's profiling of the people in the plaza of Lavapiés. Thus, not only does the film rely on black-and-white surveillance shots, but the main camera also reproduces the security apparatus throughout, by training static shots that insinuate criminality on migrant and racialized people. Through the false objectivity perpetuated by security footage, static shots imitate surveillance and thus reveal the racial biases that permeate Spanish society.

The suspicion of the other within the boundaries of Madrid justifies increased city surveillance to ensure that immigrants are behaving "appropriately." In his analysis of the global and the local in contemporary city spaces, Rodrigo Salcedo Hansen states: "The contemporary (post-modern) city is characterized by being fractured and constituted by a series of fragments or unconnected neighborhoods, where hypervigilance and social control maintain social and class separation, in both psychological and spatial terms" (104).[8] Thus, Trinidad's vigilance of Lavapiés is justified, even though the reality of searching for an unidentified immigrant in Madrid is like searching for a needle in a haystack. In addition, the film establishes an environment of state security through the sound of helicopter rotors at various junctures in the film. This sound creates a claustrophobic world of omniscient vigilance; however, neither the security cameras nor the ever-present helicopters can prevent a triple homicide or even terrorist activity, and they cannot reliably indict the perpetrators of these crimes either.

Because Urbizu shows us that the cinematic apparatus is always subjective, even when it attempts objectivity, I label his cinematic style as subjectively objective. In addition, since the subjects of a film are constructed through their representation onscreen, Urbizu's use of surveillance footage forges subjectivity through criminality. For instance, the static shot of the immigrants in Lavapiés falsely marks them as criminals precisely because it imitates the static perspective of the security camera. This same point of view shot repeats four times at the end of the film, focusing on the fire extinguisher bombs as white Spaniards filter through these spaces. The angle on these shots links all immigrants to the potential bomb plot and criminalizes them based on their foreignness. As Graham remarks, the conflation of terrorism and migration has led to "criminalizing or dehumanizing migrants' bodies as weapons against idealized homogenous, ethno-nationalist bases of national power" (16). Dehumanizing migrants perpetuates inequality and justifies spatial separation within their new country, but in *No habrá paz*, we witness this dehumanization as applied to racialized Spanish nationals. In fact, the hybridity that El Ceuti, Trinidad, and Ingrid embody threatens the idea of a homogenous Spanish national identity, and for this reason, they too must die.

Because Ingrid, Trinidad, and El Ceuti are hybrid characters, their deaths within the film mark an interesting space from which to contemplate the construction of Spanish national identity in the age of globalization. Not only are foreigners denied integration into the Spanish nation, but so too are the hybrid creatures that arise naturally within a borderland. Though the violence wrought by hybrid identities implies an undesirable instability for modern nation-states, they are inevitable in a world in which transnational social structures abound. As hybrid identities become more common, they blur the lines between the native and the threat. For this reason, *No habrá paz* heavily criticizes the concept of national security for its inability to regulate border crossings and prevent terrorist attacks, even as it racializes suspicious subjects and forces them into the margins of society. In fact, the film reminds us that hybridity in Spain occurs due to unwelcome foreign influences. Given the increasingly fluid state of national identities, a foreign-looking native must be treated as a threat. Thus, the elimination of any characters that suggest hybridity reinforces an antiquated view of a hegemonic Spanish national identity.

Characters such as El Ceuti illustrate the hybridity that defines border spaces, and his death (along with the deaths of all other hybrid characters) functions to remove different languages, accents, and races from Spanish national identity. According to Anzaldúa, "Most societies try to get rid of their deviants" (40). The killing of the Latin Americans and Africans, along with the sacrificial death of Trinidad, accomplishes this purging of "deviant" (read: racialized and foreign) behavior. This state-sanctioned violence will ultimately reconstruct the modern Spanish state in the image of its Northern European neighbors: superficially multicultural, but in reality valorizing traditional representations of whiteness, such as light skin and blue eyes. Through the fictional attack by Islamist extremists, Spain is revealed as a partner in the capitalist conspiracy of the Global North, yet the failure of this attack does little to critique this complicity, instead placing the blame squarely on the racialized others invading the country. If Spain is marked by extreme violence as the borderland between the Third World and Europe, then *No habrá paz* firmly denies for Spain its status as a borderland by rejecting hybridity as a defining feature of Spanish identity.

NOTES

1. From here on, I will refer to the film as *No habrá paz*.

2. According to Esteban Ramón, Urbizu has claimed that *No habrá paz* is not specifically about 11-M, but rather that it posits the question of how an event like 11-M could happen: "No es una película sobre el 11-M, simplemente se pregunta cómo es posible que algo así suceda."

3. "El inspector de policía Santos Trinidad siguiendo la pista de una joven desaparecida *se ve involucrado en un tiroteo*." (Emphasis added.)

4. Approximately a month after the bombings, the University Institute for Investigation regarding State Security (IUISI) of the National University for Distance Learning (UNED) put forth a publication regarding international terrorism in Spain. The article "Narcoterrorismo hispano: ETA, drogas y guerrilla latinoamericana," linked the details of 11-M that were known at the time to previous terrorist activity on Spanish soil (ETA) and its relationship with narco-trafficking. In addition, the official trial found that the perpetrators of the 11-M bombings comprised a local cell of hash traffickers of Moroccan origin. According to Bruno Cardeñosa, they acquired the explosives used through a combination of money and drugs: "[Emilio Suárez Trashorras] había contactado con un grupo de maroquíes interesados en el explosivo, quienes habrían entablado contacto con él tras conocer en prisión a un familiar de Súarez Trashorras, que a cambio de 7.000 euros y una buena cantidad de hachís—25 kilos—habría cumplimentado la operación" [Emilio Suárez Trashorras had become involved with a group of Moroccans interested in the explosive, who had gotten a hold of him after meeting a colleague of Suárez Trashorras in prison. In exchange for 7,000 euros and a large amount of hash—25 kilos—he carried out the operation] (318–19).

5. Although it may seem ironic that such a corrupt and violent character should have a name that evokes the sanctity of the Holy Trinity, one could speculate on the symbolic nature of the name Santos Trinidad (Saint Trinity). He participates in several character trinities over the course of the film, the first being the trinity of the state. Though a suspect in the murder investigation, his own search, combined with that of Detective Leiva and Judge Chacón reminds us that he still holds state power, in spite of his corruption. At the same time, his adoption of the stylistic traits of an American vigilante anti-hero links him to a trinity of hybrid characters, as discussed in the body of the article.

6. "Se volvió loco con la religion" (58:23).

7. Given the conflation of class and race in *No habrá paz*, any dark-skinned person present in the mall is automatically presumed to be poor. Ergo, participation in the world of consumption is predicated on whiteness as a symbol of wealth.

8. "La ciudad actual (post-moderna) se caracteriza por estar fracturada y constituida por una serie de fragmentos o enclaves poco relacionados entre sí, en donde la hipervigilancia y el control social mantienen las distancias sociales y de clase, tanto en términos psicológicos como espaciales."

WORKS CITED

Anzaldúa, Gloria. *Borderlands/La Frontera: The New Mestiza.* 2nd ed. San Francisco: Aunt Lute Books, 1999.

Cardeñosa, Bruno. *11-M: Claves de una conspiración: las pruebas del engaño.* Madrid: Espejo de Tinta, 2004.

Feinberg, Matthew. *Lavapiés, Madrid as Twenty-First Century Urban Spectacle.* Diss. University of Kentucky, 2011.

García Canclini, Néstor. *Hybrid Cultures: Strategies for Entering and Leaving Modernity.* Minneapolis: University of Minnesota Press, 1995.

———. *La globalización imaginada.* México, DF: Paidós, 1999.

Gaztambide, Michel and Enrique Urbizu. *No habrá paz para los malvados: Isaias, LVII. 21. Cuarta Versión.* March 31, 2010. TS.

Graham, Stephen. "The New Military Urbanism." *The Surveillance-Industrial Complex: A Political Economy of Surveillance.* Eds. Kirstie Ball and Laureen Snider. New York: Routledge, 2013, 11–26.

Kleiner-Liebau, Désirée. *Migration and the Construction of National Identitiy in Spain.* Madrid: Iberoamericana, 2009.

Lentin, Alana. "Europe and the Silence about Race." *European Journal of Social Theory* 11(4) (2008): 487–503.

Mbembe, Achille. "Necropolitics." *Public Culture* 15(1) (2003): 11–40.

Mutlu, Can, and Christopher Leite. "Dark Side of the Rock: Borders, Exceptionalism, and the Precarious Case of Ceuta and Melilla." *Eurasia Border Review* 3(2) (2012): 21–39.

Nair, Parvati. "Memory in motion: ethnicity, hybridity and globalization in self-photographs of Moroccan immigrants in Spain." *Journal of Romance Studies* 3(1) (2003): 73–86.

No habrá paz para los malvados. Dir. Enrique Urbizu. Perf. José Coronado, Helena Miquel, Juanjo Artero, Rodolfo Sancho, Abdel Ali El-Aziz. 2011.

Ramón, Esteban. "El regreso de Urbizu a su denominación de origen." RTVE, 2011. Accessed October 29, 2013. http://www.rtve.es/noticias/los-goya/no-habra-paz-para-los-malvados/.

Rubio Pardo, Mauricio. "Narcoterrorismo hispano. ETA, drogas y guerrilla latinoamericana." *España ante el terrorismo internacional.* Ed. Luisa Barón Hernández, José Villena Romera and Marcos Rubio García. Madrid: Instituto Universitario de Investigación sobre Seguridad Interior, 2004.

Salcedo Hansen, Rodrigo. "Lo local, lo global y el mall: la lógica de la exclusión y la interdependencia." *Revista de Geografía Norte Grande* 30 (2003): 103–15.

Smith, Michael Peter. *Transnational Urbanism: Locating Globalization.* Malden, MA: Blackwell Publishers, 2001.

Triandafyllidou, Anna. *Immigrants and National Identity in Europe.* New York: Routledge, 2001.

Vicherat Mattar, Daniela. "Did Walls Really Come Down? Contemporary B/ordering Walls in Europe." *Walls, Borders, Boundaries: Spatial and Cultural Practices in Europe.* Eds. Marc Silberman, Karen Till, and Janet Ward. New York: Berghahn Books, 2012, 77–93.

Wieviorka, Michel. *Violence: A New Approach.* Los Angeles: Sage, 2009.

Chapter Fifteen

When Multicultural Landscape Becomes Tragic Stage: Spanish Film and Immigration on the Verge of the Millennium

Roberto Robles Valencia

The transformation of contemporary Spanish society during the last decades, as it is well known, has been remarkable. Ironically enough, it could almost be said, mimicking the dictatorship motto, that *Spain is really different* now, as compared to what it used to be just three or four decades ago. [1] The radical changes undertaken by Spanish society have been stressed continuously by the media: the Transition to democracy, the integration to the, back then, European Community, the pageantry of the 1992 events, the Euro, the arrival of immigrants to a prosperous economic environment, among others; all of them ushered Spain, symbolically at least, into modernity and are taken as the most visual evidence of the profound changes that took place at different levels. The transformations shaped a new self-image of Spain based on the idea of modernity and the sense of belonging to a first-class-world group of nations. This was also an image interpreted as a rupture with the traditionally so-called Spanish backwardness, a historical "exceptionality" still accepted within some ideological positions. However, and especially during this turbulent present, one is prone to question the optimistic panorama offered at the beginning of the century and tempted to pose some questions about this transformation. After all, did Spain become truly different after these decades? Is this reconfiguration something more than a mirage endorsed by statistics and glamorous events that proclaim a radical modernization? Moreover, are these changes to be celebrated as a whole, or is there a need to maintain some reservations about their course? All of these are pertinent questions when talking about the progressive multicultural configuration of Spain. Likewise, it is absolutely urgent to reflect on how the country's multicultural configuration is taking shape, how it evolves, and how its cultural representations might help us to understand better its implications. There is a need to reconsider a sometimes uncritically accepted concept of multiculturalism and inquire whether this new configuration is a mere illusion as opposed to a traditional homogeneous nation. In sum, was *Spain different* back in the day for being a homogeneous nation? Is it now different for having a diversity that was never present?[2]

One of the key phenomena of Spain entering postmodernity was the arrival of immigrants attracted by the increasing opportunities of a prosperous economy—obviously, a striking transformation for a traditionally migrant society. This very single event of immigration, important as it is socially, statistically, and economically, has also enclosed a crucial representational transformation. As this volume indicates, multiculturalism is becoming a reality in a society self-defined until recently as homogeneous. One must, however, question if that reality is already settled and whether or not it is just a desired point of arrival—"toward." This chapter addresses these questions through a critical approach to three films produced at the new millennium: *Flores de otro mundo* (1999), *Poniente* (2002), and *Princesas* (2005). The following pages will propose a reading of these films as a powerful critique of the commonly accepted concept of multiculturalism.

Flores de otro mundo narrates what happens in a small Castilian village when a group of women arrive in Santa Eulalia to attend a matchmaking event organized by the single men of this rural community. Some relationships spring from the event, and as a result Damián will eventually marry Patricia, a Dominican woman, and live with her and her two small children. At the same time, Carmelo brings home her "lover" from Cuba—Milady—after having visited the isle on several vacations. The film shows the tensions in the relationships, following them until the end, when Damián and Patricia apparently succeed in their "multicultural" family project.

Poniente portrays a labor conflict between landowners and immigrant workers in a rural community to which Lucía returns after years in Madrid. Haunted by the vivid memories of her lost young daughter—drowned at sea—Lucía decides to stay, to work on her father's land against the advice of everyone, including her cousin who actually would like to purchase the property. She also establishes a romantic relationship with Curro, a returned émigré and now an administrator for her cousin and her—and also a mediator between landowners and migrant workers. The labor tensions increase until they explode in a riot provoked by the fire on Lucía's greenhouses—instigated by her own cousin, Miguel. As a consequence, a xenophobic mob attacks the immigrants with violent anger, blaming them for the fire.[3] In the aftermath, at the very end of the movie, we witness the immigrants fleeing the village while Lucía and Curro—the latter severely injured and accused of helping the immigrants—remain on a now desolated beach scene.

Princesas is, on the contrary, a crude urban narrative of prostitution, surrounding a kind of "bildungsroman" for its main character, Caye, who evolves from a cruel hostility to a better understanding of the "other," the immigrant subject, embodied in Zulema. Their shared suffering brings them together and apparently opens up a space of communication between the two separate worlds of Spaniards and immigrants. However, in the end, Zulema leaves the country, having discovered she is seriously sick, to reunite with her family while Caye seems to have found a new path that remains unknown at the film's conclusion.

These three film narratives have been read from different perspectives. On the one hand, as Cristina Carrasco has pointed out, they propose an active denouncing of the marginalization of immigrant population as well as a "reflection on racism and discrimination" (237). Consequently, they pinpoint emphatically, as some other contemporary works and media do, not only the presence of the immigrant subject but also the problematic issues raised by coexistence. From another direction, it has been argued that the narratives illustrate a representation of an already diverse society, a multicultural landscape in which the narrative action takes place, taking for granted a multicultural space, however imperfect this might be. Yet, this immediate and unproblematic acceptance of the concept of multiculturalism as a positive category is what emerges as questionable. Such a view allows, for example, Luis Prádanos to insist on the "versatile Spain" and the "multicultural Madrid" and the positive effect on the "renegotiation" of Spanish identity (Prádanos 34–39). Undoubtedly, all the films address the issue of renegotiation but, for the most part, focus on its impossibility to produce a peaceful coexistence. No matter what goodwill is invested by the characters, the final result fails to achieve such an ideal.

In the following pages I will explore the relationships established between different pairs of characters, some of them based on common experiences of inequality—Zulema and Caye in *Princesas*, Patricia and Damián/his mother in *Flores*, and Adbembi and Curro/Lucía in *Poniente*.[4] Their inability to create solid bridges of communication between the immigrant subject and the Spaniard results in the impossibility to generate a hybrid society. My contention is that this inability can be read in the terms that Žižek interprets multiculturalism: as a highly problematic "ideological operation of multicultural liberalism," rather than as a desirable point of arrival (Žižek, *Sobre la violencia* 169). The analysis of the relationships established between the characters in the films suggests a criticism on the concept of a kind of multiculturalism unable to resolve inequalities by naturalizing them when tolerated as "cultural differences."

As the best example of the failure of these attempts we can focus on a particular relevant scene. The last moments of *Poniente* show a group of immigrants hauling their belongings on their way out of the village, where the recent violent confrontation has just taken place. While they walk slowly by the shoreline, the last one, Adbembi, stops for a second to take a last look at the inland. The camera, which has offered a traveling shot of the walking line of the group—moving in the opposite direction—does not stop but continues its motion as he shortly continues his. Adbembi's gaze toward the inland, however, remains the last action seen in the film. A relaxing image of the quiet sea takes over the screen, and the image fades out after he and his gaze have already disappeared. This last condescending gaze, somehow saturated with disdain, offers an interesting insight, especially after the events narrated in the film. It does not speak the language of desire or hope. It speaks of blunt deception and suffering, but it also refers to his understanding of a drama he has witnessed only some moments earlier. It refers to the *aloofness* pointed out by Kristeva, for whom "indifference is the foreigner's shield. Insensitive, aloof, he seems, deep down, beyond the reach of attacks and rejections that he nevertheless experiences" (7). This *aloofness* allows him to perceive the drama of the Spaniards, along with the experience of his own tragedy.

In that sense, the beating of the immigrants, surely the assassination of some, appears narratively on the background, and it is just one part of the tragedy. The main characters, all of them Spaniards, are, however, the focus of the film account and suffer their own parallel catastrophe. The death of Lucía's cousin in the greenhouses is the tragic narrative event that marks the protagonist's life, by reenacting the loss of her own daughter, drowned in the sea some years ago. Moreover when it is the child's father, and Lucía's cousin, who actually causes the riots and eventually his own son's death by secretly setting on fire one of the greenhouses. Therefore, the xenophobic violence is not isolated but woven into the dramatic past of the Spaniards. That single gaze, in the end, also connects the viewer with the first scene of the film in which a blurred paradisiacal and colorful beach appears only to reveal, a minute later, a fake mini-stage carried by two boys as their school project. The real stage for the film narrative immediately appears, much less colorful, in the streets of a working class neighborhood in Madrid. The contrast of the colorful fake stage with the city streets is also the contrast between the idealized Spanish seashore and the one by which the immigrants walk at the end. Thus, the narrative is pointing to the fact that the landscape on which the immigrant arrives is not an empty or a paradisiacal one. The immigrant subject leaves it at the end having very little participation in the tragedy of the main characters. Adbembi's gaze reminds the viewer of the illusion of an empty landscape. He might leave but violence and traumatic

past remain, and his gaze becomes the viewer's device to expose both tragedies and intertwine them as a common drama.

Only in this sense can we speak about renegotiation, when referring to the
interconnected tragedies and the effect of the arrival of immigration. What
the presence of immigration causes in these films is the unveiling of a dramatic past of the main Spanish characters: the death of the child, reenacting
that of Lucía's daughter, the beating of Curro and the end of his future
project—a charming *chiringuito* by the beach—to overcome his past as an
exile. This brings to an end what, at some point, appeared as a possibility: a
happy and enriching coexistence of cultures, a short-lived image showed in
the film when Curro and Lucía share food, songs and happiness by the
immigrant shack neighborhood. That same idealized image appears in *Princesas*, when Zulema guides Caye into a street market. Latin music, colorful
clothes, exotic food enters the scene to recreate an image already present in
Spanish collective imagination—that of Lavapiés and other similar urban
areas, crowded with immigrants and their business. However, the last scenes
of *Princesas* emphasize the impossibility of a happy resolution which, sur-
prisingly, emerges also at the close of *Flores de otro mundo*. The last scene
of *Flores* portrays the arrival of another bus of single women in Santa Eulalia; the children celebrate it, following the newcomers into the entrance of the
village. There, Patricia's children, although remarkably different from the
others, join them in the game, representing a flawless coexistence and the
solution to the problematic relationship between the "multicultural" couple
of Damián and Patricia. However, it is just a possibility among others. Milady has left in search of better fortune, leaving Carmelo all on his own, dining
alone on Christmas Eve. In any case, the film has also unveiled the extreme
power of the traditional patriarchal society—Carmelo and his violent out-
rages, the humble aspirations of rural women embodied in Damian's mother—along with the diversity within Spain—the opposition urban-rural, and
the regional diversity. The renegotiation noted by Labanyi and Prádanos is,
thus, taking place within Spanish society, which has to come to terms with its
own past and its identity.[5] However, this does not necessarily imply the
immediate outcome of a multicultural society as defined, for example, by
Žižek: "the hybrid coexistence of diverse cultural life-worlds" (*Multiculturalism* 46).[6] The film narratives clearly emphasize this aspect: immigration
produces the renegotiation of the country's self-identity, but this shifting
identity does not immediately translate into a multicultural society. It does
not create a hybrid society, but rather maintains the prevailing of different
and segregated identities sharing a common space.

Moreover, these three filmic narratives call our attention to the danger of
considering multiculturalism a simplistic celebration of racial and cultural
diversity. The idealized image of a happy colorful society, as noted earlier, is
questioned by contrasting it with the dramatic ending of the films. As Will

Kymlicka has pointed out, recent criticism has commented on how "multi-culturalism is characterized as a feel-good celebration of ethno-cultural diversity, encouraging citizens to acknowledge and embrace the panoply of customs, traditions, music and cuisine that exist in a multi-ethnic society" (Kymlicka, *The Rise and Fall* 98). It is somewhat obvious that this concept has pervaded some of the recent cultural products and representations of diversity in Spain.[7] By doing so, they also stressed the idea of difference, encouraging "a conception of groups as hermetically sealed and static, each reproducing its own distinct authentic practices," as Kymlicka notes (98). This can be perceived in the films. The connection established by means of a celebratory diversity is short-lived, only present in some scenes and with no positive outcome.

Furthermore, the three narratives directly refer to one of the main criticisms mentioned by Kymlicka; what he designates as "3S picture of multiculturalism [which] . . . entirely ignores issues of economic and political inequality" (98). All three films address this disparity, first by focusing on the immigrants' status as *sin papeles*—undocumented immigrants—and then by relating their lack of legal recognition to their economically subjugated position. This legal and, hence, economic disadvantage is clear in the case of the agricultural workers in *Poniente*, as it is also evident in the case of prostitution in *Princesas*. Similarly, Patricia clarifies her position to Damián in *Flores*; she got married and stayed in Santa Eulalia because there is no other option for her to become a citizen and take care of her children. Her action confirms what was tacit before, avoiding any kind of romanticism for the viewer. Damián has to accept a loving relationship which originates in inequality and which, thus, parallels his own mother's relationship with his father in the town's patriarchal arrangement—as she acknowledges to Patricia. In doing so, the characters recognize inequalities as a first step toward challenging them, in contrast with others who remain blind to them. Caye recognizes injustice and the inferior role that, even among prostitutes, Zulema holds, and Lucía and Curro align with the undocumented workers; however, none of them has the agency to transform the status quo for the "illegal" immigrants. In this kind of Levinasian recognition of the "other," what is at stake is the process of recognition of the economic and political implications within the concept of multiculturalism, especially in the case of the undocumented immigrants. Celebrating diversity without contemplating these essential issues is doomed to failure, as the films suggest: cultural awareness is not enough.[8]

These cinematic texts also question the idea of the necessary role of goodwill: "in many parts of the world, groups are motivated by hatred and intolerance, not justice, and have no interest in treating others with goodwill" (Kymlicka, *Multicultural* 193). The narratives show, on the contrary, how goodwill does not have any significant effect on the outcome toward a just and multicultural society. It is morally admirable, but the increasing tolerance we see developing in Caye and the other prostitutes does not change the undocumented status of Zulema or any other immigrant in her situation, nor their precarious economic circumstances. Such is also the case of the underpaid field workers for whom tolerance would not change their status, which is based on an economic structure adopted by neoliberalism but clearly linked to the traditional labor conditions of *jornaleros*—day laborers—in Spain. In this sense, Žižek's corrosive criticism of tolerance as an ideological category makes perfect sense. For this author, there is a common belief that tolerance is the solution to issues of exploitation, inequality and injustice through what he calls the "culturalization of politics" (Žižek, *Sobre la violencia* 169).[9] Thus, what is perceived as cultural difference—a naturalized concept taken for granted as an essence of the subject—conceals political difference rooted in political inequality or exploitation, neutralizing any challenge to them since they have to be "tolerated" (169).

In this sense the stress placed on difference within the narratives needs to be considered. For Daniela Flesler, some of the films on immigration in contemporary Spain "strive to show Spain's difference from 'the Moors' and the Francoist past, and painstakingly try to reassure Spaniards of their unquestionable modern status" (115–16). However, it is debatable whether this is the case for the films analyzed here. Although it is undeniable that to some extent they, as Flesler writes, "reveal less about the real lives of the newcomers and more about Spain's anxiety regarding its own liminal location in Europe," this fact by itself does not necessarily imply an emphasis on difference (103). On the contrary, as we have seen, the films stress the common dramatic circumstances for nationals and immigrants and unveil the return of an unresolved past. Luis Martín-Cabrera indicates "the return of the 'colonial repressed'" displayed in *Flores de otro mundo* (53). For him, the film unveils the "epistemic violence of the discourses of Spanish modernity" and explains the "racial violence" toward the immigrants as a violence against the agents of such "return" (43). The "fracture" of "the temporality of modernity" sets the ground for the "neo-racist violence" (43–44). In this sense, the focus on Spain's own problematic identity and troubled modernity does not presuppose a reassurance of a successful integration into European modernity; on the contrary, it suggests the need to rethink modernity and Spanish historical diversity. In doing so, these films propose a critical approach to the idea of multiculturalism. To some extent they reject the appropriation of the voices of the "voiceless" excluded by giving prominence to the Spanish characters and, thus, avoiding any questionable discussion on "authenticity." At the same time, they lead us to reflect on Spain's questionable modernity, on its unique character and diverse past.

Moreover, the failure of a multicultural project in these films mirrors mostly Spain's own troubled identity and a country facing economic and exclusion problems. That is obviously the case of *Poniente*, where Curro, dragging his own exile past, stumbles upon social and economic barriers impossible to overcome. He, as well as Lucía, who returns to her own origins, does not belong to a space that now seems to be owned by an external economic agent—materialized on the "sea of plastic" of the greenhouses, portrayed repetitively in the film. The contrast between the synthetic plastic sea and the actual one appears as a persistent image. Lucía lost her child to the sea years ago; now what is at stake is creating a future for her other daughter, against this new artificial one, a metaphor for a globalized neoliberal market. The battle against the market is lost in the film. Lucía and Curro fail to fight convincingly along with the immigrants and they suffer the consequences: they all become disposable beings. Some are forced to leave; others are just defeated. However, the final "anagnorisis" suggests a possibility of political action, far from goodwill and tolerance, as moral categories. This is also the process undertaken by Caye, who finally decides to face her situation. Her traditional family—where her mother, abandoned by her husband, remains obsessed with his return—is about to find out who Caye really is, suggesting an opportunity of liberation at least from her own oppressive personal past.

On the contrary, Patricia, despite the apparently happy ending, "is also presented, through her acceptance of certain cultural norms, as a model of assimilation," as Flesler points out (114). For Flesler, this romanticized ending, in which Patricia and her children accept the practices of the village, naturalize these customs, and suggest a "disturbing" closure to the colonial and evangelical imperial project (114). In fact, this ending can be read as the mentioned "celebratory" trend of multiculturalism. It is, indeed, an acute critical approach to the social issues discussed in this chapter. However, a closer look at the narrative may offer a slightly different reading. After Patricia's assertion of her precarious situation and Damián's rejection, Patricia significantly disappears as a character from the screen. She barely comes into sight or talks during her preparations to depart. In the next scene she is about to leave in her friends' car, but Damián, silent as usual, opens the trunk and starts unloading the baggage. Patricia cries, in the most sentimental scene of the film, and, in this moment, it is certain that Patricia has lost the strong voice that she had previously possessed. Indeed, from that point on, she dissolves into group scenes—the celebration of the communion, her son's birthday—and her voice ceases to be heard. In this sense, the film bears witness to the component of disavowal involved in the process of "assimilation." After all, she now "belongs" to a patriarchal and traditional society and is probably assigned to a role similar to that of her mother-in-law: that of the silent and industrious wife. In contrast, Milady is now running away from that same outlook. Thus, the happy ending is not as perfect as it appears to be. It shows the profound fractures and strong tensions of Spanish society but also those of the process of "assimilation" or "integration," of the construction of a multicultural realm. In this way, this reading links *Flores* to the narration of failures in the construction of multiculturalism that all three films suggest.

The unsuccessful outcome in the films' accounts evokes what Žižek has indicated about multiculturalism: that it might be a mask of its opposite, "the massive presence of capitalism as 'universal' world system: it bears witness to the unprecedented homogenization of the contemporary world" (Žižek, *Multiculturalism* 46). In *Poniente*, for instance, the new agricultural landscape, alien to both the Spaniards—mainly Lucía but also the rest of landowners who persistently express their inability to raise salaries because of the market—and to the immigrants, configures this homogenized capitalist economy. The synthetic alien space emphatically opposes the image of the sea, in the same way that the idyllic fake beach at the beginning contrasts with the final scene of a sinister shoreline. On a similar note, Žižek comments on how the "hegemonic fiction (or even ideal) of multiculturalist tolerance" constitutes a fundamental part of the "'real' universality of today's globalization" (40–41). The sexual exploitation in *Princesas* does not differentiate between national origin or cultural background. Notwithstanding the dissimilar levels of oppression—Zulema suffers the abuse to obtain her legal status—both she and Caye are subjected to the domination of the same "market." That is why the prostitutes in the film unite in criticizing the newcomers for breaking the "rules" of their—now globalized—market. As a paradigmatic model, prostitution imposes the objectification of the woman's body, but, to a comparable degree, a similar reification also occurs to the undocumented workers in the plastic fields: dispensable commodities of the globalized market. As has been discussed, tolerance does not have any effect on the logic of this market; only political agency can resist such domination. It is Caye who discovers her agency and decides to act upon it after realizing her subjugated position, leaving open what the path of her action may be. Another alternative is to flee. The rural workers in *Poniente* and Milady in *Flores* choose this option. Yet another choice is "to assimilate." Patricia in *Flores* decides to do so. She may or not maintain her cultural background—celebrating her difference, her music, etc.—but she has already surrendered something more important: her political agency to question and challenge the status quo. She has to conform to the humble aspirations of a disappearing rural environment, seemingly unchanging, despite the arrival of more immigrants—as the movie's last scene implies.

In these films, the failure to realize the multicultural ideal directs our gaze to other issues: political inequality and economic exploitation. In doing so, the three texts unmask the "ideological operation of multicultural liberalism" (Žižek, *Sobre la violencia* 169). According to this philosopher, such an operation consists of naturalizing and neutralizing such inequalities under the form of "cultural differences" in what he terms the "culturization of politics" (169). By decentering the focus of the camera away from cultural differences and toward inequality and exploitation—fundamentally of the undocumented characters but also of the nationals—the films insinuate the need for a "politization of culture," as Žižek suggests, following Benjamin (Žižek, *Sobre la violencia* 169). They can be read as disputing the idea of multiculturalism advocated by Kymlicka, among others, opposing to what can be considered a "multiculturalism politics." As Kymlicka himself suggests, there is a close similarity between the political ambiguities of multiculturalism and nationalism (Kymlicka, *Contemporary* 369). Those ambiguities, however, reinforce Žižek's contention that multiculturalism co-opts political agency the way nationalism does. The appeal to tolerance, to affect, and to feelings in the films is shown as incapable of generating a viable multicultural alternative. These appeals to goodwill only manage to evoke the need for another path. It is the viewer now who decides which direction that will be.

As we have seen, these filmic representations of a society in the process of becoming multicultural suggest a more complex view than expected. It seems to be difficult to perceive "an external, separate reality to be rationally perceived and accurately represented," as John Wylie suggests writing about landscape (3). As he notes, "self and landscape, are essentially enlaced and intertwined, in a 'being-in-the-world' that precedes and preconditions rationality and objectivity" (3). This condition of being-in-the-world is a persistent image in the films: scenes of landscape, the urban and the rural, the movement from one place to another. The different "selves" portrayed are necessarily intertwined with landscape, which is mostly a stage with its own participation in the plot—the plastic fields, the rural areas, the modern city. These stages also embody the dramatic past of its inhabitants, thus becoming another character in the filmic accounts—as opposed to the empty idyllic fake landscape at the beginning of *Poniente*. When we observe that *Spain is different*, we sometimes forget the terms of comparison: different from what? Perhaps this recognition of multicultural difference is as misleading as the one that Francoism put to use some decades ago. Perhaps we are forgetting to recognize the presence of an already diverse past, homogenized by the work of Spanish nationalism. This past, materialized in landscape—stage—permeates our present and plays its role in the construction of a future society. The title's "tragic stage" evokes this idea as opposed to an optimistic landscape observed from afar which ideally would become, flawlessly, multicultural. These filmic representations complicate the depiction of immigration and multiculturalism by illuminating the interactions with the past and the inadequacy of "tolerance" as a moral category. Today the perspective is different. The context of an acute economic crisis, in which some of the patterns toward modernity seem to have reversed, provides us with a better perspective for reading these texts and the multicultural society in construction. The most recent social movements observed in Spain may also serve as an interesting insight. As Germán Labrador has recently noted, personal accounts of the crisis are circulating now as new "technologies of political imagination" (557–60). These accounts in effect articulate no difference regarding the national, cultural, or racial origin of their actors and may be taken as a more real "multicultural" expression: a stage in which collective voices are heard and where political imagination is present.

NOTES

1. Cristina Carrasco has also noticed this irony. I would like to expand this idea in order to criticize the concept of multiculturalism. See Carrasco, *Agua con sal* (245). It is also worth noting how modernity in Spain has meant, to some extent, becoming multicultural and embracing "difference," as opposed to the homogeneous self-definition of the country fabricated by radical national-catholicism.

2. For an interesting reflection on this tension between the historical homogenization of Spanish society and the anxiety in accepting the African "other" see Daniela Flesler, *The Return of the Moor*. West Lafayette, IN: Purdue University, 2008.

3. As is well known, the film is referring to the xenophobic outburst in El Ejido in 2000.

4. My analysis will follow mainly these "pairs" of characters keeping in mind always the tension between immigrant and national subject.

5. For this concept of renegotiation see: Prádanos (*op. cit*), and Labanyi "Postmodernism and the Problem of Cultural Identity." *Spanish Cultural Studies: An Introduction*. Eds. Graham Helen and Jo Labanyi. Oxford: Oxford University Press, 1995.

6. This would be Žižek's ideal definition of a multicultural society.

7. Immigrant characters are a common place in a variety of contemporary cultural products, especially in television series. As an example, we can mention the popular *Aída* (Tele5, 2005–) or films such as *La comunidad* (dir. Alex de la Iglesia 2000) or *Tapas* (dir. José Corbacho 2005). These representations—although sometimes from a sarcastic point of view—share their unproblematic stereotyped image of the immigrant, while accepting the celebration of "diversity."

8. It must be said that Kymlicka still defends the "politics of multiculturalism" in spite of these criticisms and denies the so-called retreat from multiculturalism. See, for example: Kymlicka, *The Rise and Fall*.

9. Translations from this volume are mine.

WORKS CITED

Carrasco, Cristina. "Agua con sal: Otredad y exotismo caribeño en el cine español contemporáneo." *Romance Notes* 51(2) (2011): 237–46.

Flesler, Daniela. "New Racism, Intercultural Romance, and the Immigration Question in Contemporary Spanish Cinema." *Studies in Hispanic Cinemas* 1(2) (2004): 103–18.

Flores de otro mundo. Dir. Icíar Bollaín. Filmax, 1999. DVD.

Kristeva, Julia. *Strangers to Ourselves*. New York: Columbia University Press, 1991.

Kymlicka, Will. *Contemporary Political Philosophy: an Introduction*. New York : Oxford University Press, 2002.

———. "The Rise and Fall of Multiculturalism? New Debates on Inclusion and Accommodation in Diverse Societies." *International Social Science Journal* 61(199) (2010): 97–112.

Labrador, Germán. "Las vidas 'subprime': La circulación de 'Historias de Vida' como tecnología de imaginación política en la crisis española (2007–2012)." *Hispanic Review* 80(4) (2012): 557–81.

Martín-Cabrera, Luis. "Postcolonial Memories and Racial Violence in *Flores de otro mundo.*" *Journal of Spanish Cultural Studies* 3(1) (2002): 43–55.

Poniente . Dir. Chus Gutiérrez. Olmo Films, 2002.

Prádanos, Luis I. "La mujer inmigrante latinoamericana en el cine español actual: Hacia una identidad cultural relacional en *Princesas* (2005)." *Confluencia* 27(2) (2012): 34–45.

Princesas. Dir. Fernando León de Aranoa. Warner Home Video, 2005.

Wylie, John. *Landscape*. New York: Routledge, 2007.

Žižek, Slavoj. "Multiculturalism, or the Cultural Logic of Multinational Capitalism." *New Left Review* 225 (1997): 28–51.

———. *Sobre la violencia. Seis reflexiones marginales*. Madrid: Paidós, 2008.

Index

About the Contributors

María Del Carmen Alfonso García holds a PhD from the University of Oviedo, where she obtained the PhD graduation prize in 1993. She is now a tenured professor at this university, lecturing in contemporary Spanish literature and in the gender studies programs. She is also Vice-Dean of the Faculty of Humanities. Her research focuses on contemporary Spanish literature, particularly on gender, national identity, and the discourses of self-representation. At present she takes part in a nationally funded research project on the representation of transnational cities (La ciudad fluida FFI 2010-17296). She collaborates in the following nationally funded research projects: "La ciudad fluida" (FFI 2010-17296), on the representation of transnational cities (2010–2013), and, at present, "Encuentros incorporado y conocimientos alternativos. Habitar y crear la cuidad" (FFI 2014-45642-R), on the alternative representations of cities.

Alicia Castillo Villanueva holds a PhD from the University of Limerick where she is currently lecturing in a number of areas related to the Hispanic world. Her research focuses on cultural representations of gender and violence in contemporary Spain with particular emphasis on transition to democracy and memory studies. She has published articles on women in Spain and is working toward the publication of her first book.

Ana Corbalán (PhD University of North Carolina at Chapel Hill) is associate professor of Spanish at the University of Alabama. She has published many articles and book chapters on twentieth- and twenty-first-century Spanish literature and culture. Her first book, *El cuerpo transgresor en la narrativa española contemporánea*, was published by Ediciones Libertarias (2009).

Her second book, *Memorias fragmentadas: Mirada transatlántica a la resistencia femenina contra las dictaduras*, is currently under editorial review.

Thomas Deveny (PhD University of North Carolina at Chapel Hill) is professor of Spanish and Comparative Literature at McDaniel College in Westminster, Maryland. He is author of numerous articles on Spanish literature and Hispanic film. His books include *Cain on Screen: Contemporary Spanish Cinema* (1993; paperback, 1999), *Contemporary Spanish Film from Fiction* (1999, paperback, 2003), and *Migration in Contemporary Hispanic Cinema* (2012).

Javier Entrambasaguas Monsell holds a PhD from the University of Michigan, Ann Arbor. His book manuscript, *Social Movements in Contemporary Spain*, examines cultural representations of social movements in Spain over the last forty years. Javier is interested in how social movements—such as those addressing globalization, immigration, squatters, labor rights, and the *15M*—advocate a socially active citizenship, a reformulation of urban spaces, and a reconceptualization of democracy. He is currently a visiting professor at the University of Maryland, Baltimore County.

Donna Gillespie is currently an assistant professor of Spanish at College of DuPage. She received her PhD in Romance Languages with a concentration in Spanish Literature from the University of Florida in 2012. The title of her dissertation is: *Portrayals of Women Immigrants to Spain in Fiction and Film: 1997 – 2011*. Her research interests include migration studies, multiculturalism, and studies on identity and community.

Victoria L. Ketz is an associate professor of Spanish and Chairperson of Foreign Languages at Iona College in New Rochelle, New York. She received her PhD in Spanish Literature from Columbia University in 1999. Her research interests include: contemporary theater, narrative, film, and literary theory. Dr. Ketz has published articles on pedagogy, and twentieth-century Spanish writers such as Valle-Inclán, Pérez de Ayala, Unamuno, Rodoreda, Cisneros, and others. Her current book project examines the representation of violence by female authors in Contemporary Peninsular Literature, and this year, her book on the portrayal of the African in Contemporary Spanish texts will be published.

Sohyun Lee is an assistant professor of Spanish at Texas Christian University. She has published essays in journals such as *Connections*, the *Bulletin of Hispanic Studies*, the *Global Studies Journal*, *Comparative American Studies*, and *Letras Hispanas*. Her latest publication is "La dinámica urbana de la frontera y los derechos a la ciudad: autoetnografías femeninas de Tijuana" for the special edition "Mujer y Ciudad" of *Letras Femeninas*.

Maryanne L. Leone (PhD, University of Kansas) is an associate professor of Spanish at Assumption College in Worcester, Massachusetts. Her research centers on national identity, migration, globalization, consumerism, and gender in contemporary Spain, and she currently is examining the confluence of these issues with environmental concerns. She has published articles in *Anales de la Literatura Española Contemporánea*, *Letras Hispanas*, and *Revista Canadiense de Estudios Hispánicos*.

Pilar Martínez-Quiroga is lecturer of Spanish at the University of Illinois at Urbana-Champaign. She holds a PhD in Spanish (Rutgers University, 2011). Her research deals with the construction of feminine communities in twenty-first-century Spanish narrative written by women from a multidisciplinary perspective, paying special attention to instances of resistance, social change, and citizenship .

María R. Matz is an associate professor of Latin American Studies and Culture in the department of Cultural Studies at UMass Lowell. Among her recent publications are the book *Definiendo a la mujer: Cristina Escofet y su teatro* (Puerto Rico: Penelope Academic Press, 2012) and a co-edited bilingual (English and Spanish) volume *How the Films of Pedro Almodóvar Draw upon and Influence Spanish Society* (New York: Edwin Mellen Press, 2012), as well as several articles in peer reviewed journals.

Ellen Mayock (PhD, University of Texas at Austin) is the Ernest Williams II Professor of Spanish at Washington and Lee University. She is the coeditor of *Feminist Activism in Academia* and the author of ' *The Strange Girl* ' *in Twentieth-Century Spanish Novels Written by Women* and of over thirty book chapters and articles on the production of the novel, twentieth- and twenty-first-century Spain, US-Latina writers, and feminist theory and practice.

William Nichols obtained his PhD from Michigan State University and is currently an associate professor of Spanish Literature and Culture at Georgia State University. His primary research interest focuses on exploring the perceptions of Spain's modern identity through the interrelation between politics, cultural production, and capitalism in contemporary peninsular literature and film as well as other forms of cultural expression like music and museum expositions. He has published on diverse themes like detective fiction, corporate culture, tourism, food, genre, and globalization. His manuscript, *Transatlantic Mysteries: Culture, Capital, and Crime in the " Noir Novels " of Paco Ignacio Taibo II and Manuel Vázquez Montalbán*, was published with

Bucknell University Press in 2011. He also coedited a collection of essays titled *Toward a Cultural Archive of La Movida: Back to the Future* published with Farleigh Dickinson University Press in 2014.

Diana Norton completed her master's in Spanish and Latin American languages and literatures at New York University in Madrid in 2011. She is currently working toward her doctoral degree at the University of Texas at Austin under the supervision of Professor Jill Robbins. Her primary area of interest is how foreigners are represented in twentieth-century Spanish literature and culture. Her research interests include twentieth-century Spanish cultural studies, Iberian Studies, borderland studies, transnationalism, denationalism, and cosmopolitanism.

Hayley Rabanal is associate professor in Hispanic Studies at the University of Sheffield. She is the author of *Belen Gopegui: The Pursuit of Solidarity in Post-Transition Spain* and articles on contemporary Spanish film and fiction. Her current research explores the negotiation of notions of *convivencia* and cosmopolitanism in cultural production in the interrelated contexts of immigration and multiculturalism, and discourses of cultural (historical) memory.

Roberto Robles-Valencia, assistant professor of Spanish at the University of South Alabama, holds a PhD from the University of Michigan. His main area of research focuses on Spanish nationalism of the nineteenth and twentieth centuries through the analysis of cultural artifacts. He is currently working on post-dictatorship film and urban space, as well as the present crisis and its representation.

Carole Salmon is an associate professor of French Studies and Culture in the department of Cultural Studies at UMass Lowell. She recently coedited a bilingual volume (English and Spanish) entitled *How the Films of Pedro Almodóvar Draw upon and Influence Spanish Society* (New York: Edwin Mellen Press, 2012). She regularly presents her research to national and international conferences and has published several articles in peer-reviewed journals.

Megan Saltzman earned her PhD in Spanish Cultural Studies at the University of Michigan in 2008. Currently she is an assistant professor of Spanish at West Chester University. She studies how we experience and use our everyday public space in order to create ideas and practices regarding social identity, history, and political resistence. She is currently writing a book titled *Public Everyday Space: The Deteriorating Histories of Post-Francoist Barcelona*. Megan has taught Spanish language and culture in the United States, New Zealand, and Japan.

Raquel Vega-Durán is assistant professor in the Department of Modern Languages and Literatures at Claremont McKenna College, California, where she teaches Peninsular Spanish History, literature, and film, as well as courses in Transatlantic and Mediterranean Studies. She is currently working on a book titled *Emigrant Dreams, Immigrant Borders: Transnational Encounters and the Question of Identity in Contemporary Spain.* Her work on cross-cultural connections between Spain, Africa, and Latin America has appeared in *Quaderns de Cine, Afro-Hispanic Review, Letras Femeninas,* and the volume *African Immigrants in Contemporary Spanish Texts: Crossing the Straits.*